TWENTIETH CENTURY VIEWS

The aim of this series is to present the best in contemporary critical opinion on major authors, providing a twentieth century perspective on their changing status in an era of profound revaluation.

Maynard Mack, *Series Editor*
Yale University

TOLSTOY

TOLSTOY

A COLLECTION OF CRITICAL ESSAYS

Edited by
Ralph E. Matlaw

Prentice-Hall, Inc. A SPECTRUM BOOK *Englewood Cliffs, N. J.*

To the memory
of
RENATO POGGIOLI

E s'io al vero son timido amico,
temo di perder vita tra coloro
che questo tempo chiameranno antico.

Contents

TOLSTOY

Introduction

by Ralph E. Matlaw

On July 22, 1910, when Tolstoy was in the midst of what was to be his final crisis, he went into the woods with three friends to copy and sign the testament that had been drawn up according to his instructions, hoping thereby to settle both the tormenting spiritual problems and the distasteful bickering with his wife and family that the disposition of his property and rights induced. As Tolstoy began to copy the document he misspelled "twenty," started to correct it and to reach for a fresh sheet of paper, but then smiled and said, "All right, let it be thought that I was illiterate," adding "I will put the numeral next to it so that there will be no possibility of doubt." The remark may be taken as emblematic of Tolstoy's concern for craftsmanship and precision, just as the sylvan setting might be an emblem for the deep communion with nature that informs the crucial moments of his characters' lives. For few writers, particularly in the nineteenth century, have been so much and so consistently aware of the relationship between form and content, the irreducibility of a work of art to other terms, and the technical possibilities available to the professional writer; and few writers have expressed themselves quite so fully on the topic. Yet this awareness is an aspect of Tolstoy's art that has been little investigated in the West, particularly in English, a surprising fact considering the modern critical temperament and its penchant for analyzing techniques of fiction, structure, symbols, tensions, and the like.

The reasons are not difficult to find. It is not only the sheer size (at least of the two major novels) that makes such an approach unwieldy, but also some special quality that engages the reader's imagination and leads to critical speculations of another sort. That quality is summed up in Matthew Arnold's unfortunate dictum, intended as the ultimate compliment, that *Anna Karenina* was not to be taken as a work of art but as a piece of life, and it has been eloquently particularized in Isaiah Berlin's brilliant monograph *The Hedgehog and the Fox* as follows:

> No author who has ever lived has shown such power of insight into the variety of life—the differences, the contrasts, the collisions of persons and

things and situations, each apprehended in its absolute uniqueness and conveyed with a degree of directness and a precision of concrete imagery to be found in no other writer. No one has ever excelled Tolstoy in expressing the specific flavour, the exact quality of a feeling—the degree of its "oscillation," the ebb and flow, the minute movements (which Turgenev mocked as a mere trick on his part)—the inner and outer texture and "feel" of a look, a thought, a pang of sentiment, no less than that of the specific pattern of a situation, or an entire period, continuous segments of lives of individuals, families, communities, entire nations. The celebrated life-likeness of every object and every person in his world derives from this astonishing capacity of presenting every ingredient of it in its fullest individual essence, in all its many dimensions, as it were; never as a mere datum, however vivid, within some stream of consciousness, with blurred edges, an outline, a shadow, an impressionistic representation: nor yet calling for, and dependent on, some process of reasoning in the mind of the reader; but always as a solid object, seen simultaneously from near and far, in natural, unaltering daylight from all possible angles of vision, set in an absolutely specific context in time and space—an event fully present to the senses or the imagination in all its facets, with every nuance sharply and firmly articulated.

For many critics the frequent temptation has been to show what that "life" is rather than how it is presented; to reduce it to its "essence" rather than to investigate the art that discloses it in all its fullness; to make reasonable and formulaic what Tolstoy has made tangible. Tolstoy, who expressed himself on most questions, wrote to his friend, the critic and philosopher Strakhov, that in order to convey in words everything that he wanted to say in *Anna Karenina,* he would have to write the entire novel over again, and with some irony congratulated those critics who explain in their articles what his work means, assuring them that they know more than he about it. Clearly the statement is no deterrent to those who would analyze Tolstoy's work, but it does point to an area of inquiry not sufficiently explored: the elaborate and organic design manifest in the smallest detail no less than in the grandiose conceptions and structures that makes of Tolstoy's works marvels of concision and organization rather than the "loose baggy monsters" Henry James dubbed them and other major writers considered them to be.

In replying to a critic of *Anna Karenina* Tolstoy wrote, ". . . I am very proud of its architecture—its vaults are joined so that one cannot even notice where the keystone is. And that is what I endeavored to do more than anything else. The cohesion of its structure is not based on the plot, nor on the relationships (acquaintance) of the characters, but on an inner cohesion." The architectural metaphor, curiously resembling Proust's conception of his masterpiece as a cathedral, has been elaborated on in Albert Cook's essay, "The Unity of *War and Peace*," a demonstration of the various ways and gradations by which mere placement within the plot affects or determines implications and meanings once the inner significance of each section is understood, and of the unity achieved thereby. Yet for all one learns of the enormous interrelatedness of the novel and its complexities—the buttresses of the structure, so to speak— there are also keystones to be perceived, and it can even be argued that to understand the novel one must finally come to grips with the pronoun *it* (Russian *ono*) occuring three times in this book of 1500 pages. Something similar may be observed in Tolstoy's imagery, his style, and his narrative techniques: frequently an unobtrusive detail or shift in narrative focus is used to illuminate and redefine vast areas and issues broached earlier in other ways.

Prince Andrey, for example, is presented in many different ways, and through many different eyes. But his first revelation occurs as he lies wounded at Austerlitz looking at the sky, meditating on the beauty of life; another occurs on the raft with Pierre when some of the same elements—descriptive and psychological—are again present. These extraordinary moments of liberation are all the more striking for his habitual control, the personal and social formulas that govern him and interfere with the recognition and direct expression of his desires and his love for life. Prince Andrey is associated from his first appearance with a recurrent descriptive motif that comes to be as much a part of him as his small white hands and his enormous ambition. In Anna Scherer's drawing room he is first perceived by the narrator as he enters the doorway. And in many other situations—at Austerlitz, when he sees the encampment as if through a frame; at Otradnoe, when he overhears Natasha's rapturous attempt to levitate; when his father is palpably on the other side of the door upon his return from the war; when his son has passed the crisis of his illness— in short, some of the moments that he considers the best of his life and others that are among the most important—in all these he stands framed by a window or door, not in the freedom of the earth and sky. A different set of images, involving mechanical rotation (rather than the meaningful turning of the globe, Pierre finally understands) appears in the clocks and lathe and orderly routine of the elder Bolkonsky, whose traits are passed to Prince Andrey together with the notions of fixity and duty and obligation. It is the noise of wheels that prevents him from hearing Pierre on the way to the ferry. At the crucial point in Prince Andrey's existence the images coalesce:

> The smoking shell spun like a top between him and the prostrate adjutant near a wormwood between the field and the meadow.
> "Can this be death?" thought Prince Andrey, looking with a quite new, envious glance at the grass, the wormwood, and the wisp of smoke that

curled up from the rotating black ball. "I cannot, I do not wish to die. I love life—I love this grass, this earth, this air. . . ." He thought this, and at the same time remembered that people were looking at him [and so did not throw himself to the ground].

"It's shameful, sir!" he said to the adjutant. "What. . . ."

He did not finish speaking. At one and the same moment came the sound of an explosion, a whistle of splinters as from a breaking frame, a suffocating smell of powder and Prince Andrey started to one side, raising his arm, and fell on his chest.

What follows while Andrey is dying is an elaboration and a gloss on this passage, the circularity and frame in his life shattered at last. Similar patterns of images and revelation by such detail, whether symbolic or not, exist throughout Tolstoy, from the black spot on the dead mother's face in *Childhood* to the red bag that Anna carries and that prevents her from throwing herself under the train at the first attempt, from the recalcitrant spring in the *Death of Ivan Ilych* to the doves that fly past Maslova's face at the beginning of *Resurrection,* from Irtenev's pince-nez in *The Devil* to the veiled Passion of *Master and Man,* and so on. They suggest readings and often clarify ambiguities that a more general discussion frequently cannot resolve; but tracing such patterns in Tolstoy has yet to become a central critical preoccupation.

Nor has Tolstoy's prose style been accorded enough attention. Henry James might have been surprised to learn that, like Dencombe in *The Middle Years,* Tolstoy was "a passionate corrector, a fingerer of style" who could scarcely ever reread his published work without the urge to rewrite and improve, and he could not have known that among the numerous drafts for Tolstoy's works many exist in a half-dozen or more versions, that there are fifteen extant openings of *War and Peace* and only slightly fewer for *Anna Karenina* and *Resurrection.* Studies of his changes in the text and of his style—they exist for the most part, of necessity, in Russian—indicate Tolstoy's enormous skill in refining and clarifying in order to reduce or eliminate the discrepancy between the written and the conceived. Certain features of style, however, are conveyed even in translation. These include not only the difference between the quantity and richness of descriptive passages in Tolstoy's works up to 1880 and in the so-called post-conversion works, the shift attendant upon his new vision from the complex periods of the earlier works to the terse simplicity of the latter, but also the peculiarities of style and sentence structure that accommodate so complex a view as Tolstoy's throughout his life. There is, for example, the ostensible increase of the didactic element in Tolstoy's later works. It is true that some of its forms change, from comment and explanation to exhortation, and that its direction shifts from the temporal, psychological, and ethical to the religious. But the didactic impulse was always very strong in Tolstoy and his creative work depended upon it from the first. Like other teachers, Tolstoy consistently uses certain devices: repetition, question and answer, enumeration, logical sequence. Frequently, however, the action or behavior of the characters directly contradicts their own or the narrator's rational, or at least reasonable, analysis. Prince Andrey reasons about life and cannon-fodder and Natasha, but he tarries with Pierre at the raft, avoids the men bathing in the pond, and regains his love in the exodus from Moscow—in each case ignoring the plans he had rationally formulated. In *Anna Karenina* the system is even more explicit: most things are explained with a great deal of logic and in sequence by the narrator and by certain characters. They occur "because," or "for the reason that," or "in view of"; but they are apprehended by a series of verbs that have little to do with causality or rationality: he or she "felt," "saw," "understood." Karenin enumerates the possibilities of behavior as though he were composing a protocol, but when he confronts Anna he makes an entirely different sort of appeal. His slip of the tongue when he stumbles over the word *suffer—perestradat'*, which starts first as *pele* then as *pede*—reveals another aspect of his personality only faintly suggested by the cracking of his knuckles.

There is a sense in which the later stories may contain even greater stylistic subtleties than the two great novels, where the very attempt to encompass so much frequently leads to a series of parallel clauses whose impact is that of accretion rather than of simultaneity. Perhaps the single most impressive instance occurs in the *Death of Ivan Ilych,* despite the satiric and didactic remarks that are present and even intrude throughout the story. Just before Ivan Ilych's death, when he sends his son out, the original reads: "—Uvedi . . . zhalko . . . i tebya . . . —On khotel skazat' esche 'prosti', no skazal 'propusti', i, ne v silakh uzhe buduchi popravit'-sya, makhnul rokoyu, znaya, chto poymet tot, komu nado." The passage may roughly be translated as " 'Take him away . . . pity for him . . . you too . . .'—He wanted to add 'forgive' but said 'forget' and no longer capable of correcting himself he waved his hand, knowing that He to whom it mattered would understand." The English can at best only approximate the Russian. Ivan Ilych speaks five words conveying four notions, in his weakness omitting the pronouns and repetitions that must be given in English. Most of the crucial words have at least two meanings. *Zhalko* falls somewhere between "I pity him" and "I'm sorry for him"; *prosti* usually means "forgive" but here implies finality; *propusti* means to "let through," "let pass," but it also means to "pass over" or "omit"—

to allow the son to go or to forget what has been said or done; *makhnul rokoyu* is the physical gesture of waving the arm but idiomatically also means to dismiss something; *popravit'sya* means to "correct oneself" but also to "get well." In simplest terms, the two imperatives, adverb, conjunction, and pronoun that Ivan Ilych speaks, his gesture, and his condition are a distillate of the story, repeatedly expressing in a single word two impulses—the physical and the spiritual—that contradict or complement each other. The understanding Ivan Ilych reaches and the pity that he feels are contrasted with his inability to communicate and his indifference whether he does, and the discovery that his salvation no longer depends on external expression but on inner conviction. The passage is the more striking for Tolstoy's emphasis on the hollow forms that had permeated Ivan Ilych's life before his illness, the recurrent adjectives *pleasant, decorous, acceptable, proper,* the use of imperfect tenses to convey the repetitiousness and routine of his life, and those adjectives emphasizing the uniformity of Ivan Ilych's life with all the other lives around him—*the same, equal to, just like,* and so forth.

The massive repetition of a single word and others closely related to it is characteristic of Tolstoy. The words *shame* and *horror* with their adjectival or adverbial derivatives dominate *Anna Karenina. Horror* is used ten times in the two-page chapter following Anna's seduction, and twenty other epithets related to it and to shame or guilt appear in the same space. The quasi-comic version, as always, appears with Stiva Oblonsky: *horror* is used five times in half a page when his infidelity is at issue, but it is used rather in the sense of "very much" or "terribly"; and it is used again as Vronsky breaks Frou-Frou's back, although the dominant word in that section is *neschastie*—"misfortune" or "misery." The reader without access to the original unfortunately has only a distorted view of the subtlety, precision, and tensions of Tolstoy's style, as also of the grosser effects that he, unlike his translators, did not hesitate to use. The variety of styles he uses is almost as large as the variety of life he represents—the differentiation of speech among all levels, classes, and callings, and among the representatives of the aristocracy, manorial or otherwise, that are the predominant subject of his work; the style of the folk tales, the primers, the religious stories, the polemics on theology, art, and history; the descriptions and commentary, each subordinated at every point to the larger purposes of his art.

Tolstoy's narrative techniques are equally rich and varied. Percy Lubbock, whose admiration for Tolstoy was somewhat vitiated by preconceptions about the novel form, maintained that a single point of view would have put *War and Peace* into proper perspective. But Tolstoy chose to convey as well as encompass reality and its multiple refractions wherever it may be—in Anna Scherer's salon, on the battlefields of Austerlitz and Borodino, at the hunt, in the council of war. The possibilities are immense. Kinetically they may be represented on a scale whose extremes are Prince Andrey's languid entrance at the soirée and Natasha's *grand jeté* into her mother's drawing room. The point of view constantly shifts, though the narrator's comments provide continuity and guide lines. Characters are not merely introduced or presented, they materialize before the reader through another character's eyes. The principle of organization is interrelation rather than focus. The single point of view was far too solipsistic and lacking in demonstrable reality for Tolstoy's purposes, though he was willing to attempt the form at least once in the first-person narration of *The Kreutzer Sonata*. The confessional form for ironic self-portraiture, a favorite device of Dostoevsky's, is so little attuned to Tolstoy's genius that it appears somewhat anomalous among his works. No doubt some portion of the verisimilitude achieved by Tolstoy can be directly attributed to the constant readjustment and refocusing that the shifts in point of view entail. So at the beginning of *Anna Karenina*, at the skating rink, Tolstoy presents Levin and Kitty through each other's eyes, but also through those of the attendant, the governess, Prince Shcherbatsky, and so on. Anna's triumph at the ball is the more surely communicated through Kitty's realization that something has occurred. Great art restructures a view of life, not life itself, heightening the essential at the expense of reality, as Tolstoy splendidly illustrates when he finally permits Levin and Anna to meet: Levin sees her portrait first and only after that the real figure. Anna is less dazzling than her portrait but she is alive in a way that art cannot be.

This scene accurately describes much of Tolstoy's own procedure. In the large novels multiple and diffuse presentation is essential to Tolstoy because he refused to detract from the fullness of his vision by constraining it in a ready and accepted form, which in any case could not accommodate so complex a picture of development, growth, and rebirth, of personal and national destiny. In a draft for a preface to *War and Peace,* Tolstoy maintained that every important Russian literary work has deviated from European examples and created its own form. In Tolstoy's case it may be added that the new forms attempt to destroy the logical progression and single point of view that would merely obscure his remarkably fresh confrontation of life. Even in the shorter works Tolstoy frequently avoids direct and continuous narrative as if to destroy mere plot. In *Hadji Murad* the result of an event is always revealed before presentation of the event itself and the constantly and rapidly shifting scenes reinforce the irony of mutual misunderstandings. *The Death of Ivan Ilych* reverses the temporal sequence of the two parts to emphasize the moment of illumination. Other stories, like *Two Hussars* or *Family Happiness,* mirror and contrast the opening with the closing part. Direct apprehension of reality again becomes possible. Insofar as form operates to that end, it may be viewed as another gesture in a stance central to Tolstoy's art.

The Russian formalist critic Victor Shklovsky has coined the term *ostranenie,* "estrangement" or "making it strange," to designate Tolstoy's method (and it could be extended to the stance behind it) for reasserting the reality behind the convention we have come to accept in its place. The method is simple: it refuses to accept the convention, treats it as real, and thereby exposes its conventionality. It works most strikingly when used to destroy conventions accepted by all as conventions, such as the theater or religious ritual. Throughout Natasha's visit to the opera Tolstoy ridicules the events on the stage by exposing their artificiality:

> In the second act there was scenery representing tombstones, and there was a round hole in the canvas to represent the moon, shades were raised over the footlights, and from the horns and contrabass came deep notes while many people appeared from right and left wearing black cloaks and holding things like daggers in their hands. They began waving their arms. Then some other people ran in and began dragging away the maiden who had been in white and was now in light blue. They did not drag her away at once, but sang with her for a long time, and then at last dragged her off, and behind the scenes something metallic was struck three times and everyone knelt down and sang a prayer. All these things were repeatedly interrupted by the enthusiastic shouts of the audience.

In *Resurrection* there is a striking depiction of holy communion in jail that makes explicit the perversion of Christianity implied in the juxtaposition jail-communion. Tolstoy writes of the deacon who

> sang in a merry tone of voice a song about the children eating the body of God and drinking his blood. After that the priest took the cup back with him behind the partition and finished all the remaining bits of God's flesh and drank all the remaining blood. Then he carefully sucked his moustache, wiped his beard and the cup, and came briskly out from behind the partition in the most cheerful frame of mind, his calfskin boots creaking slightly as he walked.

"Estrangement" is hardly an invention of Tolstoy's, the pose being that of the eiron whose simplicity triumphs over the guile of the shrewd and who has as a sure touchstone his spontaneous reaction to life around him; the literary antecedents are clear in works like *Gulliver's Travels* or Montesquieu's *Lettres Persanes.* But in Tolstoy's use there is a qualitative and quantitative difference, and what may itself be a convention can be conceived as the basic ingredient in Tolstoy's view and presentation of the world, as his characteristic method of apprehending truth, which, in *Sevastopol in May,* he called the unvarying hero of his tale. Gorky reports Tolstoy's remark that romanticism stems from the fear of looking into the eyes of truth. One might add that looking also requires a special talent, that Tolstoy had it to a superlative degree, from the first noting and communicating the discrepancy between expectation and event, between assumptions and actuality, between habitual and unique action. When the obscuring effect of custom evaporates, the full wonder and beauty of truth makes its impact on the viewer. It is perhaps for that reason that Tolstoy has come much closer to communicating the physical beauty and grandeur of the Caucusus than even the great Russian and English poets of the early nineteenth century. In a passage that may well convey Tolstoy's original experience the process is detailed:

"So this is where it begins," thought Olenin, and kept expecting to see the snowy mountains of which mention was so often made. Once toward evening the Nogay driver pointed with his whip to the mountains shrouded in clouds. Olenin looked eagerly, but it was dull and the mountains were almost hidden by the clouds. Olenin made out something grey and white and fleecy, but try as he would he could find nothing beautiful in the mountains of which he had so often read and heard. The mountains and the clouds appeared to him quite alike, and he thought the special beauty of the snow peaks, of which he had so often been told, was as much an invention as Bach's music and the love of women, in which he did not believe. So he gave up looking forward to seeing the mountains. But early next morning, being awakened in his cart by the freshness of the air, he glanced carelessly to the right. The morning was perfectly clear. Suddenly he saw, about twenty paces away as it seemed to him at first glance, pure white gigantic masses with delicate contours, the distinct fantastic outlines of their summits showing sharply against the far-off sky. When he had realized the distance between himself and them and the sky and the whole immensity of the mountains, and felt the infinitude of all that beauty, he became afraid it was but a phantasm or a dream. He gave himself a shake to rouse himself, but the mountains were still the same. "What's that? What is it?" he asked the driver. "Why, the mountains," the Nogay driver answered indifferently.

The opposite is equally possible, as in Nikolai Rostov's and Sonya's declaration of love, when the transvested hussar recognizes his love for Sonya, who is herself in man's clothing, wearing a moustache and smelling of the burnt cork used in her mummery. There is indeed a constant process of distortion and realignment in Tolstoy's work that forces the reader to question normal assumptions and accept the estrangement of reality.

The device is used in many ways and often far more subtly than in the examples given, and like most things in Tolstoy it exists throughout his work. There is the difference between the expectation of war and the reality in the *Sevastopol Sketches*; the use of *someone, something,* and *somewhere* in describing Baron Pest's bayonetting a Frenchman to indicate the impossibility of this having been an action one might at the moment have conceived in human and personal terms; the contrast that makes Hadji Murad's exotic dress, Tartar speech, and occasional violent cruelty seem dignified, natural, and comprehensible, while the Vorontsovs' boredom and French conversation seem quite artificial; facial expressions contradict what is said; officers picnic and enjoy themselves as the battle of Enns is about to begin; Kholstomer, a marvel of repulsive equine debility, turns out to be a once-famous trotter and in every way more useful than his master. The list could be extended at will, for Tolstoy applied the process to everything he contemplated.

In retrospect, Tolstoy's "psychological eavesdropping" may be an even more important aspect of his art as it certainly is more influential as an innovation. No one before Tolstoy had presented so scrupulously the minute and occasionally trivial fluctuations of mood and impulse, had indicated the proliferations of thought and feelings within an entirely new time scheme, or had analyzed them in such detail and with so much finesse. Tolstoy combined in an original and unique way the psychological revelations of Rousseau's *Confessions* with the associative psychology and arbitrary or relative expansion of time in Sterne, supplying precise analysis, following from inside the mind the contours of the individual's search for answers or at least for satisfactory meanings. The early fragment *A History of Yesterday* states the underlying principles—the protean changes man undergoes while maintaining his individuality, the contradictory impulses of a man whose consciousness and will are divided so that his actions and thoughts diverge, and even the theory of dreams Tolstoy formulated in which a tentative solution is found—although Tolstoy had not yet discovered the artistic means to present all these in his fiction. The elements recur in various ways and combinations, but the solution, if there is a solution, is the same. The gist of Pierre's dream before the battle of Borodino, induced by a word barely impinging on his consciousness as by his efforts throughout the novel, is "to harness," so that his natural forces will operate with unity and direction.

No subject is too trivial for Tolstoy as a starting point and none too complex at the end. Between starting point and end there are two essential lines of development. The first is perhaps the true line of psychological eavesdropping. It begins with the relatively simple questions that run through the mind of the ten-year-old protagonist at the beginning of *Childhood* as he wonders whether he may ever be forgiven, how he could have thought such cruel things, and what his feelings really are. It leads to such limited reflections as Nikolai Rostov's "will I or will I not," "am I a coward or not," and the infinitely more complex questions pondered by Pierre, Andrey, or Levin. The other line makes a startling appearance in *Sevastopol in May,* in the multiplicity of thoughts and sensations that run through a man's mind in the split second between the detonation of a shell and his death, and reappears as the interior monologue more directly related to the visible and audible world, as in Anna's trip to the railroad station at the end of Part Seven. There hardly seems to be any aspect of human behavior that Tolstoy cannot transmit either by communicating the thoughts of his characters or by indicating their gestures—each with the authority of genuine and legitimate understanding.

There were few truths Tolstoy could not contemplate directly. His critical intelligence could detect the flaw in any scheme that might have provided an acceptable version of what the world ought to be rather than what he knew it was, and his artistic sense rarely failed him, even in expressing the enormous contradictions of his own personality and life. Tolstoy was one of the most integrated of writers, expressing at every point his personality through his art, and vice-versa. It is perfectly possible to conceive his crisis, which was surely at bottom moral, psychological, and philosophical, as having a large measure of artistic crisis. It was perhaps also Tolstoy's growing realization that his earlier masterpieces could not be duplicated, that a new form, a new style, new artistic approaches would have to be devised, that led him to his dubious moral and religious positions after 1880, rather than what D. H. Lawrence called the vehement cowardice with which Tolstoy rejected all that was great in himself. Among the most significant and lasting struggles was that between his ingrained aristocracy and his futile attempt to simplify himself in dress, demands, views, and actions. He could hardly help being aware of the falseness of his position, as his final flight would indicate. But like all else in his life, that too is a constant of his work, from the chapters in his quasi-autobiographical trilogy *Childhood, Boyhood, Youth,* which dealt with the concept of *comme il faut,* to Prince Andrey, who dies of it, and Father Sergey and Nekhlyudov in *Resurrection,* who attempt to overcome it. There is one sense of aristocracy, the most superficial, which is too insignificant to obscure the inner man, and even as a youth Tolstoy overcame it. But there is another which Tolstoy never eliminated, a question of innate nobility rather than externalities, implied too in those splendid *Memoires* he inspired Gorky to write. It is no longer superficial manners, good behavior, or neatness, but an indicator of something deeper. In a draft of *War and Peace* he justifies his choice of high society as the core of his novel, finding his identification with the aristocracy as his best reason, but concludes with the most succinct and telling criticism ever made of an important aspect of Russian literature: "I am an aristocrat because I cannot believe in the high intellect, the refined taste, or the absolute honesty of a man who picks his nose and who belches." It is that view of aristocracy expressed here that permeates Tolstoy's characters, who, when they are not satirically portrayed, are completely integrated even in their shortcomings. Pierre's slovenliness is a reflection of his spiritual chaos and enthusiasms and as such is merely a fact not a judgment. Hadji Murad's religious devotion, cleanliness, certitude as to when to honor commitments or ignore them are functions of his moral probity and innate nobility. Tolstoy's wrath appears only when externals become empty forms, as with Nicholas I, Napoleon, or others he considered charlatans and worse.

It seems foolish to try to summarize what Tolstoy was and what he said. It may be impossible to do more than to suggest a few possibilities about his artistic achievement. He possessed whole areas of interest foreign to the aesthetic temperament—his interest in pedagogy, theology, political, historical, and economic theory. In part these are subjects for specialists in those fields, though no one who wishes to understand Tolstoy thoroughly can afford to ignore his theories and writings and their relevance to his development and total view, if not their relevance to the sciences in question. Tolstoy seems to have anticipated all the objections himself, refusing in the final analysis even to accept his genius. Yet it is perhaps more accurate to say that for complex reasons he was incapable of accepting even that order that he had been able to impose upon the world—"art is a lie, an arbitrary sham, harmful to people," he told Gorky. "One writes not what real life is, but simply what one thinks of life oneself. What good is that to anyone, how I see that tower or sea or Tartar—what interest or use is there in it?" Most readers find great interest in it and many find some use as well. For of all modern writers Tolstoy came closest in his search for what Henry Adams called "a historical formula that should satisfy the conditions of the stellar universe." Some readers find the work and the man behind them so extraordinary that, like Gorky, they fall into the error of designating him godlike, an epithet clearly unmerited by the person and one he would object to if it were accorded on the basis of his art; for while recognizing his artistic greatness and taking pride in it, he also knew the difference between art and theurgy. A very few have been able to follow the implications of his art without being diverted by Tolstoy's misrepresentations of his purposes or by their own predilections. Among these was Rainer Maria Rilke, who had met Tolstoy and who in 1915 wrote to a friend what may well be the deepest appreciation of Tolstoy and the closest possible rephrasing of his import and the elusive principle of integration in his work:

His enormous experience of nature (I know of hardly anyone who was initiated so passionately into nature) put him wonderfully in a position to think and write from a total standpoint, from a life sense through which death was so finely diffused that it seemed to be contained everywhere for him, like some rare and characteristic seasoning to the pungent savor of life. But it was precisely because of this that he knew such a profound and helpless fear when he realized that somewhere death in the pure state existed,—as if it were a flask full of death, or this hateful cup with the broken handle and insensate legend "Faith, Hope, and Charity," from which we are compelled to drink of the bitterness of undiluted death. This man had observed in himself and others many forms of the death-fear, for his natural self-possession enabled him to be the observer of his own terrors, and his relationship to death was such that his fear must have been marvellously permeated in the end, a regular fugue of fear, a gigantic building, a tower of fear with corridors and stairways and landings without banisters and vertiginous drops on either side—yet the intensity with which he still felt and admitted this prodigal fear of his may in the last moment—who knows?—have turned into some unapproachable reality, may suddenly have become the solid ground beneath this tower, the landscape and the sky overhead and the wind and the birds wheeling around it. . . .

Tolstoy as Man and Artist

by Renato Poggioli

More than fifty years ago, on a day in November 1910, Leo Tolstoy left his estate of Yasnaya Polyana to seek that freedom of the spirit which he was to attain only a few days later, when he met his death at the station of Astapovo. The late George Orwell found it fitting to compare Tolstoy's death to that of King Lear; Sir Isaiah Berlin—to the end of Oedipus at Colonus. These two parallels reveal different and yet similar insights: they seem to complete each other and to illuminate evenly, although from different angles, the mournful and lofty scene. Those who witnessed it saw dying, in the humble surroundings of a stationmaster's house, a rare, or rather a unique, human being: someone who had been a king, like Lear, who, like Oedipus, had become almost a saint.

The paradox of Tolstoy's death is but the last of the many paradoxes of his life. The series opens with the paradox of his birth. It would be unwise to forget that he was born a nobleman, and that he remained aristocratic in temper even after he had embraced the cause of the common man, and had started exalting the Russian peasant over all other classes and types of human beings. It took the plebeian and proletarian Gorky to guess that not even the trauma of conversion had stifled within Tolstoy the unconscious feeling of belonging to the breed of the masters: to find out that even though he would live, dress, and act like a man of the people, refusing to be addressed as "Count," the old man remained at heart a Russian *barin,* accustomed to being obeyed, served, or, at least, revered. There is no doubt that Tolstoy's personality can be fully understood and assessed only by taking into account the role that pride played in his behaviour or in his make-up: and by keeping in mind that in him the pride of the self was never wholly severed from the pride of blood and breeding.

The second paradox is that both his birth and temper made of him

"Tolstoy as Man and Artist" by Renato Poggioli. From *Oxford Slavonic Papers*, X (1962). Reprinted in *The Spirit of the Letter* by Renato Poggioli (Cambridge: Harvard University Press, 1965). Reprinted by permission of Mrs. R. Poggioli and the Oxford University Press.

a conservative, while reason and faith turned him into a radical. Tolstoy was a moral, not a social, radical: a fact which may have been not fully clear to many Tolstoyans, but which did not escape the lucid observation of Lenin. The latter maintained that Tolstoy's thinking and preaching were patriarchal and autocratic in character, and reactionary in spirit. Whether or not this is true, we must confess that the socio-psychological formula which the radical critic Nikolay Mikhaylovsky coined in order to define Tolstoy and the members of his class who followed his teachings was, at least as applied to him, rather inept. The Tolstoy who developed after the writing of *A Confession* was no "repentant nobleman": he rather resembled a feudal lord who had exchanged the sword for the cross, while preserving his haughty nature under a monk's cassock.

Tolstoy's ethical and intellectual radicalism never implied the belief that man could transform his own being and transcend himself. The only change he viewed as both necessary and possible was a "change of heart." He had himself undergone such a change and felt that his fellow men could do what he had done. He was willing and even eager to help them while they were striving towards that end: but his aid consisted more in words than in deeds. The most he would do was to set an example, and he thought that this should be enough. This is why his action was on the whole more negative than positive in character. In the Europe, or rather in the world, of the end of the nineteenth century and the beginning of the twentieth, he played the role of a supreme conscientious objector. By using our terms merely in their etymological sense, we could say that he was more of a "protestant" or a "dissenter" than a "reformer."

What Tolstoy preached was in effect that others should convert themselves as he had converted himself. In practice, as a convert and a converter, he gave nothing more, and nothing less, than a "counsel of perfection." His ideal was that each man could for ever feel as Konstantin Levin, one of his favorite heroes, did feel at a given moment of his own personal experience: "He felt himself, and did not want to be anyone else. All he wanted now was to be better than before." These words seem to prove that Tolstoy never thought seriously that human nature could be fundamentally changed. The idea of "changing life" never held for this conservative in radical dress the seductive attraction it had for many of his contemporaries, such as Nietzsche and Rimbaud, or his fellow Russian, Dostoevsky. Yet, paradoxically, it is precisely one of the commands of Nietzsche—*Werde der du bist,* "Become who you are"—which best conveys the Tolstoyan view of the conversion process:

a view which betrays the aristocratic conception of the supreme worth
of the separate person, as well as the Christian conception of the absolute value of each individual soul.

Perhaps because we know that he was a spiritual disciple of Jean-
Jacques Rousseau, or of a man who had been born a Calvinist, we are
tempted to find protestant elements in Tolstoy's beliefs. Whether or not
we are right in doing so, we can certainly point out that, outside Russia,
his religious ideas affected the English and the American spirit far more
deeply than, for instance, the French intellect, or the Latin mind in
general. At any rate, it seems evident that there are protestant components in Tolstoy's idea of the self. He viewed the self primarily as
"heart": as a heart moved by both ethos and pathos, ruled by sentiment
as well as by conscience, ceaselessly echoing the urgings of its inner voice,
which is also the voice of the spirit. He felt that man is really human
only when he listens to that voice; and thought that he who understands
it aright will never go wrong. In order to hear its promptings, man must
constantly turn toward his inner being: hence the practice of introspection, with the consequent habit, in Tolstoy's own case, of keeping
for most of his life those diaries which were the very mirrors of his soul.
In this we see another of Tolstoy's paradoxes: such lifelong preoccupation with one's psyche reveals at once the humble shame of the sinner
and the proud glory of the chosen, inextricably joining self-hatred and
self-love in a single knot.

Yet Tolstoy's idea of the self is based on a cult of the person which
avoids the pitfalls of the "cult of personality." This great Russian always
exalted the unique, native originality of every human being: a birth-
right which man could easily lose by conforming too strictly to the
conventional patterns of social life. It is obvious that Tolstoy understood that originality in a psychological, rather than in an intellectual
or cultural, key. He founded this conception not on the romantic notion
of "genius," but on the Rousseauistic and eighteenth century notion of
génie. The second of these two terms indicates not a complex organization of the highest faculties, nor an extraordinary endowment of exceptional powers, but the inarticulate virtues of simplicity and freshness,
marking a "temperament" which relies only on its innermost resources.

It was in accordance with such a view that Tolstoy moulded and
shaped practically all his creatures, his negative no less than his positive
characters, those who are untrue to their nature as well as those who
are loyal to it. He placed together on one side, without distinguishing
too much the ones from the others, the figures which are "romantic"
and those which are merely vulgar, such as Olenin and Prince Andrey,

or Aleksey Vronsky and Aleksey Karenin. He placed on the other side the all too many for whom truth is a question or a quest, and the fewer who have attained a wisdom of their own, such as Pierre Bezukhov and Konstantin Levin, or Uncle Eroshka and Hadji Murat. He loved fully only the latter, especially if they were naïve and humble, unaware of their rare worth and dignity, like Platon Karataev, or Gerasim, the faithful servant of the dying Ivan Ilich. It is in the portrayal of such characters (the more exalted the more they abase themselves) that Tolstoy seems to fulfil better than anybody else the demands of the Russian genius. It was according to such demands that Dostoevsky sought to elevate on the highest pedestal of his art the meek and saintly figures of Alyosha the novice, Zosima the "elder," and Prince Myshkin, the fool of God; yet, against his intention and beyond his will, he instead achieved the opposite feat, raising his most magnificent statues to such sombre heroes as Raskolnikov and Ivan Karamazov. Tolstoy, however, succeeded where Dostoevsky had failed: it fell to him to accomplish what D. H. Lawrence considered the chosen task of Russian literature, i.e. to depict "the phenomenal coruscation of the soul of quite commonplace people."

The man exalting the inner voice is a fanatic of a sincerity which might be defined as subjective truth. He constantly tends to confuse sincerity with objective truth, and this is why he is frequently tempted to identify both qualities with beauty, as well as with goodness. "The hero of my story," wrote the young author of *The Tales of Sebastopol,* "the one I love with all my soul, which I have tried to depict in all its beauty; which has been, is, and will for ever be beautiful—is the truth." The older Tolstoy knew how to distinguish between subjective and objective truth, and realized that the latter is rarely beautiful. Yet he never ceased to believe that the former is always good. In short, he remained for all his life a fanatic of sincerity. In this he resembled Molière's Alceste, who becomes a misanthrope precisely because he learns, through the trial of experience and the ordeal of social intercourse, that reality and sincerity rarely meet, or do so only in strife and contest.

The misanthrope *à la* Alceste is a mere disappointed and embittered lover of mankind, who ends by hating his fellow men because they are false to themselves as well as to the moral code. Despite his philanthropic bent, Tolstoy all too often behaved like a misanthrope of this kind. He turned his *saeva indignatio* primarily against society and its institutions, including religion and culture, following in this the example of Rousseau, but going farther than his master in the indictment of the sciences and the arts. His wrath did not spare individuals, especially those exercising social functions, like politicians and bureaucrats, career officers and professional people, lawyers and judges, teachers and priests, and even writers and artists. At bottom he never fully believed that man is born good, and that his only corrupter is the world. If Tolstoy remained a Christian, it was above all in his inborn suspicion of the old Adam in himself, as well as in his fellow men.

Tolstoy's misanthropy was then a matter of both his mind and his heart, being equally rooted in the lucid pessimism of his observation and in the noble idealism of his ethical vision. In view of this one should correct in at least this instance Coleridge's famous aphorism, according to which every man is either an Aristotelian or a Platonist. In Tolstoy's case one should say that he was the one and the other at the same time. One could even modernize this statement by asserting that while there is something of either Pascal or Voltaire in each human being, in Tolstoy there was something of both. The truth of this is evident in his writings of evangelical exegesis and scriptural controversy. When Tolstoy is able or willing to take a positive attitude towards a given aspect of the Christian tradition because it seems to agree with the demands of his conscience, he gives that aspect the docile and total assent of his heart, like Pascal. But when he feels that he must take a negative stand against another aspect of the same tradition because he finds it irreconcilable with the demands of his mind, then he rejects that aspect with the rebellious and uncompromising denial of his reason, which he utters with the bitter mockery of a new Voltaire.

How simple-minded and straightforward was Tolstoy's "grammar of dissent" may be shown by a single example. There is a passage in *A Critique of Dogmatic Theology* in which he attacks the credibility of the account in Genesis of the creation of the world. In this attack Tolstoy did not hesitate to employ, with the sarcastic grin of heavy irony, one of the most obvious and trivial arguments of positivistic polemics against Christianity. If "there was a morning and an evening on the first day," but "there was no sun until the fourth," said Tolstoy in a crucial phrase of that passage, then "God must have himself shaken the illuminating matter so that there might be a morning and an evening." We find it highly significant that Dostoevsky had once chosen to report the same argument, but with an opposite intention: not to challenge the word of God through the lay authority of science and reason, but to expose what religion calls a "scandal," in this case the scandal of a cheap blasphemy, of a vile incredulity. After rephrasing and refashioning it into the shape of a rhetorical question, Dostoevsky attributed the argument in his great novel *The Brothers Karamazov* to the still childish but already base which goes under the name of *Everyman* is indeed a "classical" work. There are in Tolstoy's canon many works which are classical in the same sense—works which are at once moral parables or even "morality plays" like *Everyman*. Such are *The Death of Ivan Ilich* and *Master and Servant*, both of which treat the supreme Christian theme, which is the response of Everyman to the challenge of mortality. In both Everyman finds his own transfiguration in the epiphany of death: he seems to follow literally Goethe's command—*Stirb und werde*, "Die and become," since he fulfils himself and understands the meaning of life only when his life ends. In these, and in other pieces of the same kind, Tolstoy, this classic of modern realism who distrusted all sorts of mysticism and symbolism, this Christian who doubted eternal life and disbelieved in the immortality of the soul, was able to convey an allegorical vision the like of which the western world had hardly seen since the waning of medieval culture and the decline of religious art.

This implies that Tolstoy was endowed with a lucid critical outlook, as well as with a deep poetic insight. All too few of his interpreters have given due credit to the keenness of his literary flair, to the conscious and deliberate craft with which he handles and hammers literary forms. One of the most cherished theories of that group of Russian critics who called themselves Formalists, and who briefly flourished during the early years after the Revolution, was that literary genres are born, grow, and die through the dialectics of imitation and parody. Such a process (which for them took place within the broad framework of literary history, beyond the limitations of individual writers or separate works) seems to reproduce and to repeat itself, as it were in a nutshell, in several of Tolstoy's creations. In at least one case the process appears so complex as to involve more than a single genre. This is what happens in *War and Peace*, a composition so vast and so manifold as to suggest the reworking of three different genres, each one of which ultimately defeats or transcends itself.

Tolstoy's masterpiece is in the first place a historical novel "debunking" history and denying that historical development has any purpose or sense; then an epic indicting warfare, deglamorizing military valor and the martial virtues, tearing glory's laurels from the brows of the false heroes who presume to hold the destiny of the world in their hands; finally, a national or universal drama which through the ordeal of blood, sweat, and tears ends by yielding to the sweet routine of daily life and turns into a family idyll. Most critics tend to emphasize its epic quality, and in so doing they find support in the authority of Tolstoy, who defined his masterpiece as "Homeric." After admitting the fitness of the epithet,

mind of the flunkey, Smerdyakov. It is with an impious sneer that the latter questions his devout tutor who is reading aloud from the Scriptures: "Where did the light come from on the first day if God created the sun and the stars on the fourth?"

The fact that in his quest after truth Tolstoy was never repelled by the pettiness or the bad taste of common sense reasoning is a sign of strength, not of weakness. Yet the search itself caused a perpetual conflict between his reason and his sentiment, between his intellect and his conscience. This conflict was far more serious and painful than another of his inner rifts, the one in which most of his biographers saw the supreme crisis of his life, the climax of all his contradictions and paradoxes. For the last thirty years of his long existence a steady conflict, apparently without truce or issue, seemed to arm against each other Tolstoy the preacher and Tolstoy the writer, Tolstoy the moralist and Tolstoy the artist. We think that too much has been made of this conflict. Tolstoy had always been, even before his conversion, a writer with a message; and even after his conversion he magnificently performed his artist's task, as he had himself defined it at the time when he was writing his two greatest novels: "A writer's aim is not to settle a question once and for all, but to compel the reader to see life in all its forms, which are endless."

Yet it remains true that this great and splendid writer despised literature as a profession; and that even when he took his calling seriously, he never thought that art has no end but itself. For this reason he appears to be the only exception, among the main literary creators of the modern age, to a rule once laid down by Rainer Maria Rilke that "the writer is the poet of a world which differs from the one of which he is the prophet." The world of Tolstoy the creator and the world of Tolstoy the prophet may not fully coincide, but they are closely related to each other. Even those who find that the digressions on history mar such a masterpiece as *War and Peace*, or that the tract on marriage spoils the effect of *The Kreutzer Sonata*, must admit that only by being as opinionated as he was, could Tolstoy have written what and how he did. This was obscurely felt by the same Rilke, who in his youth had visited Tolstoy. Despite his conviction that an artist must sacrifice everything to his craft, the Austrian poet admitted in one of his last letters that Tolstoy's creative figure had remained "touchingly valid and safe even when rebelling against his greatest and most evident duties."

The unity of Tolstoy is thus to be seen in a consistent interplay of all the contrasting factors of his extraordinary personality. There took place a constant dialogue and exchange, as well as a continuous controversy and debate, among the many souls dwelling within his breast. At times he was keenly aware of the problematic, as well as of the dialectical, character of his own nature: on such occasions Tolstoy the *heautontimoroumenos* would unexpectedly reveal the serenity of an almost god-like being. This happened once in a Crimean grove. The old man, who was in Gorky's company, suddenly heard, and immediately recognized, the song of a little bird. He then spoke glowingly to his younger friend of the mating habits of the tiny creature. The literal-minded disciple could not refrain from remarking that in *The Kreutzer Sonata* the master had spoken far differently of the not too dissimilar sexual *mores* of humans. To which, Gorky relates, the wise old man replied, with an Olympian smile: "But I am not a chaffinch."

If he was not a chaffinch as a creature, neither was he one as a creator. He built most of his literary creations on a maze of contradictions, at times of a labyrinthine complexity. Yet he never got lost in their meanderings or ambiguities: he always held in his hand a sort of Ariadne's thread. He knew his way out as well as his way in, being endowed with a strong sense of orientation and direction, always sensing in what part of the sky he could find his bearings. To change the metaphor, one could say that his greatest merit or virtue was that he consistently took sides, and it matters little whether they were right or wrong. They were right in most cases: at all events one could fairly claim that even in his most spontaneous writings Tolstoy was in a sense a tendentious writer who wanted to make a point and generally succeeded in making it.

Let us look for instance at an early tale, the mediocre *Two Hussars,* where the point fails to come through. This story, significantly, is composed like a diptych. The "two hussars" of the title are father and son. More or less at the same age, but at an interval in time of about thirty years, they happen to arrive in the same place, to become the guests of the same family, and to meet, in a different manner, the same incidents. The symmetry of the situation, and the sharp contrast between the two different outcomes, appear all too deliberately contrived. The writer makes the first of the two officers behave like an attractive rake, and the second like a repulsive cad. Tolstoy does so precisely because his aristocratic and conservative temper compels him to feel a sentimental indulgence for the dashing behavior of the nobles of the old generation, and an utter contempt for the mean and calculating conduct of their degenerate offspring. This is perhaps the only one of all Tolstoy's works in which he takes an outright romantic stand, based essentially on prejudice. Here Tolstoy plays with loaded dice: and we acknowledge

the retribution of poetic justice in the author's failure, in t of his entire stake.

It is evident that Tolstoy plays the same sort of high-l in another early tale, which is also a diptych, *Domestic H* there is no doubt that in this case he gets away with it wager. The first part of the story evokes the bright poetry ol love to make only more striking the representation in the se the grey prose of married life. The happiness of marriage life is for Tolstoy a reality, while romantic love is only a pas of youth. Yet that happiness may well seem without gla wrongly compared with passion, or rather with its dreams. moral of the fable: a moral which is ultimately drawn by tl partner, whom Tolstoy makes, with supreme irony, the narr story and the reluctant witness to his masculine truth. The of the *fiançailles* and the evocation of the protagonist's virgina are so astoundingly beautiful that it would be difficult to ecstatic pages in all the literature of romantic love. This is critics tend to think that the two parts contradict each other, ar artist should have been satisfied with the first, or more poetic, diptych. Such a view shows a complete misunderstanding of t and his work. D. H. Lawrence once said that one should tru writer but the tale. In this case we are forced to trust both, eve we know that *Domestic Happiness* was inspired by a personal e and dictated by a personal *parti pris*. That experience was a which failed—as Tolstoy wished to believe—through the fault o Only Tolstoy could have succeeded in creating a masterpiece out guided and wrongheaded attempt to prove that, had the marria place, it too would have failed, and again through no fault of

Notwithstanding its autobiographical basis and despite its personal bias, *Domestic Happiness* ends by winning over the rea the simple wisdom of an apologue or a parable. This fact is sig since it reveals that Tolstoy's liking for the apologue or the para a matter of taste, which later found a higher justification or s in his pedagogical theories or evangelical doctrines. It was in known passage in *What is Art?* that Tolstoy was to define the as the purest and the highest of all literary forms. Yet he had parables far earlier, even before composing his folk-tales or the fables he later collected in his school readers. It was not only as m but also as artist that Tolstoy cherished that literary vehicle. T. S once surprised and persuaded us by affirming that the medieval

we must reject the author's further claim that *War and Peace* is a new *Iliad*. It is rather a new *Odyssey*, resembling the second Homeric poem in theme and tone, and retelling the same story, which is the belated but happy return of the warrior to his land, his farm, and his home.

By spreading over an immense range of human experience, *War and Peace* gives the impression of an enormous polyptych. Yet, if we look closer, we shall see that in effect we have to do with an almost end-less series of diptychs. The novel's narrative structure is based on the regular alternation of events and scenes which contrast with each other in both subject and mood. Most observers have remarked that warlike episodes alternate with peaceful ones. Few, however, have noticed that in the sections dealing with war, actions on the battlefield suddenly break off to give place to activities unfolding in the rear, at headquarters or in the barrack-room. In the sections dealing with peace the repre-sentation of city life likewise yields in its turn to the evocation of the simpler life of the countryside. Urban life itself is depicted in parallel scenes, opposing in succession the *mores* of St. Petersburg, courtly, bureau-cratic, and European in character, to those of Moscow, oldfashioned, patriarchal, utterly Russian in spirit.

All these reciprocal oppositions are subordinated to the most inclusive and significant of all contrasts, which underlies the whole work and sets two rival worlds against each other. The first is the public world, which includes not only politics, diplomacy, and war, but also society, with its manners, its culture, and its arts. The second is the private world, exemplified by the family and its way of life, within which the individual finds his proper place, like a bird in its nest. The first of these two worlds stands for all that is artificial in the human condition; the other, for all that is natural in men and things. Despite its title this book does not celebrate the victory of Kutuzov or the defeat of Napoleon, the triumph of the Russian people or the catastrophe of the French, but the tides of being, with their ebbs and flows. In brief, this immense poem in prose sings only of the perennial resurrection of life from the ashes of the historical process. Thus even this purest of all Tolstoy's masterpieces is up to a point a tendentious work. One might claim that the whole edi-fice rests on a single rhetorical device: on the recurrence of a series of invidious comparisons which make the wars and peaces of history look vain and petty when confronted with the peaces and wars of life and nature, which are love and death.

The foundations of *Anna Karenina* are grounded on the opposition of the ethos of family life and the pathos of unlawful love. Thus the struc-ture of the second of Tolstoy's great novels is very similar to that of the first. Even here the fundamental opposition merges with parallel and lesser contrasts, such as those between "town" and "country," the new and the old capital, the frivolities of 'high life' and the labors of the fields. Here we have, however, a novel of modern life, without hopes for a better future or longings after a better past. The reader is confronted with two dramas, the one public, the other private. Socially *Anna Karenina* is a "tragedy of manners," or, as Dostoevsky would say, a "drawing-room tragedy." But morally it is another version of what the old Tolstoy, in a conversation reported by Gorky, was to call the worst of all tragedies: the "tragedy of the bedroom." But it was chiefly in the discreet treatment, and indirect representation, of the latter that Tolstoy again showed that his talent consisted in a unique fusion of literary intelligence and ethical insight.

It is evident that Tolstoy projected Anna's drama through a double perspective, based on the sublime absurdity of the Christian injunction to love the sinner and to hate his sin. He wanted the reader to be merciful, not merciless as was society, which punished Anna not for sinning but for confessing her passion before the world; yet he wanted him to be severe, as well as merciful. Anna was to be pitied but not absolved, nor was her guilt to be forgiven. Tolstoy realized, however, that in order to determine such an ideal moral balance he had to pass over in silence the fatal moment when Anna yields once and for ever to the seduction of sin. For a psychologist like Tolstoy, who looked with clear eyes at the 'facts of life', and who later dared to tear all veils from the realities of sexual love, this was not an easy thing to do. Yet, had he done otherwise, he would have hardly escaped one or the other of two pitfalls: on one hand the naturalistic portrayal, on the other the romantic idealization, of the sexual act. Tolstoy knew that Anna Karenina could not undergo the self-inflicted indignities of an Emma Bovary. He also knew that she could be neither a Francesca nor an Iseult: that neither she nor her creator could speak aloud of her sin. This is why, with great intellectual courage, he made an act of renunciation, motivated not by puritan scruples but by an artist's concern. In brief, he resisted the temptation of describing Anna's fall. Anna's fall takes place outside the novel, behind closed doors: and the author reports it, anticlimactically, as a *fait accompli*. We are informed of what has just occurred by a series of suspension dots, which open a chapter dealing only with what happens immediately afterwards.

Notwithstanding the 'domestic happiness' of Levin and Kitty, *Anna Karenina* does not end, like *War and Peace,* on a note of serenity. The second of Tolstoy's great novels conveys a sense of crisis, which seems to threaten the foundations of being and puts into question all that men live by. Yet *Anna Karenina* is not a tragedy, even though we earlier employed in connection with it such formulas as "drawing-room tragedy" and "tragedy of the bedroom." The former is in reality a tragicomedy, while the latter is too sordid to deserve that lofty name, as Tolstoy well knew. If even *Anna Karenina,* which is ruled more fully than any other creation by the 'high seriousness' of its author's inspiration, cannot be characterized as "tragic," then we must infer that Tolstoy's genius tended to that "avoidance of tragedy" which according to Erich Heller marks all that Goethe thought and wrote.

We can see the triumph of that negative tendency in *The Kreutzer Sonata,* in *The Powers of Darkness,* and in the third and last of Tolstoy's novels, *Resurrection.* It would be hard to find a more tragic subject than that of *The Kreutzer Sonata,* into which Tolstoy also introduced the Dionysian theme of the mysterious bonds between love and music. It may suffice to compare the *Sonata* with the pathetic imitation and involuntary parody on the same theme which Thomas Mann wrote in his *Tristan,* to realize that in Tolstoy there is a far deeper sense of evil than in any of the naturalistic or decadent masters of the West. Yet, by representing sex as a repulsive disease of both body and soul, he made of *The Kreutzer Sonata* a hybrid work, "contaminating" the Christian parable and the naturalistic *tranche de vie.* The same can be said of the so-called "peasant tragedy," *The Powers of Darkness,* a "morality play" written in a naturalistic key. As for *Resurrection,* the tragic curve of transgression and retribution is there replaced by the straight line of a new 'pilgrim's progress'.

There were two primary reasons why Tolstoy felt alien that tragic vision of life which was so congenial to the imagination of Dostoevsky. The first was a strong sense of the realities of nature, based on the inexorable and ineluctable law of the death of all things. The second was the eighteenth century quality of his mind which, in a sense and up to a point, was that of a *moraliste* and a *philosophe.* This last factor motivated his avoidance of the tragic even more than his evangelism. Like Alceste, he was a *raisonneur:* or, if we prefer it, a kind of modern Socrates, always refusing to heed Nietzsche's summons to the old Socrates, i.e. to "learn music." It was this rejection of "the spirit of music" that determined the nihilistic tendencies of all Tolstoy's aesthetic and critical writings: his denial of poetry and art; his condemnation of some of the most classical works of the western tradition; his libels on Beethoven and Shakespeare, and other luminaries of the human spirit.

We may resent his strictures against Beethoven and Shakespeare, but we are willing to admit that he was far from wrong in indicting some of the artistic trends of his age, which is also ours. He was certainly right in uttering his anathema against that modern heresy, the idolatry of art. Yet in order to do so he did not need to become an aesthetic iconoclast. The same can be said of his unfair mistrust of cultural values in general. Yet, if he tended to paint "the grey tree of thought" even greyer than it is, it is only because he also tended to paint "the green tree of life" with hues far brighter than its natural ones. Charles Du Bos once said that "if life could write, it would write just as Tolstoy did." We find these words misleading, even though we understand what the French critic meant by them. When he rewrites life, Tolstoy enriches and enhances it. He always conveys our sense of being with greater intensity and fullness than we apprehend it in reality.

The midsummer-night dream of a girl, retelling that dream to her friend, while they gaze from the window of a villa at the starry sky and at the darkness of the empty fields; the intimate conversations of two friends, broken by spells of silence sealing the reciprocal understanding of their souls while they are crossing a river on a ferry at dusk; the wild sledge ride of a Christmas party of young men and women, caressed by the cold wind and lulled by their bliss: all of us have experienced such moments at least once in our lives. Yet neither our perception of them, nor their rehearsal through imagination and memory, seems to possess the magic quality which marks their reflection in the mirror of Tolstoy's art.

Most critics overemphasize the median and moderate temper of Tolstoy's realism, without realizing that this miracle-worker makes art more real than nature and more vivid than life. When Tolstoy looks with smiling love at the things surrounding him, he turns what he likes into something bewitching and fanciful. He himself seems to have hinted at miracles of this kind in a charming episode in *Childhood.* The boy-protagonist tells the reader how he decided once to draw a hunting scene. He had at his disposal only blue paint and wondered whether he could paint a hare in that color. He then consulted his father, who resolved his childish doubts by reassuring him that there are also blue hares in the world. We now know that blue hares do indeed exist in the world of Tolstoy's art, and that the bluer they are, the truer they look.

Yet Tolstoy is Tolstoy not merely because he loved and re-enacted all the most vital aspects of human experience, or because he created more than anybody else—after God, and, of course, Shakespeare. Even among modern writers there are after all many creators who have loved the human and the real, perhaps more unwisely, but no less well. As a matter of fact it was one of them who once declared, in the jargon of the prize-fighter, that he felt ready to challenge all the champions of European realism, for example Turgenev and Flaubert, but that he would never dare to meet Tolstoy in the ring. The writer who spoke these words must have obscurely realized that love of life alone cannot lead to that summit which Tolstoy, alone among the moderns, seems to have attained.

Another man of letters of our time stated once, lucidly and epigrammatically, that it is literature that makes a work literature, but that something else makes it great. This "something else" may well be the urge, on the writer's part, to seek the meaning of the life he recreates through the wonders of imagination and the portents of love. This is perhaps the truth contained in the statements just cited, which belong respectively to an eminent novelist, Ernest Hemingway, and to an outstanding poet and critic, T. S. Eliot. The case of Tolstoy, at once exemplary and unique, seems the most convincing proof of such a truth: no other artist loved both life and the meaning of life with so much joy and despair as he.

Tolstoy and Enlightenment

by Isaiah Berlin

I

"Two things are always said about Tolstoy," wrote the celebrated Russian critic Mikhailovsky, in a largely forgotten essay published in the eighties, "that he is an outstandingly good writer of fiction and a bad thinker. This has become an axiom needing no demonstration." This almost universal verdict has reigned, virtually unchallenged, for something like a hundred years; and Mikhailovsky's attempt to question it remained relatively isolated. Tolstoy dismissed his left-wing ally as a routine radical hack, and expressed surprise that anyone should take interest in him. This was characteristic but unjust. The essay, which its author called "The Right Hand and the Left Hand of Leo Tolstoy," is a brilliant and convincing defence of Tolstoy on both intellectual and moral grounds, directed mainly against those who saw in the novelist's ethical doctrines, and in particular in his glorification of the peasants and of natural instinct and his constant disparagement of scientific culture, merely a perverse and sophisticated obscurantism which discredited the liberal cause, and played into the hands of priests and reactionaries. Mikhailovsky rejected this view, and in the course of his long and careful attempt to sift the enlightened grain from the reactionary chaff in Tolstoy's opinions, reached the conclusion that there was an unresolved and unavowed conflict in the great novelist's conceptions both of human nature and of the problems facing Russian and Western civilization. Mikhailovsky maintained that, so far from being a "bad thinker," Tolstoy was no less acute, clear-eyed and convincing in his analysis of ideas than of motive, character and action. In his zeal for his paradoxical thesis—paradoxical certainly at the time at which he wrote it—Mikhailovsky sometimes goes too far. My own remarks are

"Tolstoy and Enlightenment" by Isaiah Berlin. From *Mightier than the Sword* (London: Macmillan & Co., Ltd., 1964). Copyright © 1964 The English Centre of International P.E.N. An abbreviated version of this P.E.N. Hermon Ould Memorial Lecture, 1960, appeared in *Encounter* (February, 1961). Reprinted by permission of the author, The English Centre of International P.E.N., and *Encounter*.

no more than an extended gloss on his thesis; for in substance it seems to me to be correct, or at any rate more right than wrong. Tolstoy's opinions are always subjective and can be (as for example in his writings on Shakespeare or Dante or Wagner) wildly perverse. But the questions which in his more didactic essays he tries to answer nearly always turn on cardinal questions of principle, and his analysis is always first hand, and cuts far deeper, in the deliberately simplified and naked form in which he usually presents it, than those of more balanced, concrete and "objective" thinkers. Direct vision often tends to be disturbing: Tolstoy used this gift to the full to destroy both his own peace and that of his readers. It was this habit of asking exaggeratedly simple but fundamental questions, to which he did not himself—at any rate in the sixties and seventies—claim to possess the answers, that gave Tolstoy the reputation of being a "nihilist." Yet he certainly had no wish to destroy for the sake of destruction. He only wanted, more than anything else in the world, to know the truth. How annihilating this passion can be, is shown by others who have chosen to probe below the limits set by the wisdom of their generation: the author of the *Book of Job*, Machiavelli, Pascal, Rousseau. Like them, Tolstoy cannot be fitted into any of the public movements of his own, or indeed any other, age. The only company to which he belongs is the subversive one of questioners to whom no answer has been, or seems likely to be, given—at least no answer which they or those who understand them will begin to accept.

As for Tolstoy's positive ideas—and they varied less during his long life than has sometimes been represented—they are his own but not unique: they have something in common with the French enlightenment of the eighteenth century; something with those of the twentieth; little with those of his own times. He belonged to neither of the great ideological streams which divided educated Russian opinion during his youth. He was not a radical intellectual with his eyes turned to the West, nor a Slavophil, that is to say, a believer in a Christian and nationalist monarchy. His views cut across these categories. Like the radicals, he had always condemned political repression, arbitrary violence, economic exploitation and all that creates and perpetuates inequality among men. But the rest of the "westernizing" outlook—the overwhelming sense of civic responsibility, the belief in natural science as the door to all truth, in social and political reform, in democracy, material progress, secularism—this celebrated amalgam, the heart of the ideology of the intelligentsia—Tolstoy rejected early in life. He believed in individual liberty and indeed in progress too, but in a queer sense of his own.[1] He looked with contempt on liberals and socialists, and with even greater hatred on the right-wing parties of his time. His closest affinity, as has often been remarked, is with Rousseau; he liked and admired Rousseau's views more than those of any other modern writer. Like Rousseau, he rejected the doctrine of original sin, and believed that man was born innocent and had been ruined by his own bad institutions; especially by what passed for education among civilized men. Like Rousseau again, he put the blame for this process of decadence largely on the intellectuals and the institutions which they support—in particular the self-appointed *élites* of experts, sophisticated *côteries*, remote from common humanity, self-estranged from natural life. These men are damned because they have all but lost the most precious of all human possessions, the capacity with which all men are born—to see the truth, the immutable, eternal truth, which only charlatans and sophists represent as varying in different circumstances and times and places—the truth which is visible fully only to the innocent eye of those whose hearts have not been corrupted—children, peasants, those not blinded by vanity and pride, the simple, the good. Education, as the West understands it ruins innocence. That is why children resist it bitterly and instinctively: that is why it has to be rammed down their throats, and, like all coercion and violence, maims the victim and at times destroys him beyond redress. Men crave for truth by nature; therefore true education must be of such a kind that children and unsophisticated, ignorant people will absorb it readily and eagerly. But to understand this, and to discover how to apply this knowledge, the educated must put away their intellectual arrogance and make a new beginning. They must purge their minds of theories, of false, quasi-scientific analogies between the world of men and the world of animals, or of men and inanimate things. Only then will they be able to re-establish a personal relationship with the uneducated—a relationship which only humanity and love can achieve. In modern times only Rousseau, and perhaps Dickens, seem to him to have seen this. Certainly the people's condition will never be improved until not only the Czarist bureaucracy, but the "progressists," as Tolstoy called them, the vain and doctrinaire intelligentsia, are "prised off the people's necks"—the common people's, and the children's too. So long as fanatical theorists bedevil education, little is to be hoped for. Even the old-fashioned village priest—so Tolstoy maintains in one of his early

---

[1] Education is for him "a human activity based on a desire for equality, and a constant tendency to advance in knowledge." Equality, that is, between the teacher and the taught. This desire for equality on the part of both is itself for him the spring of progress—progress in the "advance of knowledge" of what men are and what they should do.

tracts—was less harmful: he knew little and was clumsy, idle and stupid; but he treated his pupils as God's creatures, not as scientists treat specimens in a laboratory; he did what he could; he was often corrupt, ill tempered, ignorant, unjust, but these were human—"natural"—vices, and therefore their effects, unlike those of machine-made modern instruction, inflicted no permanent injury.

With these opinions it is not surprising to find that Tolstoy was personally happier among the Slavophil reactionaries. He rejected their ideas, but at least they seemed to him to have some contact with reality—the land, the peasants, traditional ways of life. At least they believed in the primacy of spiritual values, and in the futility of trying to change men by changing the superficial sides of their life by means of political or constitutional reforms. But the Slavophils also believed in the Orthodox Church, in the unique historical destiny of the Russian people, in the sanctity of history as a divinely ordained process and therefore as the justification of many anomalies because they were native and ancient, and thus instruments in the divine tactic; they lived by a Christian faith in the mystical body—at once community and church—of the generations of the faithful, past, present and yet unborn. Intellectually, Tolstoy utterly repudiated all this; temperamentally he responded to it all too strongly. As a writer he truly understood only the nobility and the peasants: and the former better than the latter. He shared many of the instinctive beliefs of his country neighbours: like them he had a natural aversion from all forms of middle-class liberalism: the *bourgeoisie* scarcely appears in his novels: his attitude to parliamentary democracy, the rights of women, universal suffrage, was not very different from that of Cobbett or Carlyle or Proudhon or D. H. Lawrence. He shared deeply the Slavophil suspicion of all scientific and theoretical generalizations as such, and this created a bridge which made personal relations with the Moscow Slavophils congenial to him. But his intellect was not at one with his instinctive convictions. As a thinker he had profound affinities with the eighteenth century *philosophes*. Like them, he looked upon the patriarchal Russian State and Church, idealized by the Slavophils (and the implication that common ideals united the educated ruling minority and the uneducated masses) as organized, hypocritical conspiracies. Like the moralists of the Enlightenment, he looked for true values not in history, nor the sacred missions of nations or cultures or churches, but in the individual's own personal experience. Like them, too, he believed in eternal (and not in historically evolving) ends of life, and rejected with both hands the romantic notion of race or nation or culture as creative agencies, still more the Hegelian conception of history as the self-realization of self-perfecting reason incarnated in men, or movements, or institutions (ideas which had deeply influenced the Slavophils); all his life he looked on this as cloudy metaphysical nonsense.

Tolstoy's cold, clear, uncompromising realism is quite explicit in the notes, diaries and letters of his early life. The reminiscences of those who knew him as a boy or as a student in the University of Kazan, reinforce this impression. His character was deeply conservative, with a streak of caprice and irrationality; but his mind remained calm, logical and un-swerving; he followed the argument easily and fearlessly to whatever ex-treme it led and then embraced it—a typically Russian, and sometimes fatal, combination of qualities. What did not satisfy his critical sense, he rejected, he left the University of Kazan because he decided that the pro-fessors were incompetent and dealt with trivial issues. Like Helvétius and his friends in the mid-eighteenth century, Tolstoy denounced theology, history, the teaching of dead languages and literatures—the entire classical curriculum—as an accumulation of data and rules that no reasonable man could wish to know. History particularly irritated him as a systematic attempt to answer trivial or non-existent questions, with all the real issues carefully left out. "History is like a deaf man answering questions which nobody has put to him," he announced to a startled fellow student while they were both locked in the University detention room for some minor act of insubordination. The first extended statement of his full "ideo-logical" position belongs to the sixties. The occasion for it was his decision to compose a treatise on education. All his intellectual strength and all his prejudice went into this attempt.

II

In 1860 Tolstoy, then thirty-two years old, found himself in one of his periodic moral crises. He had acquired some fame as a writer: *Sebastopol, Childhood, Adolescence and Youth* and two or three shorter tales had been praised by the critics. He was on terms of friendship with some of the most gifted of an exceptionally talented generation of writers in his country—Turgenev, Nekrassov, Goncharov, Panaev, Pisemsky, Fet. His writing struck everyone by its freshness, sharpness, marvellous descriptive power and the precision and originality of its images. His style was at times criticized as awkward and even barbarous; but he was the most promising of the younger prose writers; he had a future; and yet his literary friends felt reservations about him. He paid visits to the literary *salons*, both right- and left-wing, but he seemed at ease in none of them. He was bold, imaginative and independent; but he was not a man of letters, not fundamentally concerned with problems of literature and writing, still less of writers; he had wandered in from another, less intellectual, more aristocratic and more primitive world. He was a well-born dilettante; but that was nothing new: the poetry of Pushkin and his contemporaries—unequalled in the history of Russian literature—had been created by amateurs of genius. It was not his origin but his unconcealed indifference to the literary life as such—to the habits and problems of professional writers, editors, publicists—that made his friends among the men of letters feel uneasy in his presence. This worldly, clever young officer could be exceedingly agreeable; his love of writing was genuine and very deep; but he was too contemptuous, too formidable and reserved, he did not dream of opening his heart in a *milieu* dedicated to intimate, unending self-revelation. He was inscrutable, disdainful, disconcerting, a little frightening. It was true that he no longer lived the life of an aristocratic officer. The wild nights on which the young radicals looked with hatred or contempt as characteristic of the dissipated lives of the reactionary *jeunesse dorée* no longer amused him. He had married, he had settled down, he was in love with his wife, he became for a time a model (if at times exasperating) husband. But he did not trouble to conceal the fact that he had infinitely more respect for all forms of real life—whether of the free Cossacks in the Caucasus, or of the rich young Guards officers in Moscow with their racehorses and balls and gypsies—than for the world of books, reviews, critics, professors, political discussions and talk about ideals, or philosophy and literary values. Moreover, he was opinionated, quarrelsome, and at times unexpectedly savage; with the result that his literary friends treated him with nervous respect, and, in the end, drew away from him; or perhaps he abandoned them. Apart from the poet Fet, who was an eccentric and deeply conservative country squire himself, Tolstoy had scarcely any intimates among the writers of his own generation. His breach with Turgenev is well known. He was even remoter from other *littérateurs*. There were times when he was fond of Vassili Botkin; he liked Nekrassov better than his poetry; but then Nekrassov was an editor of genius and had admired and encouraged him from his earliest beginnings.

The sense of the contrast between life and literature haunted Tolstoy all his life, and made him doubt his own vocation as a writer. Like other young men of birth and fortune, he was conscience stricken by the appalling condition of the peasants. Mere reflection or denunciation seemed to him a form of evasion. He must act, he must start at home. Like the eighteenth century radicals, he was convinced that men were born equal, and were made unequal by the way in which they were brought up. He established a school for the boys of his own village; and, dissatisfied with the educational theories then in vogue in Russia, decided to go abroad to study Western methods in theory and in practice. He derived a great deal from his visits to England, France, Switzerland, Belgium, Germany—including the title of his greatest novel. But his conversations with the most advanced Western authorities on education, and his observation of their methods, had convinced him that they were at best worthless, at worst harmful, to the children upon whom they were practised. He did not stay long in England and paid little attention to its "antiquated" schools. In France he found that learning was almost entirely mechanical—by rote; prepared questions, lists of dates, for example, were answered competently, because they had been learnt by heart. But the same children, when asked for the same facts from some unexpected angle, often produced absurd replies, which showed that their knowledge meant nothing to them. The schoolboy who replied that the murderer of Henry IV of France was Julius Caesar seemed to him typical: the boy neither understood nor took an interest in the facts he had stored up: all that was gained, at most, was a mechanical memory. But, the true home of theory was Germany. The pages which Tolstoy devotes to describing teaching and teachers in Germany rival and anticipate the celebrated pages in *War and Peace* in which he makes savage fun of admired experts in another field—the German strategists employed by the Russian Army—whom he represents as grotesque and pompous dolts.

In *Yasnaya Polyana*, the journal called after his estate, which he had had privately printed in 1859-61, Tolstoy speaks of his educational visits to various schools[2] in the West and, by way of example gives a hair-raising (and exceedingly entertaining) account of the latest methods of elementary teaching used by a specialist trained in one of the most advanced of the German teachers' seminaries. He describes the pedantic, immensely self-satisfied schoolmaster, as he enters the room and notes with approval that the children are seated at their desks, crushed and obedient, in total silence, as prescribed by German rules of behaviour. "He casts a look round the class and is quite clear in his mind about what they ought to understand; he knows it all already, he knows what the children's souls are made of and a good many other things that the

---

[2] These were the very years of Matthew Arnold's tours of inspection of the French and German educational systems. A comparison of their impressions might prove illuminating; they admired each other's writings and outlooks, but did not, so far as is known, know one another.

seminary has taught him." The schoolmaster enters, armed with the latest and most progressive pedagogic volume, called *Das Fischbuch*. It contains pictures of a fish.

"What is this, dear children?" "A fish," replies the brightest. "No, no. Think. Think!" And he will not rest until some child says that what they see is not a fish, but a book. That is better. "And what do books contain?" "Letters," says the bravest boy. "No, no," says the schoolmaster sadly. "You really *must* think of what you are saying." By this time the children are beginning to be hopelessly demoralized: they have no notion of what they are meant to say. They have a confused and perfectly correct feeling that the schoolmaster wants them to say something unintelligible —that the fish is not a fish; they feel that whatever it is that he wants them to say is something that they will never think of. Their thoughts begin to stray. They wonder (this is very Tolstoyan) why the master is wearing spectacles, why he is looking through them instead of taking them off, and so on. The master urges them to concentrate; he harries and tortures them until he manages to make them say that what they see is not a fish, but a picture, and then, after more torture, that the picture represents a fish. If that is what he wants them to say, would it not be easier, Tolstoy asks, to make them learn this piece of profound wisdom by heart, instead of tormenting them with the idiotic Fishbook method, which so far from causing them to think "creatively," merely stupefies them? The genuinely intelligent children know that their answers are always wrong; they cannot tell why, they only know that this is so; while the stupid, who occasionally provide the right answers, do not understand why they are praised. All that the German pedogogue is doing is to feed dead human material—or rather living human beings —into a grotesque mechanical contraption invented by fanatical fools who think that this is a way of applying scientific method to the education of men. Tolstoy assures us that his account (of which I have quoted only a short fragment) is not a parody, but a faithful reproduction of what he saw and heard in the advanced schools of Germany and in "those schools in England which have been fortunate enough to acquire these wonderful modern methods."

Disillusioned and indignant, Tolstoy returned to his Russian estate and began to teach the village children himself. He built schools, continued to study and reject and denounce current doctrines of education, published periodicals and pamphlets, invented new methods of learning geography, zoology, physics; composed an entire manual of arithmetic of his own, inveighed against all methods of coercion, especially those which consisted of forcing children against their will to memorize facts and dates and figures. In short, he behaved like an energetic, opinionated, somewhat eccentric eighteenth century land-owner, who had become a convert to the doctrines of Rousseau or the abbé Mably. His accounts of his theories and experiments fill two stout volumes in the pre-revolutionary editions of his collected works. They are still fascinating, if only because they contain some of the best descriptions of village life, and especially of children, both comical and lyrical, that even he had ever composed. He wrote them in the sixties and seventies, when he was at the height of his creative powers. The reader tends to lose sight of Tolstoy's overriding didactic purpose before the unrivalled insight into the twisting, criss-crossing pattern of the thoughts and feelings of individual village children, and the marvellous concreteness and imagination of the descriptions of their talk and their behaviour and of physical nature round them—of trees, meadows, sky, light and darkness and winter in a village in Central Russia. Yet side by side with this expression of a direct vision of human experience there run the clear, firm dogmas of a fanatically doctrinaire eighteenth century rationalist—doctrines not fused with the life that he describes, but superimposed upon it, like windows with rigorously symmetrical patterns drawn upon them, unrelated to the world on which they open, and yet achieving a kind of illusory artistic and intellectual unity with it, owing to the unbounded vitality and constructive genius of the writing itself. It is one of the most extraordinary performances in the history of literature.

The enemy is always the same: experts, professionals, men who claim special authority over other men. Universities and professors are a frequent target for attack. There are intimations of this already in the section entitled *Youth* of his earlier autobiographical novel. There is something eighteenth century, reminiscent both of Voltaire and of Bentham, about Tolstoy's devastating accounts of the dull and incompetent professors and the desperately bored and obsequious students in Russia in his youth. The tone is unusual in the nineteenth century: dry, ironical, didactic, mordant, at once withering and entertaining; the whole based on the contrast between the harmonious simplicity of nature and the self-destructive complications created by the malice or stupidity of men—men from whom the author feels himself detached, whom he affects not to understand and mocks at from a distance.[3] We are at the earliest

---

[3] This is one of the best examples of what the excellent Soviet critic Victor Shklovsky has called the descriptive method of ostraneniye—"rendering strange"—not to be confounded with either Hegelian or Brechtian "alienation"—founded on a pretended inability to discover any rational explanation for behaviour which the author seeks to deride.

beginnings of a theme which grew obsessive in Tolstoy's later life, that the solution to all our perplexities stares us in the face—that the answer is about us everywhere, like the light of day, if only we would not close our eyes or look everywhere but at what is there, before our very eyes, the clear, simple irresistible truth.

Like Rousseau and Kant and the believers in Natural law, Tolstoy was convinced that men have certain basic material and spiritual needs in all places, at all times. If these needs are fulfilled, they lead harmonious lives, which is the goal of their nature. Moral, aesthetic and other spiritual values are objective and eternal, and man's inner harmony depends upon his correct relationship to these. Moreover, Tolstoy constantly defended the proposition that human beings are more harmonious in childhood than under the corrupting influence of eduation in later life;[4] and also something that he believed much more deeply and expressed in everything he wrote or said—that simple people, peasants, Cossacks, and the like have a more "natural" and correct attitude than civilized men towards these basic values and that they are free and independent in a sense in which civilized men are not. For (he insists on this over and over again) peasant communities are in a position to supply their own material and spiritual needs out of their own resources, provided that they are not robbed or enslaved by oppressors and exploiters; whereas civilized men need for their survival the forced labour of others —serfs, slaves, the exploited masses, ironically called "dependents" because their masters depend on *them*. The masters are parasitic upon others: they are degraded not merely by the fact that to enslave and exploit others is a denial of such objective values as justice, equality, human dignity, love—values which men crave to realize because they must, because they are men—but for the further and, to him, even more important reason, that to live on robbed or borrowed goods and so fail to be self-subsistent, falsifies "natural" feelings and perceptions, corrodes men morally, and makes them both wicked and miserable. The human ideal is a society of free and equal men, who live and think by the light of what is true and right, and so are not in conflict with each other or themselves. This is a form—a very simple one—of the classical doctrine of Natural law, whether in its theological or secular, liberal-anarchist form. To it Tolstoy adhered all his life, as much in his "secular" period as after his "conversion." His early stories express this vividly. The Cossacks Lukashka or Uncle Yeroshka in *The Cossacks* are morally su-

---

[4] "Man," he wrote in 1862, "is born perfect—that is the great word spoken by Rousseau, and it will, like a rock, remain strong and true."

perior as well as happier and aesthetically more harmonious beings than
Olenin. Olenin knows this; indeed that is the heart of the situation.
Pierre in *War and Peace* and Levin in *Anna Karenina* sense this in
simple peasants and soldiers; so does Nekhlyudov in *The Morning of a
Landowner*. This conviction fills Tolstoy's mind to a greater and greater
degree, until it overshadows all other issues in his later works; *Resurrection* and *The Death of Ivan Ilyich* are not intelligible without it.

Tolstoy's critical thought constantly revolves round this central conflict
—nature and artifice, truth and invention. When in the nineties he laid
down conditions of excellence in art (in the course of an introduction to
a Russian translation of some of Maupassant's stories), he demanded of
all writers, in the first place, the possession of sufficient talent; in the
second, that the subject itself must be morally important; and finally,
that they must truly love and hate what they describe—"commit" themselves—retain the direct moral vision of childhood, and not maim their
natures by practising self-imposed, self-lacerating and always illusory ob-
jectivity and detachment. Talent is not given equally to all men; but
everyone can, if he tries, discover what is good and what is bad, what is
important and what is trivial. Only false—"made up"—theories blind
men and writers to this, and so distort their lives and creative activity.
He applies his criteria quite literally. Thus Nekrassov, according to
Tolstoy, treated subjects of profound importance, and possessed superb
skill as a writer; but he failed because his attitude towards his suffering
peasants and crushed idealists remained chilly and unreal. Dostoevsky's
subjects, Tolstoy concedes, lack nothing in seriousness, and his concern
is profound and genuine; but the first condition is not fulfilled: he is
diffuse and repetitive, he does not know how to tell the truth clearly,
and then to stop—one can, after the first hundred pages or so, predict
all the rest. Turgenev writes well and stands in a real, morally adequate,
relationship to his subjects; but he fails fearfully on the second count:
the level is too superficial—the issues are too trivial—and for this no
degree of integrity or skill can compensate. For, Tolstoy insists again and
again, content determines form, never form content; and if the topic is
too small, nothing will save the work of the artist. To hold the opposite
of this—to believe in the primacy of form—is to sacrifice truth: to end
by producing works that are contrived. There is no harsher word in
Tolstoy's entire critical vocabulary than "made up"—indicating that the
writer did not truly experience or imagine, but merely "composed," "contrived," "made up" that which he is purporting to describe. So, too,
Tolstoy maintained that Maupassant, whose gifts he admired greatly
(and perhaps overestimated), betrayed his genius precisely owing to false

and vulgar theories of this kind; yet he was judged, none the less, to be a good writer to the degree to which, like Balaam, although he might have meant to curse the good, he could not help discerning it: and this perception inevitably attracted his love to it and forced him against his own will towards the truth. Talent is vision, vision reveals the truth, truth is eternal and objective. To see the truth about nature or about conduct, to see it directly and vividly as only a man of genius (or a simple human being or a child) can see it, and then, in cold blood, to deny or tamper with the vision, no matter with what motive, is always monstrous, unnatural, a symptom of a deeply, perhaps fatally, diseased condition.

III

Truth, for Tolstoy, is always discoverable, to follow it is to be good, inwardly sound, harmonious. Yet it is clear that our society is not harmonious or composed of internally harmonious individuals. The interests of the educated minority—what he calls "the professors, the barons and the bankers"—are opposed to those of the majority—the peasants, the poor. Each side is indifferent to, or mocks, the values of the other. Even those who, like Olenin, Pierre, Nekhlyudov, Levin, realize the spuriousness of the values of the professors, barons and bankers, and the moral decay in which their false education has involved them, even those who are truly contrite, cannot, despite Slavophil pretensions, go native and "merge" with the mass of the common people. Are they too corrupt ever to recover their innocence? Is their case hopeless? Can it be that civilized men have acquired (or discovered) certain true values of their own, which barbarians and children may know nothing of, but which they— the civilized—cannot lose or forget, even if, by some impossible means, they could transform themselves into peasants or the free and happy Cossacks of the Don and the Terek? This is one of the central and most tormenting problems in Tolstoy's life, to which he goes back again and again, and to which he returns conflicting answers.

Tolstoy knows that he himself clearly belongs to the minority of barons, bankers, professors. He knows the symptoms of his condition only too well. He cannot, for example, deny his passionate love for the music of Mozart or Chopin or the poetry of Pushkin or Tyutchev—the ripest fruits of civilization. He needs—he cannot do without—the printed word and all the elaborate paraphernalia of the culture in which such lives are lived and such works of art are created. But what is the use of Pushkin to village boys, when his words are not intelligible to them? What real benefits has the invention of printing brought the peasants? We are told, Tolstoy observes, that books educate societies ("that is, make them more corrupt"), that it was the written word that has promoted the emancipation of the serfs in Russia. Tolstoy denies this: the government would have done the same without books or pamphlets. Pushkin's *Boris Godunov* pleases him, Tolstoy, deeply, but to the peasants means nothing. The triumphs of civilization? The telegraph informs him about his sister's health, or about the political prospects of King Otto I of Greece; but what benefit do the masses gain from it? Yet it is they who pay and have always paid for it all, and they know this well. When peasants in the "cholera riots" kill doctors because they regard them as poisoners, what they do is no doubt wrong, yet these murders are no accident: the instinct which tells the peasants who their oppressors are is sound, and the doctors belong to that class. When Wanda Landowska played to the villagers of Yasnaya Polyana, the great majority of them remained unresponsive. Yet can it be doubted that it is these simple people who lead the least broken lives, immeasurably superior to the warped and tormented lives of the rich and educated? The common people, Tolstoy asserts in his early educational tracts, are self-subsistent not only materially but spiritually—folksong, ballads, the *Iliad,* the Bible, spring from the people itself, and are therefore intelligible to all men everywhere, as Tyutchev's magnificent poem *Silentium,* or *Don Giovanni,* or the Ninth Symphony are not. If there is an ideal of human life, it lies not in the future but in the past. Once upon a time there was the Garden of Eden, and in it dwelt the uncorrupted human soul—as the Bible and Rousseau conceived it—and then came the Fall, corruption, suffering, falsehood. It is mere blindness (Tolstoy says over and over again) to believe, as liberals or socialists—"the progressives"—believe, that the golden age is still to come, that history is the story of improvement, that advances in natural science or material skills coincide with real moral progress. The truth is the reverse of this.

The child is closer to the ideal harmony than the man, and the simple peasant than the torn, "alienated," morally and spiritually unanchored, self-destructive parasites who form the civilized *élite*. From this doctrine springs Tolstoy's notable anti-individualism; and in particular his diagnosis of the individual's will as the source of misdirection and perversion of "natural" human tendencies, and hence the conviction (derived largely from Schopenhauer's doctrine of the will as the source of frustration) that to plan, organize, rely on science, try to create ordered patterns of life in accordance with rational theories, is to swim against the stream of nature, to close one's eyes to the saving truth within us, to torture facts to fit artificial schemes, and torture human beings to fit social and economic systems against which their natures cry out. From the same source, too, comes the obverse of this moral: Tolstoy's faith in the intuitively grasped direction of things as being not merely inevitable but objectively—providentially—good; and therefore belief in the need to submit to it: his quietism.

This is one aspect of his teaching, the most familiar, the central idea of the Tolstoyan movement. It runs through all his mature works, imaginative, critical, didactic, from *The Cossacks* and *Family Happiness,* to his last religious tracts; this is the doctrine which both liberals and Marxists duly condemned. It is in this mood that Tolstoy (like Marx, whom he neither respected nor understood) maintains that to imagine that heroic personalities determine events is a piece of colossal megalomania and self-deception. His narrative is designed to show the insignificance of Napoleon or Alexander, or of aristocratic and bureaucratic society in *Anna Karenina,* or of the judges and official persons in *Resurrection;* or again, the emptiness and intellectual impotence of historians and philosophers who try to explain events by employing concepts like "power" attributed to great men, or "influence" ascribed to writers, orators, preachers—words, abstractions, which, in his view, explain nothing, being themselves more obscure than the facts for which they purport to account. He maintains that we do not begin to understand, and therefore cannot explain or analyse, what it is to wield authority or strength, to influence, to dominate. Explanations that do not explain, are, for Tolstoy, a symptom of the destructive and self-inflated intellect, the faculty that kills innocence and leads to false notions and the ruin of human life.

That is one strain, inspired by Rousseau and present in that early romanticism which inspired primitivism in art and in life, not in Russia alone. Tolstoy imagines that this state can be achieved by observing the lives of simple people and by the study of the Gospels.

His other strain (interwoven with the first) is the direct opposite of this. Mikhailovsky in his essay on Tolstoy says, justly enough, that Olenin cannot, charmed as he is by the Caucasus and the Cossack idyll, transform himself into a Lukashka, return to the childlike harmony, which in his case has long been broken. Levin knows that if he tried to become a peasant this could only be a grotesque farce, which the peasants would be the first to perceive and deride; he and Pierre and Nicolai Rostov know obscurely that in some sense they have something to give that the peasants have not. In the famous essay entitled *What is Art?* Tolstoy unexpectedly tells the educated reader that the peasant "needs what your life of ten generations uncrushed by hard labour has given you. You had the leisure to search, to think, to suffer—then give him that for whose sake you suffered; he is in need of it . . . do not bury in the earth the talent given you by history . . ." Leisure, then, need not be merely destructive. Progress can occur; we can learn from what happened in the past, as those who lived in that past could not. It is true that we live in an unjust order. But this itself creates direct moral obligations. Those who are members of the civilized *élite,* cut off as they tragically are from the mass of the people, have the duty to attempt to rebuild broken humanity, to stop exploiting other men, to give them what they most need—education, knowledge, material help, a capacity for living better lives. Levin in *Anna Karenina,* as Mikhailovsky remarks, takes up where Nicolai Rostov in *War and Peace* leaves off; they are not quietists, yet what they do is right. The emancipation of the peasants, in Tolstoy's view, although it did not go far enough, was nevertheless a powerful act of will—good will—on the part of the government, and now it is necessary to teach peasants to read and write and grasp the rules of arithmetic, which the peasants cannot do for themselves; to equip them for the use of freedom. I may be unable to merge myself with the mass of peasants; but I can at least use the fruit of the unjustly obtained leisure of myself and my ancestors—my education, knowledge, skills—for the benefit of those whose labour made it possible. This is the talent which I may not bury. I must work to promote a just society in accordance with those objective standards which all men, except the hopelessly corrupt, see and accept, whether they live by them or not. The simple see them more clearly, the sophisticated more dimly, but all men can see them if they try; indeed, to be able to see them is part of what it is to be a man. When injustice is perpetrated, I have an obligation to speak out and act against it; nor may artists, any more than other men, sit with folded hands. What makes good writers good is first and foremost, ability to see truth—social and individual, material and spiritual—and so present it that it cannot be escaped. Tolstoy holds that Maupassant, for example, is doing exactly this, despite all his aesthetic fallacies. Maupassant may, because he is a corrupt human being, take the side of the bad against the good, write about a worthless Paris seducer with greater sympathy than he feels for his victims. But provided that he tells the truth at a level that is sufficiently profound (and men of talent cannot avoid doing this) he will face the reader with fundamental moral questions—even though this may not be his intention—questions which the reader can neither escape nor answer without severe and painful self-examination. This, for Tolstoy, opens the path to regeneration, and is the proper function of art. Vocation, talent, artistic conscience—all these are obedience to an inescapable inner need: to satisfy it is the artist's purpose and duty. Nothing therefore, is more false than the view of the artist as a purveyor or a craftsman whose sole function is to create a beautiful thing, as the aesthetes—Flaubert, or Renan or Maupassant[5] (or Mr. Evelyn Waugh) maintain. There is only one true human goal, and it is equally binding on all men—landowners, doctors, barons, professors, bankers, peasants: to tell the truth and act according to it, that is, to do good and persuade others to do so. That God exists, or that the *Iliad* is beautiful, or that men have a right to be free and to be equal, are all eternal and absolute truths. Therefore, we must persuade men to read the *Iliad* and not pornographic French novels, and to work for an equal society, not a theocratic or political hierarchy. Coercion is evil; this is self-evident and men have always known it to be true; therefore they must work for a society in which there will be no wars, no prisons, no executions, in any circumstances, for any reason—for a society in which there is the highest attainable degree of individual freedom. By his own route Tolstoy arrived at a programme of Christian anarchism which had much in common with that of the "realist" school of painters and composers—Mussorgsky, Repin, Stassov—and with that of their political allies, the Russian Populists, although he rejected their belief in natural science and their doctrinaire socialism and faith in the methods of terrorism. For what he now appeared to be advocating was a programme of action, not of quietism; this programme underlay the educational reforms that Tolstoy attempted to carry out. *L'éducation peut tout* said Helvétius a hundred years before, and Tolstoy in effect agreed. Ignorance is responsible for misery, inequality, wars. He writes with indignation about the prevalent "inequality of education," and in particular "the disproportion of the educated and uneducated, or more exactly the savage and the literate."

If it were not for ignorance, human beings could not be exploited or coerced. "One man cannot compel others—only a dominant majority can do that, united in its lack of education. It only looks as if Napoleon III concluded the peace of Villafranca, suppresses newspapers or wants to conquer Savoy, actually all this is done by the Félixes and Victors who cannot read newspapers" (*ibid.*, p. 329). This is the seed of the doctrine that henceforth determines all his thoughts—that the real agents of his-

---

[5] Tolstoy is moved to indignation by Maupassant's celebrated dictum (which he quotes) that the business of the artist is not to entertain, delight, move, astonish, cause his reader to dream, reflect, smile, weep or shudder, but "faire quelque chose de beau dans la forme qui vous conviendra le mieux d'après votre tempérament."

tory are the masses—the collection of obscure individuals, the Félixes and Victors, although responsibility for them is mistakenly attributed to leaders and great men. If the Félixes and Victors refused to march, there would be no wars; if they were educated and could read newspapers— and if these newspapers contained truth instead of falsehood—they would not march. This is eighteenth century rationalist doctrine in its clearest form. For Tolstoy, at this stage, all social movements can be analysed into the specific behaviour of specific individuals. Peoples, governments, nations, armies, are only collective nouns, not genuine entities—to attribute to them the characteristics of human beings, to speak of them as literally active or powerful, as authors of this achievement or that feature —is not misleading only if it is remembered that they can (and not in principle only) be analysed into their constituent elements. This positivist conviction Tolstoy holds in a stronger form than Marx or Comte—as strongly as the most extreme empiricists of our own time: like them, he denounces as myth, as metaphysical obfuscation, anything that implies that collective behaviour is not analysable into the behaviour of the individuals who compose the collective; and to this he adds the corollary that the real activity of a man is the "inner" activity of his spirit, and not the "outer" activity as expressed in social or political life. And he quotes the activist and revolutionary Herzen towards whom his attitude was at all times highly ambivalent in support of this position.[6] It is hardly necessary to add that the whole of *War and Peace* and much of *Anna Karenina* and *Resurrection* is an incarnation of this central idea. All the results of advancing civilization—the telegraph, steamers, theatres, academies, literature, etc.—are useless so long as only one per cent of the people are receiving education. "All this (i.e. universities, etc.) is useful, but useful as a dinner in the English Club might be useful if all of it were eaten by the manager and the cook. These things are created by all the seventy million Russians, but are of use only to thousands." Who shall determine what is the right kind of education? When in doubt Tolstoy returns to Rousseau. "The will of the people is the sole factor by which our (educational) activity should be guided."

> If we offer the people certain kinds of knowledge . . . and find that they have a bad influence on it, I conclude not that the people is bad because it doesn't absorb this knowledge, nor that the people, unlike ourselves, is not adult enough to do so . . . but that this kind of knowledge is bad, abnormal, and that with the help of the people we must work out new sorts of knowledge more suitable for us all—that is both for the educated and for the common people. . . .

[6] *Literaturnoye Nasledstvo*, No. 41-42, 1941, p. 517.

Someone might ask: Why should we assume that the arts and sciences of our own educated class are false? Why should you infer their falsity from the mere fact that the people does not take to it? This question is answered very easily: because there are thousands of us, but millions of them.

This democratic programme is Tolstoy's answer to the hated "liberals" and "progressives" and the specialists and civilized *élites* to whom they look for salvation. Faithful to Rousseau (and if he had but known it), to Kant, he strove to discover, collect, expound eternal truths; awaken the spontaneous interest, the imagination, love, curiosity, of children or simple folk; above all liberate their 'natural' moral, emotional and intellectual powers, which he did not doubt, as Rousseau did not doubt, would achieve harmony within men and between them, provided that we took care to eliminate whatever might cramp, maim, and kill them.[7]

IV

This programme—that of making possible the free self-development of all human faculties—rests on one vast assumption: that there exists at least one path of development which ensures that these faculties will neither conflict with each other, nor develop disproportionately—a sure path to the complete harmony in which everything fits and is at peace; with the corollary that we can find it—that knowledge of man's nature gained from observation or introspection or moral intuition, or from the study of the lives and writings of the best and wisest men of all ages or of the simple hearts of the "millions" and not of the "thousands," will show it to us. This is not the place for considering how far this doctrine is compatible with ancient religious teachings or modern psychology. The point I wish to stress is that it is, above all, a programme of action, a call for universal education and re-education, a declaration of war against current social values, against the tyranny of states, societies, churches, against brutality, injustice, ignorance, stupidity, hypocrisy, weakness, above all, against vanity and moral blindness. A man who has fought a good fight in this war will thereby expiate the sin of having been a hedonist and an exploiter, and the son and beneficiary of robbers and oppressors.

This is what Tolstoy believed, preached and practised. His "conversion" altered his view of what was good and what was evil. It did not weaken

[7] These quotations come from Tolstoy's writings in 1862, most of which are to be found in vol. 8 of the Jubilee Edition of his works. Informative remarks on this topic may be found in an article by E. N. Kupreyanova in *Yasnopolyanski Sbornik* (Tula, July, 1955).

his faith in the need for action. His belief in the principles themselves
henceforth never wavered. The enemy entered by another door: Tolstoy's
sense of reality was too inexorable to keep out a terrible doubt about how
these principles—no matter how true themselves—should be applied.
Even though *I* believe some things to be beautiful or good, and others
to be ugly and evil, what right have *I* to bring up others in the light of
my convictions, when I know that, do what I might, I cannot help liking
Chopin and Maupassant, while these far better beings—peasants or
children—do not? Have I, who stand at the end of a long period of decadence—of generations of civilized, unnatural living—have *I* the right to
touch *their* souls?

To seek to influence someone, however mysterious the process, is to
engage in a dark, morally suspect enterprise. This is obvious in the case
of the crude manipulation of one man by another. But in principle it
holds equally of education. All educators seek to shape the minds and
lives of human beings in the direction of a given goal, or in the light of a
specific ideal model. But if we—the sophisticated members of a deeply
corrupt society—are ourselves unhappy, inharmonious, gone astray, what
can we be doing but trying to change children who are born healthy into
our own sick semblance, to make of them cripples like ourselves? We are
what we have become; we cannot help our love of Pushkin's verses, of
Chopin's music; we discover that children and peasants find them unintelligible or tedious. What do we do? We persist, we "educate" them, until
they too, appear to enjoy these works, or, at least, grasp why we enjoy
them. What have we done? We find the works of Mozart and Chopin
beautiful only because Mozart and Chopin were themselves children of
our degenerate culture, and therefore their words speak to our diseased
minds; but what right have we to infect others, to make them as corrupt
as ourselves? ("The works of Pushkin, Gogol, Turgenev, Derzhavin
. . . are not needed by the people and will bring it no benefit.") We see
the blemishes of other systems. We see all too clearly how the human
personality is destroyed by Protestant insistence on blind obedience, by
Catholic belief in social emulation, by the appeal to material self-interest
and the value of social rank and position on which Russian education,
according to Tolstoy, is based. Is it not, then, either monstrous arrogance
or a perverse inconsistency to behave as if our own system of education—
something recommended by Pestalozzi, or by the inventors of the Lan-
caster method, or by some other expert, systems that reflect their inventors' civilized and consequently perverted, personalities—as if such ideas
were necessarily superior, or even less destructive than what we condemn

so readily and justly in the superficial French or the stupid and pompous Germans?

How is this to be avoided? Tolstoy repeats the lessons of Rousseau's *Emile*. Nature, only nature will save us. We must seek to find what is "natural," spontaneous, uncorrupt, sound, in harmony with itself and other objects in the world, and then to clear paths for development on these lines; not seek to alter, to force into a mould. We must listen to the dictates of our stifled original nature—not look on it as mere raw material on which to impose our unique individual personalities and powerful wills. To defy, to be Promethean, to create goals and build worlds in rivalry with what our moral sense knows to be eternal truths, given once and for all to all men, truths, knowledge of which alone renders them men and not beasts—that is the monstrous sin of pride, committed by all reformers, all revolutionaries, all men judged by the world to be great and effective. It is committed in just as large a measure by those in authority—by legislators, bureaucrats, judges, country squires who, out of liberal convictions or simply caprice or boredom, dictate, bully and interfere with the lives of peasants.[8] Do not teach: learn; that is the central notion of Tolstoy's essay, written nearly a hundred years ago, *"Should we teach the peasants' children how to write, or should they teach us?"* and it goes through all the notes on education, published in the sixties and seventies and written with his customary freshness, attention to detail and unapproachable power of direct perception. In one of these he gives examples of stories written by the children in his village, and speaks of the awe which he felt, face to face with the act of pure creation in which, he assures us, he played no part himself; these stories would only be spoilt by his "corrections"; they seem to him far deeper than anything by Goethe. He speaks of how deeply ashamed they made him feel of his own superficiality, vanity, stupidity, narrowness, lack of moral and aesthetic sense. If, he tells us, one can help children and peasants at all, it is only by making it easier for them to advance freely along their own instinctive path; to direct is to spoil; men are good and only need freedom to realize their goodness.

"We speak," writes Tolstoy in the seventies, "of bringing a man up to be a scoundrel, a hypocrite, a good man: of the Spartans as bringing up brave men, of French education as producing one-sided and self-satisfied

---

[8] Mikhailovsky maintains that in *Polikushka*, one of Tolstoy's best stories, composed during the months in which he wrote his educational tracts, he represents the tragic death of the hero as being ultimately caused by the wilful interference with the lives of her peasants by the well meaning, but vain and stupid, landowner. His argument seems to me exceedingly convincing.

persons, and so on." But this is speaking of, and using, human beings as so much raw material for us to model, this is what "to bring up" to be like this or like that, means. We are evidently ready to alter the direction spontaneously followed by the souls and wills of others, to deny them independence—in favour of what? Of our own corrupt, false, or, at best, uncertain values? "Education," Tolstoy says elsewhere, "is the action of one person on another with a view to causing the other to acquire certain moral habits"; but this always involves some degree of moral tyranny. And in a wild moment of panic, he adds "Is not the ultimate motive of the educator *envy*—envy of the purity of the child; desire to make the child more like himself, that is to say, more corrupt?" he goes on to add, "What has the entire history of education been?" he answers: "All philosophers of education, from Plato to Kant, professed to want one thing: to free education from the chains of the evil past—from its ignorance and its errors—to find out what men truly need, and adjust the new schools to that." They struck off one yoke only to put another in its place. Certain scholastic philosophers insisted on Greek, because that was the language of Aristotle who knew the truth. Luther, Tolstoy continues, denied the authority of the Fathers and insisted on inculcating the original Hebrew, because he *knew* that that was the language in which God had revealed eternal truths to men. Bacon looked to empirical knowledge of nature, and his theories contradicted those of Aristotle. Rousseau proclaimed his faith in life—life as he conceived it—and not in theories. But about one thing they were all agreed: that one must liberate the young from the blind despotism of the old; and each immediately substituted his own fanatical, enslaving dogma in its place. If I am sure that I know the truth and that all else is error, does that alone entitle me to superintend the education of another? Is such certainty enough? Whether or not it disagrees with the certainties of others? Have I the right to put a wall round the pupil, exclude all external influences, and try to mould him as I please, in my own, or somebody else's, image? The answer to this question, Tolstoy passionately says to the "progressives," "must be 'yes' or 'no' . . ., if it is yes, then the church schools and the Jews' schools have as much right to exist as our universities." He declares that he sees no moral difference, at least in principle, between the compulsory Latin of the traditional establishments and the compulsory materialism with which the radical professors indoctrinate their captive audiences. There might indeed, be something to be said for the things that the liberals delight in denouncing: education at home, for example; for it is surely natural that parents should wish their children to resemble them. Again there is a case for a religious upbringing, since it is natural that believers should want to save all other human beings from what they are certain must be eternal damnation. Similarly the Government is entitled to train men, for society cannot survive without some sort of government, and governments cannot exist without some qualified specialists to serve them. But what is the moral basis of "liberal education" in schools and universities, staffed by men who do not even claim to be sure that what they teach is true? Empiricism? The lessons of history? The only lesson that history teaches us is that all previous educational systems have proved to be despotisms founded on falsehoods, and later roundly condemned. Why should the twenty-first century not look back on us in the nineteenth with the same scorn and amusement as that with which we now look on mediaeval schools and universities? If the history of education is the history merely of tyranny and error, why should we, and what right have we, to carry on this abominable farce? And if we are told that it has always been so, that it is nothing new, that we cannot help it and must do our best—is this not like saying that murders have always taken place, so that we might as well go on murdering even though we have now discovered what it is that makes men murder? In these circumstances, we should be villains if we did not say at least this much: that since, unlike the Pope or Luther or modern positivists, we do not ourselves claim to base our education (or other forms of interference with human beings) on knowledge of absolute truth, we must at least stop torturing others in the name of something that we do not know. All we can know for certain is what men actually want. Let us at least have the courage of our admitted ignorance, of our doubts and uncertainties. At least, we can try to discover what others—children or adults—require, by taking off the spectacles of tradition, prejudice, dogma, and making it possible for ourselves to know men as they truly are, by listening to them carefully and sympathetically, and understanding them and their lives and their needs, one by one, individually. Let us at least try to provide them with what they ask for, and leave them as free as possible. Give them *Bildung* (for which Tolstoy produces an equivalent Russian word—pointing out with pride that it has none in French or English), that is to say, seek to influence them by precept and by the example of your own lives; but not apply 'education' to them, which is essentially a method of coercion and destroys what is most natural and sacred in man—the capacity for knowing and acting for oneself in accordance with what one thinks to be true and good—the power and the right of self-direction.

But he cannot let the matter rest there, as many a liberal has tried to do. For the question immediately arises; how are we to contrive to leave the schoolboy and the student free? By being morally neutral? By imparting only factual knowledge, not ethical, or aesthetic, or social or religious doctrine? By placing the "facts" before the pupil, and letting him form his own conclusions, without seeking to influence him in any direction, for fear that we might infect him with our own diseased outlooks? But is it really possible for such neutral communications to occur between men? Is not every human communication a conscious or unconscious impression of one temperament, attitude to life, scale of values, upon another? Are men ever so thoroughly insulated from each other that the careful avoidance of more than the minimum degree of social intercourse will leave them unsullied, absolutely free to see truth and falsehood, good and evil, beauty and ugliness, with their own, and only their own eyes? But this is an absurd conception of individuals as creatures who can be kept pure from all social influence, and seemed absurd in the world even of Tolstoy's middle years, even, that is, without the new knowledge of human beings that we have acquired today as the result of the labours of psychologists, sociologists, philosophers. We live in a degenerate society; only the pure, Tolstoy says, can rescue us. But who, he reasonably asks, will educate the educators? Who is so pure as to know how, let alone be able, to heal our world or anyone in it?

Between these poles—on one side the facts, nature, what there is; on the other duty, justice, what there should be; on one side innocence, on the other education; between the claims of spontaneity and those of obligation, of the injustice of coercing others, and of the injustice of leaving them to their own ways, Tolstoy wavered and struggled all his life. And not only he, but all those populists and socialists, the doctors, engineers, agricultural experts, painters and composers and idealistic students in Russia who "went to the people" and could not decide whether they had gone to teach or to learn, whether the 'good of the people' for which they were ready to sacrifice their lives, was what "the people" in fact desired, or something that the reformers and they alone knew to be good for it—something which the "people" should desire—would desire if only they were as educated and wise as their champions—but, in fact, in their benighted state, often spurned and violently resisted. These contradictions, and his unswerving recognition of his failure to reconcile or modify them, are, in a sense, what gives its special meaning both to Tolstoy's life and to the morally agonized, didactic pages of his art. He furiously rejected the compromises and alibis of his liberal contemporaries as mere feebleness and evasion. Yet he believed that a final solution to the problem of how to apply the principles of Jesus must exist, even though neither he nor any one else had wholly discovered it. He rejected the very possibility that some of the tendencies and goals of which he speaks might be literally both valid and incompatible. Historicism versus moral responsibility; quietism versus the duty to resist evil; teleology or a causal order against the play of chance and irrational force; on the one hand, spiritual harmony, simplicity, the mass of the people, and on the other, the irresistible attraction of the culture of minorities and their sciences, and arts, the conflict between corruption of the civilized portion of society and its direct duty to raise the masses of the people to its own level; the dynamism and falsifying influence of passionate, simple, one-sided faith, as against the clear-sighted sense of the complex facts and inevitable weakness in action which flows from enlightened scepticism— all these strains are given full play in the thought of Tolstoy. His adhesion to them appears as a series of inconsistencies in his system, because the conflicts may, after all, exist in fact and lead to collisions in real life.[9] Tolstoy is incapable of suppressing, or falsifying, or explaining away or "transcending" by reference to dialectical or other "deeper" levels of thought, any truth when it presents itself to him, no matter what this entails, where it leads, how much it destroys of what he most passionately longs to believe. Everyone knows that Tolstoy placed truth highest of all the virtues. Others have made such declarations and have celebrated her no less memorably. But Tolstoy is among the few who have truly earned that rare right: for he sacrificed all he had upon her altar—happiness, friendship, love, peace, moral and intellectual certainty, and, in the end, his life. And all she gave him in return was doubt, insecurity, self-contempt, insoluble contradictions. In this sense (although he would have repudiated this most violently) he is a martyr and a hero in the central tradition of the European enlightenment. This seems a paradox: but then his entire life is in this sense a great paradox, inasmuch as it bears constant witness to a proposition to the denial of which his last years were dedicated—that the truth is seldom wholly simple or clear, or as obvious as it may sometimes seem to the eye of the ordinary, sensible man.

[9] Some Marxist critics, for instance Lukács, represent these contradictions as the expression in art of the crisis of the semi-feudal social structure in Russia, and in particular of the condition of the peasants whose predicament Tolstoy's writing is held to reflect. This seems to me too optimistic: the destruction of Tolstoy's social world should have rendered his dilemmas obsolete. The reader can judge for himself whether this is so.

On Tolstoy's Crises

by B. M. Eikhenbaum

Tolstoy began as the liquidator of Romantic poetics and the destroyer of established canons. He changed the matter, the devices, and the form of art. In place of a refined metaphoric style, in place of emphatic musical syntax, Tolstoy used a plain but complex, almost awkward sentence; in place of a rambling stream of feelings and emotionally colored descriptions, the detailed description of minutiae and the analysis and exfoliation of spiritual life; in place of complex plots, the parallelism of several lines, barely connected but not intertwined.

From the very beginning Tolstoy was conscious of himself against a background of disintegrating romantic art. Bypassing the generation of the fathers, he went back to the grandfathers, to the eighteenth century. His mentors and inspirers were Sterne, Rousseau, Bernadin de Saint-Pierre, Franklin, Buffon, and Goldsmith. *Childhood* reflects the influence of Töpfer, brought up during that very eighteenth century; in the *Sevastopol Sketches* Tolstoy follows in the wake of Stendhal—"the last man of the eighteenth century." A great deal of Tolstoy is determined by the battle with romantic clichés. "Realism" is only a motivation for that battle. It is a motto continually repeated when literary schools change, and continually changing its meaning. Tolstoy wanted to write in a way different from that of his fathers. In the early diaries he already laughed at romantic descriptions:

> It is said that when one looks at a beautiful scene one thinks of the grandeur of God and the insignificance of man; lovers see their beloved in water, others say that mountains apparently said this, and that leaves said that, and that trees called somewhere. How can one have such thoughts? You have to work hard to beat such nonsense into your head.

And Tolstoy consistently destroyed Romantic clichés. The image of the Romantic daredevil in Marlinsky's and Lermontov's manner is lowered and parodied. The traditional "poetic" Caucasus is lowered:

"On Tolstoy's Crises" by B. M. Eikhenbaum. From *Skvoz' literaturu* (Leningrad, 1924), pp. 67-72. Translated for this volume by Ralph E. Matlaw.

After all, in Russia the Caucasus are described somehow majestically, with
eternal virgin ice-caps, wild torrents, daggers, felt cloaks, Cherkassian girls—
it's all a little terrifying, but in reality there is nothing gay about it. If they
at least knew that we've never been in the virgin ice-caps, and that there's
nothing gay about being there, or that the Caucasus are divided into administrative states: Stavropol, Tiflis, etc. [*The Wood Felling*]

It is interesting that for a long time Tolstoy remained silent about the
most "poetic" subject—love—and the critics impatiently waited for him
to write a novel with a love interest. And finally it appeared—*Family
Happiness*. But the protagonist is an elderly man, who does not want to
declare his love in the ordinary novelistic way: "When I read novels,"
he says,

I think what an embarrassed face Lieutenant Strelsky or Alfred must have
when he says "I love you, Elenore!" and thinks that something unusual will
suddenly happen. And nothing happens, neither with her nor with him, the
same eyes and nose remain and everything remains the same.

Marriage is the starting point of the plot, rather than the denouément (as
it ordinarily is in love stories). This is an intentional deviation. In his
Reminiscences, V. Lazursky adduces Tolstoy's words that "those who finish their novels with a wedding, as if that were so good that there is no
reason to write any further—they all babble sheer nonsense."

Tolstoy rejects the very genre of the Romantic tale with its central
hero and love interest. He is drawn toward large forms, and everything
written before *War and Peace* seems to be only preliminary studies,
working out individual situations, individual scenes, individual devices.
After exhausting his devices of "minutiae" in the large forms he moves to
new ones—to the folk tale. Those two moments in his work are accompanied by stormy crises. Tolstoy's work is to the present day considered to fall into two sharply divided periods, up to the *Confession* and
after it. To the present day it is thought that after *Confession* Tolstoy
became a moralist.

That is not true. Crises accompany Tolstoy's entire work. And this is
not at all a peculiarity of his nature. Art itself underwent these crises.
Romantic poetics were worn out. Art had to look anew at life in order
to justify itself anew. From the very beginning Tolstoy interrupted his
artistic work with completely extraneous plans and this background is
vital to him. In 1855 Tolstoy already attained that "great, colossal"
thought to accomplish which he was ready to dedicate his whole life,
the idea of founding "a religion that corresponds to the development of
mankind, the religion of Christ, but purified of faith and mystery."

The real basis for all of these crises in Tolstoy was the search for new artistic forms and a new justification for them. For that reason the *Confession* was followed by the tract on art, on which Tolstoy worked during the course of fifteen years. That tract was prepared for by another crisis, the crisis of the 1860s, unjustifiably forgotten when the "break" of the 1870s is discussed. The crisis of the 1860s developed from the end of the 1850s, when Tolstoy appeared among St. Petersburg's literary men. He stunned everyone with his sharp paradoxes and his impatience. He found no canons, authorities and traditions acceptable. For a while, Druzhinin took charge of him and made sure that Tolstoy "scribbled by the dozen" the words *what, who,* and *that.* But several years passed and Tolstoy accomplished a fantastic, a stunning jump from literature to pedagogy, from St. Petersburg literary men to the Fedkas and Semkas. It seemed to his friends that he had given up literature. Druzhinin was grief-stricken and tried to prevail on him:

> Every writer has minutes of doubt and dissatisfaction with himself, and no matter how strong and valid that feeling, no one has yet ended his connection with literature because of it; but everyone has continued to write to the end.

In reality Tolstoy's work in the school developed on the basis of a deeply hidden artistic quest. As though unexpectedly for Tolstoy himself he turned from schoolteacher into experimenter. His article "Who Should Teach Whom to Write: We the Peasant Children or the Peasant Children Us?" (1862) is no less significant an artistic pamphlet than the future tract on art. Tolstoy sets Semka's and Fedka's work against Russian literature, finding nothing comparable in it. He is ecstatic about the artistic details they imprint in the word. He is agitated and jolted by the power of that primitive creation that depends upon no tradition whatsoever.

Tolstoy's later turn to primitivism is already marked here. In place of subjects, Tolstoy gives his pupils proverbs that serve as the canvas, so to speak, for the weaving of a design, for intertwining details into a simple and clear decoration. At that time Tolstoy himself already dreamt of such primitives: "among a number of unattainable dreams I always think of a series of works neither stories nor yet descriptions, based on proverbs." The transition to intentional primitivism is finally declared later, in the tract *What is Art.* Here Tolstoy opposed that very "triviality," those details that critics formerly took him to task for, calling that device imitation.

In verbal art that device of imitation consists in describing to the smallest detail the external appearance of a character, clothes, gestures, sounds, lodgings with all those peculiarities which are found in life. . . . If you eliminate details from our best contemporary novels, what would remain?

He is attracted by "the realm of folk child art," that had not been deemed a worthy subject of art: jokes, proverbs, riddles, songs, dances, childrens' entertainments, imitations. It is characteristic that such primitivism seems to him to be a far more *difficult* task for art than a verse narrative about Cleopatra's time, or a painting of Nero setting Rome afire, or a symphony in the style of Brahms or Richard Strauss, or a Wagnerian opera. Tolstoy keenly felt the impossibility of using traditionally "poetic" material: maidens, warriors, shepherds, hermits, angels, devils of all sorts, moonlight, thunderstorms, mountains, the sea, abysses, long hair, lions, lambs, doves, nightingales—these are the clichés he enumerates that people consider poetic because "they have been used more frequently than others by earlier artists in their works." Small wonder that to the novels of Zola, Bourget, and Huysmans, "with their highly provocative subjects" he opposes a story from a children's journal about a hen and her brood scattering the white flour prepared by a poor widow for Easter cake and how she consoles the children with the proverb "Ryebread we bake is as good as a cake." Moreover, he contrasts Rossi's performance of Hamlet to a description of the Voguls' theatre, where the entire play consists of a hunter's pursuit of deer.

Tolstoy denotes the crisis of Russian artistic prose. No wonder that a new flowering of poetry began after him, where maidens, moonlight, thunderstorms, the sea, flowers and nightingales underwent a new poetization. Tolstoy is the destroyer and the consumator. But do we not return to him in the search for a new, "unpoetic" art?

Tolstoy, Seer of the Flesh

by Dmitri Merezhkovsky

In all literature there is no writer equal to Tolstoy in depicting the human body. Though he misuses repetitions, he usually attains what he needs by them, and he never suffers from the *longueurs* so common to other vigorous masters. He is accurate, simple, and as short as possible, selecting only the few, small, unnoticed facial or personal features and producing them, not all at once, but gradually and one by one, distributing them over the whole course of the story, weaving them into the living web of the action. Thus at the first appearance of old Prince Bolkonski we get only a fleeting sketch, in four or five lines, "the short figure of the old man with the powdered wig, small *dry hands* and grey, overhanging brows that sometimes, when he was roused, dimmed the flash of the clever youthful eyes." When he sits down to the lathe "by the movement of his small foot, the firm pressure of his thin veined hand" (we already know his hands are dry, but Tolstoy loves to go back to the hands of his heroes), "you could still see in the Prince the obstinate and long-enduring force of hale old age." When he talks to his daughter, Princess Maria, "he shows in a cold smile, his strong but yellowish teeth." When he sits at the table and bends over her, beginning the usual lesson in geometry, she "feels herself surrounded with the snuffy, old-age, acrid savour of her father," which had long been a sign to her. There he is all before us as if alive, height, build, hands, feet, eyes, gestures, brows, even the peculiar savour belonging to each man.

Or take the effect on Vronski when he first sees Anna Karenina. You could see at a glance she belonged to the well-born; that she was very beautiful, that she had red lips, flashing grey eyes, which looked dark from the thickness of the lashes, and that "an excess of life had so filled her being that in spite of herself it showed, now in the flash of her eyes, now in her smile." And again as the story progresses, gradually, imperceptibly,

"Tolstoy, Seer of the Flesh" by Dmitri Merezhkovsky. From *Tolstoi as Man and Artist, With an Essay on Dostoievski*, trans. F. H. Trench (London: Archibald Constable & Co., 1902). All rights reserved, 1902. Reprinted by permission of Archibald Constable & Co.

trait is added to trait, feature to feature: when she gives her hand to Vronski he is delighted "as by something exceptional with the vigorous clasp with which she boldly shook his own." When she is talking to her sister-in-law Dolly, Anna takes her hand in "her own vigorous little one." The wrist of this hand is "thin and tiny," we see the "slender tapering fingers," off which the rings slip easily.

In the hands of Karenina, as in those of other characters (it may be because the hands are the only part of the human body always bare and near elemental nature, and unconscious as the animal), there is yet greater expressiveness than in the face. In the hands of Anna lies the whole charm of her person, the union of strength and delicacy. We learn when she is standing in the crowd at the ball "that she always held herself exceptionally erect"; when she leaves the railway carriage or walks through the room she has "a quick, decisive gait, carrying with strange ease her full and perfectly proportioned body." When she dances she has "a distinguishing grace, sureness and lightness of movement"; when, having gone on a visit to Dolly, she takes off her hat, her black hair, that catches in everything, "ripples into waves all over," and on another occasion "the unruly short waves of her curly hair keep fluttering at the nape and on the temples."

In these unruly curls, so easily becoming unkempt, there is the same tension, "the excess of something" ever ready for passion, as in the too bright flash of the eyes, or the smile, breaking out involuntarily and "fluctuating between the eyes and the lips." And lastly, when she goes to the ball, we see her skin. "The black, low-cut velvet bodice showed her full shoulders and breast like polished old ivory, and *rounded* arms." This polishedness, firmness, and *roundness* of the body, as with Platon Karataev, is to Tolstoy very important and subtle, a mysterious trait. All these scattered, single features complete and tally with one another, as in beautiful statues the shape of one limb always corresponds to the shape of another. The traits are so harmonized that they naturally and involuntarily unite, in the fancy of the reader, into one living, personal whole: so that when we finish the book we cannot but recognize Anna Karenina.

This gift of *insight into the body* at times, though seldom, leads Tolstoy into excess. It is easy and pleasant to him to describe living bodies and their movements. He depicts exactly how a horse begins to start when touched by the spur: "Yarkov touched his horse with the spurs and it thrice in irritation shifted its legs, not knowing with which to begin, reared and leaped." In the first lines of *Anna Karenina* Tolstoy is in a hurry to tell us how Stepan Arcadievich Oblonski, of whom we as yet know nothing, "draws plenty of air into his broad pectoral structure," and how he walks with "his usual brisk step, turning out the feet which so lightly carry his full frame." This last feature is significant, because it records the family likeness of the brother Stepan with his sister Anna. Even if all this seems extravagant, yet extravagance in art is not excess, it is even in many cases the most needful of all things. But here is a character of third-rate importance, one of those which vanish almost as soon as they appear, some paltry regimental commander in [*War and Peace*], who has no sooner flitted before us than we have already seen that he "is broader from the chest to the back than from one shoulder to the other," and he stalks before the front "with a gait that shakes at every step and his back slightly bent." This shaky walk is repeated four times in five pages. Perhaps the observation is both true and picturesque, but it is here an inappropriate touch and in excess. Anna Karenina's fingers, "taper at the ends," are important; but we should not have lost much if he had not told us that the Tartar footman who hands dinner to Levin and Oblonski were broadhipped. Sometimes the distinguishing quality of an artist is shown, not so much by what he has in due proportion as by the gift which he has to excess.

The language of gesture, if less varied than words, is more direct, expressive and suggestive. It is easier to lie in words than by gesture or facial expression. One glance, one wrinkle, one quiver of a muscle in the face, may express the unutterable. Succeeding series of these unconscious, involuntary movements, impressing and stratifying themselves on the face and physique, form the expression of the face and the countenance of the body. Certain feelings impel us to corresponding movements, and, on the other hand, certain habitual movements impel to the corresponding *internal* states. The man who prays, folds his hands and bends his knees, and the man too who folds his hands and bends his knees is near to the praying frame of mind. Thus there exists an uninterrupted current, not only from the internal to the external, but from the external to the internal.

Tolstoy, with inimitable art, uses this convertible connection between the external and the internal. By the same law of mechanical sympathy which makes a stationary tense chord vibrate in answer to a neighbouring chord, the sight of another crying or laughing awakes in us the desire to cry or laugh; we experience when we read similar descriptions in the nerves and muscles. And so by the motions of muscles or nerves we enter shortly and directly into the internal world of his characters, begin to live with them, and in them.

When we learn that Ivan Ilyich cried out three days for pain "Uh, U-uh, Uh!" because when he began to cry "I don't want to!" he pro-

longed the sound "o-o-o," it is easy for us, not only to picture to ourselves, but ourselves physically [to] experience this terrible transition
from human speech to a senseless animal howl. And what an endlessly
complex, variegated sense at times a single movement, a single attitude
of human limbs receives at his hands!

After the battle of Borodino, in the marquee for the wounded, the
doctor, in his blood-stained apron with hands covered with blood "holds
in one of them a cigar between the middle and fore-finger, so as not to
mess it." This position of the fingers implies both the uninterruptedness
of his terrible employment, and the absence of repugnance for it; indifference to wounds and blood, owing to long habit, weariness, and desire to forget. The complexity of these internal states is concentrated in
one little physical detail, in the position of the two fingers, the description of which fills half a line.

When Prince Andrey, learning that Kutuzov is sending Bagration's
force to certain death, feels a doubt whether the commander-in-chief has
the right to sacrifice, in this self-confident way, the lives of thousands of
men, he "looks at Kutuzov, and what involuntarily strikes his eye at a
yard's distance is the clean-washed sutures of the scar on Kutuzov's tem-
ple, where the bullet at Ismail penetrated his head, and his lost eye."
"Yes, he has the right," thinks Bolkonski.

More than anything which science tells Ivan Ilyich about his illness
by the mouth of the doctors, more than all his own wonted conventional
ideas about death, does a chance look reveal the actual horror of his
state. "Ivan Ilyich began to brush his hair and looked in the mirror: he
was horrified by the way that his hair clung closely to his long forehead."
No words would suffice to express animal fear of death, as this state of
the hair noticed in the mirror. The indifference of the healthy to the
sick, or the living to the dying, is realized by Ivan Ilyich, not from the
words people use, but only by "the brawny, full-veined neck, closely girt
by its white collar, and the powerful limbs habited in tight black
breeches, of Fedor Petrovich" (his daughter's betrothed).

Between Pierre and Prince Vasili the relations are very strained and
delicate. Prince Vasili wishes to give Pierre his daughter Ellen and is
waiting impatiently for Pierre to make her an offer. The latter cannot
make up his mind. One day, finding himself alone with the father and
daughter, he rises and is for going away, saying it is late.

> Prince Vasili looked at him with stern inquiry, as if the remark was so
> strange that it was impossible to believe his ears. But presently the look of
> sternness changed. He took Pierre by the arm, put him in a chair and smiled
> caressingly, "Well, what of Lelia?" he said, turning at once to his daughter

and then again to Pierre, reminding him, not at all to the point, of a stupid anecdote of a certain Sergey Kuzmich. Pierre smiled, *but it was plain from his smile* that he knew that it was not the story of Sergey Kuzmich that interested Prince Vasili at the moment: and Prince Vasili was aware that Pierre saw this. The former suddenly muttered something and left the room. It seemed to Pierre that Prince Vasili, too, felt confused. He looked at Ellen, and she too seemed embarrassed, and her eye said, "Well you yourself are to blame."

What complex and many-sided significance evoked by a single smile! It is repeated and mirrored in the minds of those around, in a series of scarcely perceptible half-conscious thoughts and feelings, like a ray or a sound.

Pierre sees Natasha after a long separation, and the death of her first betrothed, Prince Andrey. She is so changed that he does not recognize her.

"But no, it cannot be," he thinks. "This stern, thin, pale, aged face? It cannot be she. It is only the memory of a face." But at that moment Princess Maria says, "Natasha." And the face with the observant eyes, with difficulty, with an effort, as a stuck door is opened, smiled at him and from this opened door suddenly, startlingly, came the breath, floating round Pierre, of that long forgotten happiness. It came and took hold of and swallowed him whole. When she smiled, there could no longer be a doubt; it was Natasha, and he loved her.

During this scene, one of the most important and decisive in the action of this novel, only [five] words are pronounced by Princess Maria, "Then you don't recognize her?" But the silent smile of Natasha is stronger than words; it decides the fate of Pierre.

Tolstoy depicts by gesture such intangible peculiarity of sensation as a bar of music, or of a song.

The drummer and choir leader looked sternly over the soldiers of his band and frowned. Then having convinced himself that all eyes were fixed on him, he appeared carefully to raise in both hands some unseen precious object above their heads, held it there some seconds and suddenly threw it away desperately. "Ah! alackaday, my tent, my tent! my new tent!" took up twenty men's voices.

He has equally at command the primal elemental masses and the lightest molecules scattered, like dust, over our inward atmosphere, the very atoms of feeling. The same hand which moves mountains guides these atoms as well. And perhaps the second operation is more wonderful than the first. Putting aside all that is general, literary, conventional, and artificial, Tolstoy explores in sensation what is most private, personal, and particular; takes subtle shafts of feeling, and whets and sharpens these shafts to an almost excessive sharpness, so that they penetrate and pierce like ineradicable needles; the peculiarity of his sensation will become for ever our own peculiarity. We feel Tolstoy afterwards, when we return to real life. We may say that the nervous susceptibility of people who have read the books of Tolstoy becomes different from what it was before reading them.

The secret of his effects consists, amongst other things, in his noticing what others do not, as too commonplace and which, when illumined by consciousness, precisely in consequence of this commonplace character seems unusual. Thus he first made the discovery, apparently so simple and easy, but which for thousands of years had evaded all observers, that the smile is reflected, not only on the face, but in the sound of the voice, that the voice as well as the face can be smiling. Platon Karataev at night, when Pierre cannot see his face, says something to him, "in a voice changed by a smile." The living web of art consists in such small but striking observations and discoveries. He was the first to notice that the sound of horse-hoofs is, as it were, a "transparent sound."

His language, usually simple and measured, does not suffer from an excess of epithet. When the sensation to be described is so subtle and new that by no combination of words can it possibly be expressed, he uses concatenations of onomatopoeic sounds, which serve children and primitive people in the construction of language.

In his delirium, Prince Andrey heard a low, whispering voice, ceaselessly affirming in time "I piti piti piti," and then "i ti ti," and again "i piti piti piti," and once more "i ti ti." At the same time at the sound of this whispered music Prince Andrey felt that over his face, over the very middle of it, moved some strange airy edifice of fine needles or chips. He felt, although it was hard for him, that he must assiduously maintain his equilibrium in order that this delicate fabric might not fall down. But still it did fall down, and slowly rose again to the sounds of the rhythmically whispering music. "It rises, it rises! It falls to pieces and yet spreads," said he to himself. "I piti piti piti, i ti ti, i piti piti—bang, a fly has knocked against it."

Ivan Ilyich, remembering before his death the stewed plums "which they advise me to eat now," remembered also the "dry, crinkled French prunes when I was a child." It would seem the detail was sufficiently definite. But the artist enforces it still more. Ivan remembered the peculiar taste of plums and "the abundance of saliva when you got to the stones." With this sensation of saliva from plum stones is connected in his mind a whole series of memories, of his nurse, his brother, his toys, of his whole childhood, and these memories in their turn evoke in him a comparison of the then happiness of his life with his present despair and dread of death. "No need for that, too painful," he says to himself. Such are the generalizations to which, in us all, trifling details lead.

Sonia, when in love with Nicolai Rostov, kisses him. Pushkin would have stopped at recording the kiss. But Tolstoy, not content, looks for more exactness. The thing took place at Christmas, Sonia was disguised as a hussar, and moustaches had been marked on her lips with burnt cork. And so Nicolai remembers "the smell of cork, mixed with the feel of the kiss."

The most intangible gradations and peculiarities of sensation are distinguished by him to correspond with the character, sex, age, bringing up, and status of the person experiencing them. It seems that in this region there are no hidden ways for him. His sensual experience is inexhaustible, as if he had lived hundreds of lives in various shapes of men and animals. He fathoms the unusual sensation of her bared body to a young girl, before going to her first ball. So, too, the feelings of a woman growing old and worn out with child bearing, who "shudders as she remembers the pain of her quivering breasts, experienced with almost every child." Also of a nursing mother, who has not yet severed the mysterious connection of her body with that of her child, and who "knows for a certainty, by the excess of milk in her, that the child is insufficiently fed." Lastly, the sensations and thoughts of animals, for instance the sporting dog of Levin, to whom the face of her master seems "familiar," but his eyes "always strange."

Not only the old Greeks and Romans, but in all probability the people of the eighteenth century, would not have understood the meaning of the "transparent" sound of horsehoofs, or how there can be "a savour of burnt cork mixed with the feel of a kiss," or dishes "reflect" an expression of the human countenance, a pleasant smile, or how there can be "a roundness" in the savour of a man. If our critics, the Draconian judges of the new so-called "decadence" of Art, were consistent throughout, should they not accuse even Tolstoy of "morbid obliquity"? But the truth is that to determine the fixed units of the healthy and the morbid in Art is much more difficult than it seems to the guardians of the Classical canons. Is not the "obliquity" they presuppose only an *intensifying,* the natural and inevitable development, refinement, and deepening of healthy sensuality? Perhaps our children, with their unimpaired susceptibility, will understand what is unintelligible to our critics and will justify Tolstoy. Children are well aware of what some fathers have forgotten, viz.:

that the different branches of what are called "the five senses" are by no means so sharply divided from one another, but blend, interweave, cover and supplement one another, so that sounds may seem bright and coloured ("the bright voice of the nightingale," Pushkin has it) and concatenations of movements, colours, or even scents may have the effect of music (what is called "eurhythmia"), the harmony of movement, as of colours in painting. It is usually thought that the physical sensations, as opposed to mental, are a constant quantity throughout time in the historical development of mankind. In reality, the care of physical sensation changes with the development of intellect. We see and hear what our ancestors did not see or hear. However much the admirers of classical antiquity may complain of the physical degeneracy of the men of to-day, it is scarcely possible to doubt that we are creatures more keen-sighted, keen of hearing and physically acute, than the heroes of the *Iliad* and the *Odyssey*. Does not science, too, conjecture that certain sensations, for instance, the last colours of the spectrum, have become the general achievement of men, only at a comparatively recent and historical stage of their existence, and that perhaps even Homer confused green with dark blue in one epithet, for the hue of seawater? Does there not still go on a similar natural growth and *intensification* in other branches of human sentience? Will not our children's children see and hear what we as yet do not see and hear? Will not the unseen be seen to them, though undreamed of by our fathers, our critics, men of worn-out sensitiveness to impression, nay, even to the boldest and most advanced of ourselves? Will not our present "decadent" over-refinement, which so alarms the old believers of the day on Art, then seem in its turn obvious, primitive, Homeric healthiness and coarseness? In this unchecked development, movement and flow, where is the fixed standard for dividing the lawful from the unlawful, wholesome from morbid, natural from corrupt? Yesterday's exception becomes to-day's rule. And who shall dare to say to the living body, the living spirit, "Here shall you stop, no further may you go"? Why particularly here? Why not farther on?

However this may be, the special glory of Tolstoy lies exactly in the fact that he was the first to express (and with what fearless sincerity!), new branches, unexhausted and inexhaustible,—of oversubtilizing physical and mental consciousness. We may say that he gave us new bodily sensations, new vessels for new wine.

The Apostle Paul divides human existence into three branches, borrowing the division from the philosophers of the Alexandrian School, the physical man, the spiritual and the natural. The last is the connecting link between the first two, something intermediate, double, transitional,

like twilight; neither Flesh nor Spirit, that in which the Flesh is completed and the Spirit begins, in the language of psycho-physiology the
physico-spiritual phenomenon.

Tolstoy is the greatest depictor of this physico-spiritual region in the
natural man; that side of the flesh which approaches the spirit, and that
side of the spirit which approaches the flesh, the mysterious border-region
where the struggle between the animal and the God in man takes place.
Therein lies the struggle and the tragedy of his own life. He is a "man
of the senses," half-heathen, half-Christian; neither to the full.

In proportion as he recedes from this neutral ground in either direction, it matters not whether towards the region of the cold "pre-animal"
Nature, that region which *seems* inorganic, insentient, inanimate, "material" (the terrible and beatific calm of which Turgeniev and Pushkin
have told so well); or as he essays the opposite region; human spirituality,
almost set free from the body, released from animal nature, the region of
pure thought (the passionate workings of which are so well embodied by
Dostoevsky and Tiutchev) the power of artistic delineation in Tolstoy
decreases, and in the end collapses, so that there are limits which are for
him wholly unattainable. But within the limits of the purely natural man
he is the supreme artist of the world.

In other provinces of Art, for instance the painting of the Italian Ren-
aissance and the sculpture of the ancient Greeks, there have been artists
who with greater completeness than Tolstoy depicted the bodily man.
The music of the present day, and in part the literature, penetrate us
more deeply. But nowhere, and at no time, has the "natural man" appeared with such startling truth and nakedness as he appears in the creations of Tolstoy.

Tolstoy's Art

by Käte Hamburger

When we said that the autobiographical nature of Tolstoy's first work, the trilogy *Childhood, Boyhood, Youth* (1852-1857) was not an accidental phenomenon, that, in fact, the work is of vital significance for that reason, the statement at first seems to be exaggerated. It is no rarity that a novelist or dramatist forms the material of his works from the dates, milieu, personages, and events of his life or partially incorporates them in it. We know that the substance of *Buddenbrooks* is the story of Thomas Mann's family, that Dickens represented himself in *David Copperfield* as did Byron in *Childe Harold* and Keller in *Der grüne Heinrich,* and in the broadest possible sense every poetic work has its autobiographical sources, whether material or psychological.

We mean something else when we emphasize the autobiographical element as the determining impetus in Tolstoy's literary work. The point in question here is not the more-or-less trivial fact that the work is an expression of Tolstoy's life and experience, but rather that it is the *functional relationship* in that the autobiographical impetus is related to the inner principle of form in the Tolstoyan epic, of which the poet himself is essentially unconscious. The analysis of this principle of form will show that the functional relationship takes root in the notion of natural life and the conception of truth appropriate to it, and also how it operates.

When we compare *Childhood, Boyhood, Youth* with other famous confessions in literature—the *Confessions* of Augustine and Rousseau, or Goethe's *Dichtung und Wahrheit*—the first difference between Tolstoy's and the other works is marked by its temporal position in the life of the author. The three autobiographies of world literature cited are retrospective portraits of their youth by mature, indeed, aged men; *Childhood, Boyhood, Youth,* however, is the work of a young man at the beginning

"Tolstoy's Art" by Käte Hamburger. From *Tolstoy, Gestalt und Problem*, 2nd, revised edition, in the paperback Kleine Vandenhoeck-Reihe, 159/160/161 (Göttingen: Vandenhoeck & Ruprecht, 1963). Copyright © 1963 by Vandenhoeck & Ruprecht. Reprinted by permission of Vandenhoeck & Ruprecht and of the author. Translated for this volume by B. Korpan.

of his development, on the brink of manhood, who is sufficiently close to his boyhood years to be able to relive and render the emotional life of childhood in its direct freshness and authenticity. The very existence of such an autobiography, drawn directly from recent, original experience is significant for Tolstoy's feeling for life and his creative art. This direct touch with life (which brings Tolstoy's first work closer to *Werther* than to *Dichtung und Wahrheit*) can be understood as an unconscious expression of a man who is concerned more with self-knowledge than with the creation of an objectively self-contained independent artistic structure. And even if one were to object that *Childhood, Boyhood, Youth* in spite of everything is different from the aforementioned autobiographies because it nevertheless has an objective artistic form, then a more thorough consideration of the structure would reveal that the autobiographical theme proper is directly linked to the self-portrait in the diaries of his youth.

The objective form of the artistic work is to a certain degree only minimal: by providing the first person narrator with another name and by stripping the remaining figures, circumstances, and relationships to family and friends of their external biographical characters through appropriate alterations. The same is not true, however, for the internal autobiographical content. The self-analyses, which were only sketched in the early diary, are carried farther and develop in greater detail and in more elaborately presented scenes what was sketched there: how in young Tolstoy (Irtenev) there was a strong drive toward immediate, unreflecting participation in life, toward the natural patency of being and existence, and at the same time a drive toward moral self-discipline and even self-torment. There are chapters, constituting the permanent magic of the work, that depict the personages, rooms, landscapes, and events of the world of childhood with all the sensuous freshness of that which is experienced and seen: images of a tender mother figure, radiant as in life, of a kind father who enjoys life, and of a fashionably majestic grandmother who instills respect; the portrait, full of love and humor, of the good-natured German tutor Karl Ivanovitch, and the contrasting portrait of the elegant French instructor, drawn with aversion, old servants and maids, beggars and half-demented pilgrims, who are housed on the estate and treated almost as saints; brothers, friends, and girls, moved by the first stirrings of love; school, hunts, children's balls, country excursions and formal visits—in short, the life of a boy belonging to the Russian aristocracy of the nineteenth century, who, on his estates and in his townhouse leads the life appropriate to his station. But as in the diary, the objective faithfulness to life embodied in the poetic depiction of the world around him is simultaneously endowed with the critical observation of his moral relationship to this life. After the magnificent rendering of a spring storm, conveying the smells of woods, birches, violets, decayed winter foliage, morels, and the wet branches of a blossoming alder, there follows immediately a chapter entitled "A New View," namely, the first sudden realization that there are other lives in the world besides one's own, the experience of one's fellow creatures, that lies at the roots of Tolstoyanism. And the name by which Tolstoy henceforth personified his moral "I," Prince Nekhlyudov, already occurs in this first work. He is depicted here as the youth's friend, whose still vague ideal conviction that it is the duty of each human being to strive for moral perfection determines Tolstoyan life decisively from the very beginning.

Nevertheless we note again that the question of the moral idea as such does not occur in this context. It had to be mentioned here as evidence of the dependence on autobiography in this first work—and not in this work alone, but in all the writings of the following years. More or less all of them are extensions of *Childhood, Boyhood, Youth*—that is, stamped by a biographical quality: the Caucasian stories "The Raid," "The Wood Felling," *The Cossacks*, "Sevastopol," "The Snowstorm"; the tales "Lucerne," "The Morning of a Landowner," and "Notes of a Billiard-Marker." They are biographical in the sense of external depiction of experience as much as in the sense of confession, above all insofar as the moral idea in them is personified in Nekhlyudov—and further, in respect to Tolstoy's Nekhlyudov–"I," *Resurrection,* the work of his old age, which completes the ring begun with *Childhood, Boyhood, Youth,* can be added to the series of early works of the 1850s.

One need hardly mention that this representation of the self is not to be derived merely from the name. Olenin, the hero of *The Cossacks,* Prince Bolkonski and Pierre Bezukhov in *War and Peace,* Levin in *Anna Karenina,* Pozdnyshev in the *Kreutzer Sonata,* Sarryntsov in *A Light Shines in the Darkness,* Fedya Protasov in *The Living Corpse*—all are Tolstoyan "I"–heroes, representatives of his own problems, more or less precise embodiments of his own situations. So far as the mere material is concerned, the tales of the 1850s belong to the same pattern of autobiographical representation as *Childhood, Boyhood, Youth.* One need hardly offer proof to show that "Lucerne," "Sevastopol," "The Morning of a Landowner," "The Wood Felling," and "The Raid" are direct renderings of personally experienced situations and events. In any case, the invented elements of the stories are so few in number and significance that they do not damage the nature of the personal experience in the external matter. This is also true for *The Cossacks,* in which it is less obvious as such, and only for the sake of completeness should it be mentioned here that *War and Peace* as well as *Anna Karenina* contains an abundance of such autobiographical material, namely extremely faithful portraits of parents and relatives, adherent to the family and social world to which Tolstoy belonged.

But it is neither the autobiographical content of the stories nor the more-or-less veiled self-portraiture of the Nekhlyudov figures and their counterparts that constitute the specific peculiarity of the autobiographical impetus in Tolstoy's creation. We have noted that both elements are frequently found in literature, and if we are to establish the autobiographical impetus as an unconsciously created *principle of form* in Tolstoy's art, it cannot be sought in them. Certainly this impetus did not make its appearance at once. It is deeply linked with what we might call the direct relation to life, which as such is the innermost cause of the narrative technique that is so strongly autobiographically oriented or, in other terms, the cause of the thin line between autobiography and fiction. We will therefore designate the autobiographical impetus that serves the function of a principle of form as the tendency toward *open form*. It is stamped on the early writings mentioned, undergoes a particular and peculiar formation in the poetic masterpiece *War and Peace* that terminates and crowns the early period, investing that work with its permanent magic, is in part toned down though still on the whole retained in *Anna Karenina,* and it is not by chance that it finally breaks through again as the main mode in the principal work of his old age, *Resurrection.*

The open form is most easily recognized and apparent in *Childhood, Boyhood, Youth.* The publisher, with some justice, refused to accept Tolstoy's designation of the work as a novel and wanted to point to the autobiographical nature of the work in the title. A novel, no matter how diffusely narrated, is a closed form of narration, a story that builds up an external or internal event and leads it to a definite conclusion. But the description of youth in *Childhood* is not linked to the structural and suspense-arousing elements of the story. Instead, all three parts are composed of small pictures of life in a series that is in itself, as it were, endlessly open and that can be regarded as continuing at will from the point where it by chance concludes. It is clear that this structure is intrinsically connected with its autobiographical character, in fact, in a broader sense with the direct approach to life mentioned above, from which the biography of his youth proceeds.

It is worth noting, nonetheless, how the tendency toward open form in the writings of this period unconsciously continues. The basic feature of all the tales of the 1850s is not so much that of the story as it is that of the picture—and indeed of a picture that can be extended with many more optional details and in many further directions at will. As for the distinctness of this structure, after *Childhood, Boyhood, Youth* one must cite in first place the depiction of the siege at Sevastopol, to which the stories "The Raid" and "The Wood Felling" belong thematically. It is the representation of war—on which the great painter of battles in *War and Peace* is already practicing his skill—not the war seen in official reports, but the daily life of the soldiers and officers, the dirt of communication trenches, the torments and screams in primitive field hospitals, death that threatens the lives of men in the advanced bastions every minute—pictures of life, even when filled with horror, linked to one another in the same technique of pictures and episodes as in *Childhood, Boyhood, Youth*.

At first glance works like "The Morning of a Landowner" and *The Cossacks* seem to be different. In "Landowner" and *The Cossacks* a story is developed to the extent that both deal with a protagonist who sets a particular undertaking in motion: in the "Landowner" it concerns young Prince Nekhlyudov, who gives up his university studies and devotes himself to improving the position of the peasants; in *The Cossacks* it concerns Olenin, a spoiled young man who, weary of the corrupt life of luxury in the big city, seeks to mend his soul in the mighty setting of the Caucasus and among the primitive beings of the mountain villages. But the effect that these novels create stems neither from moments of suspense in the action nor from special interest in the experiences of their protagonist. To a greater extent here, too, scenes from life form the actual content and charm of the work: the life and types of Russian peasants on estates in the "Landowner," the unfamiliar and alluring milieu of the cossacks and Circassians on the banks of the Terek—and much as the heroes of these novels continually participate in that life, they still remain outsiders and observers, who are ultimately identical with the author himself, who relates his own experience through them. Despite external appearances, this holds for the hero of *The Cossacks* too. For although he seems more closely linked to the milieu and the people of the Caucasian village through his love for the pretty cossack girl Marianka than the young landowner Nekhlyudov is to his peasants, whom he only visits and superintends, no real novelistic plot results from this circumstance either. In the final analysis the girl Marianka belongs only to the picture of the village, which Olenin observes as something foreign and allows to pass before him. The love for Marianka plays no larger a role emotionally than his participation in the military expeditions of the Circassians, his friendship with the young Lukashka, or his conversations with Uncle

Eroshka, and in no way represents a center around which the narrative
could be constructed as is usually done in love stories. For this reason
The Cossacks as well as *Childhood, Boyhood, Youth* or "Sevastopol" can
dispense with a real climactic moment.

Nor is such a climax produced through the moral meaning from which
the narratives finally stem in *The Cossacks* or in "Landowner," or even
in the late work *Resurrection,* which is closely related to the works of the
early period. Indeed, it is precisely that moral meaning which, transferred
to the "moral" heroes, gives those pictures and episodes their open form
as pure description. For the life of the cossacks, the peasants, and the
prisoners runs its course independent of the moral hero, who remains
outside the events, does not participate in them, whether he is an observer and sentimental yearner like Olenin, or whether he desires to take
part by helping and changing things like Prince Nekhlyudov in the early
tales and the later works. When in the end Olenin arrives at the resigned
conclusion that his sentimental yearning for a "return to nature" must
remain unrealizable for him, the intellectual man of culture, when the
young landowner Nekhlyudov, in spite of all his moral efforts and attempts at social reform, ultimately envies the young peasant lad Ilyushka
his simplicity and lack of moral constraint in his existence, or the
Nekhlyudov of *Resurrection* realizes that the basic flaw of the social order
is that all men are evil-doers before God and therefore no one may punish
other evil-doers—all these are experiences and insights of outsiders, who
are in no way engaged in the fates and lives of the cossacks, the peasants,
or the prisoners. The life of these groups of men—in all three cases they
are represented with the power of naturalistic observation, the truth and
the freshness of direct contact with life that already designated the author
of *Childhood, Boyhood, Youth* as one of the greatest epic poets in world
literature—these depictions of life to a certain degree unfold with little
concern for the fact that they are themselves objects of artistic creation,
unconcerned as natural life itself, which submits to no laws other than
those which develop out of life itself. The naturalness and inner laws of
life are ultimately the only reasons for what we feel to be the lack of
suspense of these novels and tales.[1] This in itself is an example of the
principle of open form, that for its part was recognized as the unconscious
artistic expression of the natural truth of life that directed Tolstoy's
creative impulse. And even if not all Tolstoy's poetic works are marked

---

[1] This lack of suspense by no means necessarily creates the feeling of boredom in
the reader, although it cannot be denied that *The Cossacks,* above all, suffers from
a certain boredom and probably the unfortunate criticism that is very often made of
Resurrection stems from this impulse.

by this principle of form,[2] it became operative in the great novel that concludes the early period, *War and Peace,* if only in a special way and in such a manner that a perfected epic art form was created.

It was with *War and Peace* that Tolstoy first achieved the height of his epic mastery and entered world literature. This means at the same time that the impulse to lack of suspense and to the purely descriptive character of pictures and episodes that produced the open form in the aforementioned works is no longer to be found in this masterpiece. There are no moral heroes here who stand outside the actual happenings and whose inner experiences have nothing to do with these events. Here each of the numerous figures who live, experience, act, and suffer is inextricably woven into the events and life that unfold inexhaustibly here—to such a degree that *War and Peace* is incomparable not only within Tolstoy's own work, but in world literature.

The inexhaustibility, the richness of life this novel presents is, however, realized through nothing other than the principle of open form, if one analyses the structure more deeply. Only here it was achieved in the actual *process of forming* itself, in a totally different way than in the works mentioned above, which were too restricted by autobiography, and that the idea of natural life became for the first time an art form reposing in itself.

We will designate the methodological principle that produces the special open form of the large novel as *decentralization.* It is characterized not by a central figure who is led through various milieus and spheres of people and objects in order that they be represented through his eyes, so to say, as is customary in traditional narrative style, but rather the masses of subject matter are divided into various spheres of life in such a way that a particular group belongs to each sphere. These groups are undoubtedly not completely isolated from each other, in the sense of Jules Romains' technique and method of *unanimisme;* they touch each other and link up in part by family relations and friendships as life brings them together by chance, by circumstances through which people encounter each other, live together for a while, and then separate from each other again. It is, however, essential that in this novel, as in life, each person be the center of his own life, which may well touch or cross the paths of other persons, but must not do so of necessity. Therefore there is no real central figure in *War and Peace,* around whom all events,

[2] Of the writings of the early period this is valid for "Polikushka," "Kholstomer," "Family Happiness." In the late period there are, other than the short moral tales and legends, the three dramas, which by their very nature are not characterized by the epic principle of open form.

persons, and places can be arranged. Neither Prince Andrey nor Pierre Bezukhov, neither Nikolai Rostov nor Natasha nor Princess Mary is the "hero" of the novel. Instead the poet accompanies first one then the other of these and countless other personages on part of their life course, only to depart and let him recede into the background for a while again. When we are with young Count Nikolai Rostov in his regiment, for example, or on a wolf hunt on his father's estate, we participate in his love story and his other problems of life, and meanwhile we forget to a certain extent all other men and their destinies until one of them emerges into the foreground of the novelistic stage and for a period of time becomes in turn the center of our interest. For no one particular plot or one special problem constitutes the theme of the novel, but rather nothing more and nothing less than a segment of life—the life of Russians, of the Russian land and its folk and above all of its upper class, in a particular historical epoch, in war and peace, in their homes, in army headquarters and in the offices of diplomats, at balls, hunts, and on the battle fields, in their most private destinies and in their stake in their fatherland.

It is this technique of decentralization that creates the illusion of the open, the unbound, and continually moving on, which is the essence of life. The novel does not end with any concluding episode: death, failure, or even a betrothal. Instead, after the death of a person, no matter what deep and painful traces he leaves behind, as in the case of Prince Andrey, life continues for those who remain alive, and Natasha finds new happiness. Reconstruction follows economic ruin, as in the case of Count Rostov, and it is not an engagement, that is, a novelistic "happy ending," that concludes the story of Pierre and Natasha and of Nikolai and Mary, but a picture of their daily home life that one may conceive as continuing with passing time until their deaths. The technique of decentralization, which permits an effortless transition from one milieu to another, from one person or group of persons to another, simultaneously eliminates the scaffolding of art, or at least of artistic technique—and in this sea of life, men, events, and experiences there seems to be no structure or law other than the structure and law of life itself.

If we compare Tolstoy's second principal poetic work, *Anna Karenina*, with *War and Peace* from this point of view, it would seem obvious that the principle of open form as well as the method of decentralization no longer applied. The story of Anna Karenina presents an action complete in itself, since despite the breadth of its movement and despite the slowness and numerous retarding moments in its development, it seems from its beginning—the encounter of Anna and Vronsky at the Moscow ball to the final catastrophe, Anna's suicide under the wheels of the train—to be built according to the traditional form of the novel.

But the Anna Karenina-plot does not constitute the entire content of the novel. The story of Levin and Kitty occupies equal space—and when we examine it more closely, we see that the open form emerges in it once again to a certain degree unconsciously. It could of course be objected that this is not the case inasmuch as the Levin-plot is constructed and intended as a contrasting parallel action to the Anna-plot: namely the legitimate marriage as the opposite of the illegitimate union that leads to ruin, the ethically oriented god-seeking man Levin in contrast to the adultress who is possessed by the demonic natural force of love. But aside from the fact that, upon closer investigation, the assertion of such a contrast everywhere leads to discrepancies, one can conclude from the entire character and all the spheres of life of the novel that such a morality was far removed from Tolstoy—and not in vain did he affix to his work as motto the Biblical words: "Mine is the vengeance." We penetrate deeper into Tolstoy's essence when we interpret the Kitty-Levin-plot as springing from Tolstoy's unconsciously working drive to depict "life." Even though Vronsky and Anna are not related to his own life and to his problems of life, the figures of Levin and Kitty are flesh of his flesh and spirit of his spirit. It is also known that he depicted his own marriage and in part its early history in this couple. By means of the Levin-plot Tolstoy built his own life into the Anna Karenina novel, and here again an autobiographical impulse works toward the open form, which was seen as the artistic precipitate of the urge to portray natural life in its true colors.

For if viewed formally, the Levin-plot exists like the persons and groups of persons in *War and Peace*. It represents a life that—in contrast to Anna's and Vronsky's—unfolds without dramatically climactic events, and which must be conceived as continuing at the point where the novel ends. Levin's engagement to Kitty Shcherbatsky, which comes about only after several difficulties, takes place in the first half of the novel and does not present a conclusion, and even though the marriage is troubled at one time or another by minor disturbances, it is carried out in accordance to bourgeois life, which in that epoch meant normal life and is conceived as continuing to some natural conclusion. So far as Levin's moral and religious and social problems are concerned, however, he experiences at the very end a kind of answer from the mouth of a simple peasant, namely, that man should live for the sake of his soul and think of God, which means to love thy neighbor—but one cannot say that this realization contains any decisive, life-reforming force for Levin or, so far as it applies to this realization, that it is made evident as such. For life—and this is Tolstoy's unconscious insight into truth and the reality of life coming into the open—life does not undergo change so easily, no matter how decisive the realizations are that we come to about it. It is neither dramatic nor lyrical-poetic, but natural when Kitty, to whom he wants to open his heart at that moment—"She understands it," he thought. "She knows what I'm thinking about"—unsuspecting, interrupts him with the prosaic request to check if everything is in order in the guest room for Sergey Ivanovitch. In fact, Levin's life will continue as before,—he will, despite his perception of the meaning of life as love for one's neighbor, get angry at Ivan the coachman as before, become involved in quarrels with other people as before, and will feel a wall separating himself from them, including his young wife. Thus ends the story of Levin, and it is not arbitrary to have the entire novel end with that and not with Anna's death or its aftermath, Vronsky's inner breakdown and departure for the Serbian war. By concluding with Levin's unconcluded story, it gains the aspect of infinity, or what is the same thing of the *future*, for all life, inasmuch as it is life, receives its meaning through the future. And we might say that in *Anna Karenina* too, the structural principle of open form that is natural to Tolstoy and that is the form of life, operates in a modified way.

It operates also in the construction of the novel, upon closer examination, and if possible in a still sharper and more pronounced fashion than in *War and Peace*. In *Anna Karenina* too the subject matter is decentralized. Three family groups, the Shcherbatski-Levins, the Karenins, and the Oblonskys, who are linked together only through accidental family relationships, live each for themselves in their own circle, each occupied with their own personal problems, corresponding to the reality of natural life: the Karenins are occupied with the story of adultery; the Oblonskys with their economic problems and marital difficulties; the Shcherbatskys with Kitty's marriage, and Levin, who becomes a part of this family as son-in-law, with the affairs of his agriculture as well as with those of his conscience, and in a fashion similar to that of *War and Peace* the reader spends some time first with one group, then with another. Not one of these family groups in relation to the others, each of the people belonging for the time being to one of them, is linked to the others except through the sympathy that exists among relatives and friends; that is, they are not linked together through and in a unity of action. Each of these groups could contribute its material to its own more or less exciting novelistic plot, and if the novel is entitled after the Anna Karenina-plot, this might have occurred because this plot is the most dramatic-sensational of the three. In short, the aspect of natural life, which only seldom rises to dramatic heights, and seldom tears people out of their ordinary existences, is preserved in *Anna Karenina* as it is in *War and Peace* and, as in the latter, is created through the technique of open form and decentralization.

We have attempted to understand Tolstoy's singular method and technique, which departs from traditional novelistic style, and to derive it from the veracity of his striving for perception and configuration. This aesthetic "theory of imitation"—the imagination as a mirror of nature or natural life and genius as reproducing and copying rather than as creating anew—lies at the root of the healthy Naturalism of Tolstoy's art, as little as it itself dares to express the essence of life.

The naturalism of Tolstoy's *style* and *diction* is nothing more than another expression of his striving for veracity. It corresponds to the principle of open form insofar as it is a direct offspring of the attempt to represent life in its actuality. When the critic Nekrasov emphasized truth as a special trait of the first tale *Childhood,* it must have been above all, indeed in the first place, the narrative style that led him to use such an epithet.

Indeed, this early work points to Tolstoy's unique style practically fully developed as that which distinguishes his novels from the mass of European narrative literature of his time and lends them their peculiar modernity. When we say "modernity," we are not referring to content and problems. *War and Peace* is a historical novel, and the love-and-marriage conflict of *Anna Karenina* is (as we shall see more precisely later) in a particularly important way connected with its time and is outdated by contemporary points of view. The modernity of these novels derives from another source: from a striking immediacy, naturalness, and directness in the manner of representation, which appear to stem from an attitude toward his material different from that of the traditional novelistic style of the nineteenth century. It is, so to say, a non-literary, a non-artistic attitude. One receives the impression that the poet views his figures far less as literary objects than as people who belong to his own life, people whom he does not describe, analyze, "sketch," or "outline" in any way, but rather with whom he mingles in his daily life, in an ordinary and not festive way, often jokingly and humorously.

In Tolstoy's novels and tales nothing remains of the favorite nineteenth century narrative and stylistic forms, no remnants of the frame-narratives that to a certain extent display artificiality, but that were, for example, typical for Turgenev, the most famous Russian novelist of that time, and in which Theodor Storm excelled in Germany. Tolstoy never presents such unnatural situations as, for example, that in Turgenev's "First Love," where the guests at an evening gathering are suddenly requested to tell the story of their first love, or, as in another tale of the same writer, "Andrej Kolosov," to tell something about the most remarkable person they had encountered.

Nothing of this romanticizing technique, of these often heightened, constructed situations that were characteristic of the mid-nineteenth century is to be found in Tolstoy. It is significant for the "naturalistic" naturalness of his feeling for style and striving for style, that at a reading of a Pushkin story that begins with the words, "The guests assembled at the estate of Count L.," Tolstoy called out enthusiastically: "How good, how simple it is! *In medias res.* That's how one must begin. Pushkin is my teacher"—and these trivial words inspired him to begin writing the first chapter of *Anna Karenina.* "On that very evening," reports Countess Tolstoy, "he wrote the opening sentence of this novel: 'Everything was in confusion in the Oblonsky household' "—a sentence no less trivial than the one in the Pushkin story, one must concede, from which, however, later the great and true pictures of life in the novel developed that have preserved its eternal freshness.

To this representational method of natural truth—or more meaningfully, the truth of the natural—corresponds the direct, unpretentious narrative style *per se*—a style that molds persons and things, thoughts and feelings with enormous plasticity, without arabesques, metaphors, and comparisons, but in a direct view, so to say. It does not lie within the scope of this presentation, there is no place to demonstrate it through an analysis of style and language, and we cannot undertake it here. One example alone, a reference from *Childhood, Boyhood, Youth,* might serve to stimulate such a view of Tolstoy's narrative style, which unites itself immediately to the world he describes:

> You would go into the apple orchard, perhaps you have crept into the very midst of the tall, thick, overgrown raspberry bush. Above you is the clear hot sky, around you the pale green prickly verdure of the raspberry bushes mingled with weeds. . . . Green, needle-like grass and young burrs forced their way through last year's foliage and besprinkled with dew, turn succulent green in the perpetual shade, as if they knew nothing of how brilliantly the sun shines on the leaves of the apple tree. . . . In this thicket it is always damp; it smells of permanent, dense shade, of spiders' webs, of fallen apples, already turned black and lying around on the mouldy earth, of raspberries, often also of the woodlice that you swallow unnoticed with a berry, whereupon you eat another berry as quickly as possible. . . .

There seems to be no artistic impulse at work in this style. Every picturesque, musical, or otherwise aesthetically designed effect is avoided. The aim of the narrative is to approach the being of things as adequately and accurately as possible—and the result is that the actual object, here the raspberry bush thicket beneath the apple trees, stands forth in its total sensuous real liveliness. Tolstoy's style, when one attempts to grasp its most inner essence—this style alone makes it comprehensible that his calling to be a poet never stood at the center of his consciousness and striving, not even during the time of his first poetic creativity. His poetic genius was not soil in which his feeling for existence took root and from which it grew, instead it was directed and determined by the moral drive to seek out the real bases of human life. We may stress again that this is not to be understood here in the sense of moral contents as such—to what extent they are present in the early works is another question—rather solely in the sense of the unveiled naturalism that characterizes Tolstoy's style. This means, as we may point out again in this connection, that the foundations and roots of Tolstoy's feeling for existence displace these—if one seeks to separate completely his artistry from his moralism, in fact, his spirituality—as an unconsciously and inadequately perceived violation of his poetic genius. When Merezhkovsky, for instance, supported by the utterances of Countess Tolstoy or the eldest son Leo, is given to attributing the discomfort that Tolstoy experienced during the time of the "Crisis"—that is, the final decision to seek the truth—to such a violation, then he fails to recognize the spiritual events that occurred here. That the reverse is really much more the case, that the spiritual unrest was caused by the realization that he was not on the "right path" for his artistic creativity, namely the realization of the moral idea, is quite apparent in his *Confession,* written toward the end of the 1870s. Here Tolstoy says that when he was feted in Petersburg literary circles as a genius three years after his debut as a writer and shared with his colleagues belief in the meaning and importance of art for life, he had begun to doubt that "theory."

Inasmuch as Tolstoy created works of art, to a certain extent against his own will and innermost convictions—torn by the power of the artist-creator that was given to him, so to say—*physei,* the ethos that lives in them and forms them from within is the ethos of the absolute respect for the truth of life. The two great novels that are morally the least tendencious of his works are also marked by this ethos purely formally, as we have attempted to illustrate.

Tolstoy and the Development of Realism

by Georg Lukács

I

. . . The epic presentation of the totality of life—unlike the dramatic—must inevitably include the presentation of the externals of life, the epic-poetic transformation of the most important objects making up some sphere of human life and most typical events necessarily occurring in such a sphere. Hegel calls this first postulate of epic presentation "the totality of objects." This postulate is not a theoretical invention. Every novelist instinctively feels that his work cannot claim to be complete if it lacks this "totality of objects," that is, if it does not include every important object, event and sphere of life belonging to the theme. The crucial difference between the genuine epics of the old realists and the disintegration of form in the declining newer literature is manifested in the way in which this "totality of objects" is linked with the individual destinies of the characters.

The modern writer, the looker-on, can very well achieve such an awareness of this totality of objects. And if he is a great writer, he may conjure it up before us by the force, the suggestive power of his descriptions. Every reader will remember, for instance, Zola's markets, stock exchanges, underworld haunts, theatres, racetracks, etc. So far as the encyclopaedic character of his contents and the artistic quality of his descriptions is concerned, Zola, too, possessed this "totality of objects." But these objects have a being entirely independent of the fate of the characters. They form a mighty but indifferent background to human destinies with which they have no real connection; at best they are the more or less accidental scenery among which these human destinies are enacted.

How different are the classics!

Homer tells us about the weapons of Achilles, weapons made by the gods. But he does not do so as soon as Achilles takes the stage. Only when Achilles has angrily retired to his tent, when the Trojans have triumphed, when Patrocles has been killed in the borrowed armour of Achilles, when Achilles himself is preparing for the mortal combat with Hector—a combat mortal in every sense of the word, for Achilles knows that he himself must die soon after Hector's death—it is just before this dramatic moment of the combat with Hector, when the weapons of the two champions decide the fate of two nations and the better weapons of Achilles, apart from his god-like strength, become a factor deciding the outcome of the duel—only then does Homer describe how Hephaistos forged these weapons for Achilles.

Thus the description of the weapons of Achilles is truly epic, not only because the poet describes their *making* and not their *appearance* (Lessing points this out in the famous chapter in his *Laokoon*), but also from the point of view of the composition as a whole, for it occurs exactly where these weapons of Achilles play a decisive part in the story, in the characterization and fate of the heroes. Thus these arms of Achilles are not objects independent of the characters in the story but an integrating factor of the story itself.

The really great novelists are in this respect always true-born sons of Homer. True, the world of objects and the relationship between them and men has changed, has become more intricate, less spontaneously poetic. But the art of the great novelists manifests itself precisely in the ability to overcome the unpoetic nature of their world, through sharing and experiencing the life and evolution of the society they lived in. It is by sending out their spontaneously typical heroes to fulfil their inherently necessary destinies that the great writers have mastered with such sovereign power the changeful texture of the external and internal, great and little moments that make up life. Their heroes set out on their career and encounter quite naturally the specific objects and events of their sphere of life. Precisely because the characters are typical in the most profound sense of the word, they must of necessity meet the most important objects of their sphere of life more than once in the course of their typical career. The writer is free to introduce these objects when and where they have become typical and necessary requisites in the drama of life he is describing.

There is perhaps no other modern author in whose works the 'totality of objects' is so rich, so complete as in Tolstoy. We need not think only of *War and Peace* in which every detail of the war is shown, from the court and the general staff down to the guerilla fighters and prisoners of

war and every phase of peaceful private life from birth to death. We can
recall the dances, clubs, parties, social calls, conferences, work in the fields,
horse-races and card games described in *Anna Karenina* and the court
and prison scenes in *Resurrection*. But if we subject to a closer analysis
any of these pictures—which Tolstoy paints with such pleasure, so
broadly and in such detail that each of them becomes a separate picture
within the framework of the whole—we cannot fail to see how different
they are from the pictures painted by modern realists and how similar to
those we find in the old epics.

These pictures of Tolstoy are never mere scenery, never merely pictures
and descriptions, never merely contributions to the "totality of objects."
The Christmas fancy-dress procession in *War and Peace* marks a crisis in
the love of Nikolai Rostov and Sonia; the victorious cavalry charge
signals a crisis in the life of Nikolai Rostov; the horse-race is a turning-
point in the relations between Anna Karenina and Vronski; the trial of
Katyusha leads to the fateful meeting between her and Nekhlyudov and
so on. Each such separately presented section of the "totality of objects"
contains some decisive point which makes it a necessary factor in the
evolution of one or more of the characters in the novel.

In reality the interconnections and relationships in Tolstoy's novels are
much more intricate and varied then merely such points of contact between objective happenings and the subjective experiences of the characters, as have been referred to in the preceding; such points of intersection
also mark more or less important turning-points of the whole story. Every
phase of such crises, every thought and emotion of the characters is in-
separably intertwined with the turning-point, with the event which pro-
vides the opportunity for the crisis in the story. For instance: when it is
already inevitable that a crisis in the relationship of Anna and Vronski
to Karenin should arise, the race and Vronski's accident is nevertheless
not merely an opportunity for the crisis to become manifest, it also determines the nature of the crisis. It reveals traits in each of the three
characters which in other circumstances would not have manifested themselves in the same way and with the same typicality. Because of the
internal threads which link the horse-race with the characters and the
plot, the race entirely ceases to be a mere picture—it grows into the
fateful culminating scene of a great drama, and the fact that riding in
races is a typical pastime of Vronski, that attending horse-races at which
royalty is present is a typical habit of the bureaucrat Karenin, renders
the manifold relationships between individual destinies and the 'totality
of objects' even more manifold and typical by the intervention of social
factors.

Such a presentation of the "totality of objects" dispenses Tolstoy—like every truly great epic poet—from giving dry and tedious descriptions of a setting, the connection between which and individual destinies is always general and abstract and hence always remains coincidental. The 'totality of objects' in Tolstoy always expresses, in immediate, spontaneous and palpable form, the close bond between individual destinies and the surrounding world.

II

Such a manner of presenting the 'totality of objects' is a condition *sine qua non* of depicting truly typical characters. Engels stressed the importance of typical circumstances in close connection with the typicality of characters, as a prerequisite of true realism. But typical circumstances may be depicted abstractly or concretely, even if they are correctly described, so far as their social nature is concerned. In the works of the newer realists such descriptions increasingly tend to be abstract. If the characters in a work of art, their mutual relationships, the stories of their lives, etc., cannot be shown in such a manner that the relationships between them and their environment appear as the natural results of the characterization; if the settings and instruments of the story are from the viewpoint of the individual merely accidental (i.e., if artistically they make the impression of mere scenery), then it is impossible for the artist to depict typical circumstances in a really convincing manner. For it is one thing for the intelligence to admit that a certain *milieu,* complete with all the phenomena pertaining to it, has been perfectly described, and quite another to become a participant in the profoundly moving experience of seeing how the destinies of individual men and women grow out of an infinite wealth of circumstances they have encountered and how the turning-points in their lives are indissolubly linked with the typical conditions prevailing in their sphere of life.

It is obvious that changes in the style of presentation are reflections of the changes in social reality itself, that they mirror the fact that capitalism is increasingly becoming the dominant factor in every form of human existence.

Hegel very clearly recognized the harmful effect of this change, on art in general and on epic literature in particular. He says about this: "What man requires for his external life, house and home, tent, chair, bed, sword and spear, the ship with which he crosses the ocean, the chariot which carries him into battle, boiling and roasting, slaughtering, eating and drinking—nothing of all this must have become merely a dead means

to an end for him; he must feel alive in all these with his whose sense and
self in order that what is in itself merely external be given a humanly
inspired individual character by such close connection with the human
individual. Our present-day machinery and factories together with the
products they turn out and in general our means of satisfying our external
needs would in this respect—exactly like modern state organisation—be
out of tune with the background of life which the original epic requires."

With this Hegel has accurately stated the central problem of style
confronting the modern *bourgeois* novel. The great novelists have ever
fought a heroic battle to overcome, in the sphere of art, that coldness and
harshness in *bourgeois* existence and in the relationships of men with
each other and with nature, which opposes such a rigid resistance to poetic
presentation. But the poet can overcome this resistance only by seeking
out the surviving live elements of these relationships in reality itself, by
culling from his own rich and real experience and expressing in concentrated form the moments in which such still living tendencies manifest
themselves as relationships between individuals. For the mechanical and
'finished' character of the capitalist world, described by Hegel and so
often repeated after him, is, it is true, an existing and growing evolutionary tendency in capitalism, but it must never be forgotten that it is still
only a tendency, that society is objectively never "finished," fulfilled, dead,
petrified reality.

Thus the decisive artistic problem of *bourgeois* realism was this: is the
writer to swim against the current or should he allow himself to be carried
by the stream of capitalism?

In the first case he may create live images, which it is of course extremely
difficult to hew out of the refractory material but which are nevertheless
true and real, for they depict the still existing spark of life, the struggle
against the "finished" world. Their truth rests on the fact that what they
depict, in an extremely exaggerated form, is substantially correct in its
social content.

In the second case—and this is the method followed by newer realism
since Flaubert—there is less and less swimming against the current. But
it would be quite wrong and superficial to say that this brought literature
into closer contact with daily life; that it was the way of life that had
changed and literature had merely adapted itself to the change. For
writers who, in their own literary activity, yield to the undeniably existing
social evolutionary tendency referred to in the preceding, must in their
works inevitably turn what is merely a tendency into a generalized, all-
embracing reality. Their writings, which cannot strike a spark of life from
capitalist reality, thus become even more petrified, even more 'finished'

than reality itself and are even more dull, hopeless and commonplace than the world they purport to depict.

It is naturally impossible to preserve among the realities of capitalist society the Homeric intensity of the relations between men and the outer world. It was a piece of good fortune quite exceptional in the history of the modern novel that Defoe, in his *Robinson Crusoe,* succeeded in turning all the tools required for the satisfaction of elementary human needs into components of a thrilling story and by means of this vital connection with human destinies, endow them with a significance poetic in the highest sense of the word. And although *Robinson Crusoe* is an isolated, unrepeatable instance, it is yet most instructive because it indicates the *direction* in which the imagination of the writer should move if it is to find an artistic solution to the problem of overcoming the prose of capitalist reality. It is futile for a writer to adorn his descriptions with the choicest, most brilliant, most adequate words, futile to make his characters feel the deepest sorrow and the greatest indignation at the emptiness, hopelessness, inhumanity and "petrification" of reality. It is all in vain, even if this sorrow is expressed with the greatest sincerity and in the most beautiful lyrical form. The example of *Robinson Crusoe* shows that the struggle against the prose of capitalist reality can be successful only if the author invents situations which are not in themselves impossible within the framework of this reality (although they may never really occur) and then, given this invented situation, allows his characters to develop freely all the essential factors of their social existence.

Tolstoy's unique epic greatness rests on such a power of invention. His stories roll on with apparent slowness, without vehement turnings, seemingly following in a straight line along the track of the ordinary lives of his figures. But always and everywhere along this track Tolstoy invents situations arising with internal poetic necessity from the concrete stage of development reached by the characters, situations in which they are brought into a living relationship with nature. *War and Peace* in particular is full of such significant and magnificently living pictures. Think for instance of the splendid hunting party organized by the Rostov family and the idyllic evening with the old uncle with the sequel to it. In *Anna Karenina* the relationship to nature has already become much more problematic. All the more admirable is the genius with which Tolstoy creates such pictures as Levin's mowing of a field, letting them grow out of the problematic nature of Levin's relationship with his peasants and his sentimental attitude to physical labour.

It would be a mistake, however, to limit this problem of the poetic animation of the world depicted by Tolstoy to the relationship between man and nature. The increasing division of labour between town and countryside, the growing social weight of the towns necessarily shifts the action more and more to the urban scene, and to the modern great city and even in such cities no poetic invention can restore a Homeric relationship between man and nature, between man and the objects now turned into commodities. That does not imply, of course, that the realist writer must surrender without a battle to the "finished" prose of this urban world. The great realists have never capitulated, on this point least of all. But here again the writer is compelled to invent situations in which the world of the great city is endowed with life and poetry. Such poetry can here be born only if the human figures themselves are deeply imbued with life and their relationships with each other are rendered profoundly dramatic. If the writer succeeds in inventing such situations, situations in which the struggles and mutual relationships between the characters widen into a great dramatic spectacle, then the objects in which these mutual human relationships find expression and which are the vehicle for them, will—precisely as a result of this their function—be endowed with a poetic magic. How conscious the great realists were of this, is shown by a passage in Balzac's *Splendeur et Misère des Courtisanes,* when the duel between Vautrin "the Cromwell of the hulks" and Corentin, the greatest police spy of his time, has reached its culminating point. Corentin's assistant, Peyrade, feels that he is in constant danger.

> Thus the terror, which is spread in the depths of the American forests by the ruses of hostile tribes and from which Cooper has derived so much advantage, enveloped with its glamour the tiniest details of Parisian life. Passers-by, shops, carriages, some man at a window—all this aroused in the human numbers entrusted with protecting old Peyrade (for whom this was a matter of life and death) the same engrossing interest which the trunk of a tree, a beaver lodge, a pelt, a buffalo robe, a motionless boat or an overhanging tree at the water's edge possesses in Cooper's novels.

Naturally this glamour is no longer the clear, bright, simple magic of the infancy of the human race, such as we find in Homer. The striving of the great realists to remain true to the realities of life has for its inevitable result that when they portray life under capitalism and particularly life in the great cities, they must turn into poetry all the dark uncanniness, all the horrible inhumanity of it. But this poetry is real poetry: it comes poetically to life precisely because of its unrelieved horror. This discovery and revelation of poetic beauty in the dreadful ugliness of capitalist life is worlds apart from those photographic copies of the surface which use the hopelessness and desolation of the subject as the medium of presentation. An instance of this is the masterpiece of Tolstoy's late period *The Death of Ivan Ilyich*. Superficially, what is painted here is the everyday story of an average human being, such as any modern realist might have painted. But Tolstoy's gift of invention turns the inevitable isolation of the dying Ivan Ilyich into an almost Robinson Crusoe-like desert island—an island of horror, of a horrible death after a meaningless life—and inspires with a terrible dark poetry all the figures and all the objects through which the human relationships are conveyed. The fading world of court sittings, card-parties, visits to the theatre, ugly furniture, down to the nauseating filth of the dying man's bodily functions, is here integrated to a most vivid and animated world in which each object eloquently and poetically expresses the soul-destroying emptiness and futility of human life in a capitalist society.

In this their poetic quality the late works of Tolstoy have strong affinities with the creative methods of the great realists of the nineteenth century, although the artistic and historical differences are very considerable. Balzac and Stendhal got over the "finished" unpoetic nature of *bourgeois* society by resolving social life into a struggle, an interplay of mutual passionate relationships between individuals; thus society does not confront the human beings living in it as a "finished" force, as a dead machine, as something fateful and inalterable. Not only is society—objectively as well as in the picture given of it in these writings—undergoing constant change (the period in question is that between 1789 and 1848) but the characters depicted by Balzac and Stendhal do actually "make their own history." In a Balzac novel a court of law is not simply an institution with certain social functions, as in the books written after 1848. It is a battlefield of various social struggles, and every interrogation of a suspect, every drawing-up of a document, every court sentence is the result of intricate social tugs-of-war whose every phase we are invited to witness.

One of the principal themes of Tolstoy's *oeuvre* is the transformation of the social scene. In writing about Tolstoy Lenin quotes these words of Levin: "How everything has been turned upside down with us now, and is only just getting settled again." One could scarcely describe the period between 1861 and 1905 more strikingly. Everyone—or at least every Russian—knows what was "turned upside down" then. It was serfdom and the whole old régime tied up with it. But what is "only just getting settled again" is quite unknown, strange, and incomprehensible to the masses of the people! The extraordinary poetic sensitivity to all the human implications connected with this 'turning upside down' of old Russia was one of the essential elements of Tolstoy's greatness as a writer.

However wrong or reactionary his political and other opinions about this development may have been, he had certainly seen with extraordinary clarity the changes wrought in the various strata of society by this transformation of old Russia and seen them in motion, in all their mobility, never as an established condition, as a static, rigid state.

Let us consider the figure of Oblonski in *Anna Karenina*. Tolstoy shows him, not as a naturalistically conceived landowner-bureaucrat who has reached a certain level of capitalist development; what he shows is the increasing degree of capitalist transformation as it affects Oblonski's own personal life. As a human type, Oblonski is much more of an old-world country squire, who much prefers a comfortable, leisurely, broad foundation for a life of ease and pleasure to a however brilliant career at court, in the administration, or in the army. That is why his metamorphosis into a half-capitalist, capitalistically-corrupted type is so interesting. Oblonski's officialdom has purely material motives: on the income of his estates alone he can no longer live the life he wants to live. The transition to closer ties with capitalism (a seat on a board of directors, etc.) is the natural consequence of his evolution, the natural widening of the new parasitic foundations of his life. On this basis the old pleasure-loving outlook of the landowner evolves in Oblonski into a superficially good-natured, superficially epicurean Liberalism. He takes over from a modern *bourgeois* world-view all that can ideologically justify and support his undisturbed enjoyment of life. But he still remains the old country gentleman when he instinctively despises the ruthless place-seeking of his colleagues-in-office and interprets and practises the Liberal "laissez-faire" in his own good-humouredly egoistic way as "live and let live," "après-moi le déluge," and the like.

But what is decisive for the difference between Tolstoy's last principles of composition and the great realists of the early nineteenth century is that the social formations, institutions and the like are much more "finished," lifeless, inhuman and machinelike in Tolstoy than they ever were in either Balzac or Stendhal. The essential reason for this conception springs from the very fountainhead of Tolstoy's genius: that he regards society from the viewpoint of the exploited peasantry. In Balzac's world, too, the social and political institutions are transformed into militant mutual relationships solely for the representatives of the classes immediately participating in the struggle for power; for the plebeian social groups these institutions, too, are a "finished" world, complete in itself and confronting them with machinelike apathy. Only the gigantic figure of Vautrin rises up to fight, with changing fortunes, a battle against the powers of the state; the other criminals lead a miserable existence in the pores of society and the police confronts them as an impersonal and irresistible force. Naturally this applies even more to the peasants and the lower middle class. Hence, needless to say it is obvious that Tolstoy, who regarded the world from the angle of the Russian peasant, could not but have a similar conception of society and the state.

But this does not completely explain the attitude of Tolstoy to all these problems. For even the members of the ruling class take up a different attitude to state and social institutions in Tolstoy and in Balzac. Tolstoy's characters, even if they belong to the upper classes, regard these institutions as a "finished" objectivized world in itself. The reasons for this are obvious enough. The first of them was the character of Tsarist autocracy, which permitted intervention by individuals in social and political events only in the form of intrigue, corruption, backstairs influence—or revolt. No one of any high intellectual and moral quality could regard the Tsarist state as something in which he had a part, not even to the extent to which the characters of Balzac and Stendhal could do so in respect of the several states of their time. This 'finished,' this dead quality of the Tsarist state and its social institutions assumed ever greater rigidity in Tolstoy's writings, running parallel in this with the increasing estrangement between the forces of the state and the life of Russian society. From the remote distance of the historic past single figures still protrude into Tolstoy's world, figures of whom he thinks that they might possibly still have some influence over the state. Such is old Prince Bolkonski in *War and Peace*. But even he has retired, angry and disappointed, to his estates and the career of his son already consists of nothing but a chain of disappointments, a progressive destruction of the illusion that a decent and gifted man might actively participate in the military or political life of Tsarist Russia. This chain of disillusionment is shown by Tolstoy not merely as the individual destiny of Andrey Bolkonski or Pierre Bezukhov. On the contrary it very clearly reflects the ideological repercussions in Tsarist Russia of the French revolution and of the Napoleonic period, i.e., those human and psychological motives, those human and psychological conflicts, which drove the flower of the Russian nobility of the time to the Decembrist insurrection. Whether Pierre Bezukhov's road would have led to such a consummation is a point left open by Tolstoy. But the fact that for some length of time Tolstoy considered the plan of writing a novel about the Decembrists shows that the perspective was at least not foreign to his conception of such aristocratic rebels.

True, the political and social world, as Tolstoy saw it in his youth and early manhood, was a fairly loose structure. The semi-patriarchal form of bondage existing in the world of *War and Peace* gave elbow-room enough for free movement, for independence and autonomy in the local and personal sphere. One need only think of the life led by the independent country squires, the activities of the partisans and the like. There can be no doubt that Tolstoy observed and reproduced these traits with complete historical fidelity. But the eyes with which he regarded them were themselves conditioned by the level of his own development, and by the stage reached in the evolution of Russian society at the time when he wrote these books. With the transformations brought about by historical development and hence with the change in Tolstoy's views on the state and on society, his manner of presentation changes too. His *The Cossacks* and other early Caucasian stories show, in their central conception of society, traits very similar to those found in *War and Peace,* while the late and unfinished *Hadji Murat,* although related to the previous in subject, has a much firmer structure, with less opportunities for private human activities.

The driving force in this transformation of reality was the growth of capitalism. But in order to understand Tolstoy's world it is very important to see clearly that capitalism in the form in which it emerged in Russia, was—in Lenin's words—an Asiatic, and 'Octobrist' capitalism.

This form of capitalist development aggravated even further the social conditions unpropitious to art and literature and increased the deadness and rigidity of the resulting social formations. What Marx had in his time said of German developments applied no less to the Russia of Tolstoy's later years:

> In all other spheres we are tormented . . . not only by the development of capitalist production but also by the lack of its development; side by side with modern troubles we are oppressed by many inherited troubles arising from the survival of ancient and antiquated methods of production with their accompaniment of out-of-date social and political conditions. We suffer not only from the living but also from the dead.

Precisely because Tolstoy's immediate attention was directed mainly towards describing the upper classes, he expressed in the most vivid and plastic fashion this "Asiatic" character of nascent Russian capitalism and its tendency not to destroy or eliminate the worst aspects of an autocracy already superseded by historical development but merely to adapt them to the requirements of capitalist interests. In *Anna Karenina* Tolstoy already created superb types showing this "capitalization" and corresponding bureaucratization of the Russian nobility. Here is Oblonski, in whom Tolstoy has painted a wonderfully rich and subtly modelled picture of the Liberal tendencies at work within this social group; here, also, we find the type of the modern aristocrat in the person of Vronski. Vronski changes his mode of life as a result of his passion for Anna; he gives up his military career and develops into a capitalist landowner, who transforms the traditional husbandry of his estates into a capitalist enterprise, champions Liberalism and progress in the political counsels of the nobility and attempts to revive the "independence" of the nobles' way of life on a capitalist basis. Thus the effect, from the social point of view, of an accidental passion is to induce in Vronski a typical evolution proper to his class. To round off the picture, there is a third character, the type of the already completely bureaucratized, reactionary, obscurantist, hypocritical and empty administrative official in the person of Karenin. Capitalist division of labour increasingly permeates all human relationships, it becomes the way of life, the decisive determinant of thoughts and emotions; Tolstoy depicts with an increasingly bitter irony how in this world of divided labour human beings are transformed into parts of an inhuman machine. This division of labour is a most suitable instrument for the oppression and exploitation of the working masses and Tolstoy hates it precisely because it is an instrument of oppression and exploitation. But as the great and universal genius that he is, Tolstoy presents this *whole* process as it affects *all* classes of the population; he reveals its inner dialectic, the way in which this capitalist-bureaucratic division of labour not only dehumanizes and transforms into mere malignant robots the human beings (even those of the ruling class) which it has enmeshed, but also how this whole process turns against these same human beings at every point in their lives, whenever they attempt to defend their own elementary vital interests or manifest a remnant of humanity still surviving within themselves.

An instance of this is the wonderful scene between Ivan Ilyich and his doctor. Ivan Ilyich has become the complete bureaucrat, a paragon of a judge, who strips his cases of all humanity with consummate bureaucratic skill and who has turned himself into a perfectly functioning cog in the great Tsarist machinery of oppression. In vain do the accused, caught in the wheels of this machine, plead the special, the human implications of their case—the expert judge calmly and politely shepherds them back to the path of the paragraphs on which they are crushed by the juggernaut of the law in accordance with the requirements of the Tsarist system. But now Ivan Ilyich himself is dangerously ill and wants to find out from his doctor what his condition and expectations are. The doctor, however, is just such another superior bureaucrat, just such another perfect piece of machinery as Ivan Ilyich himself; he treats Ivan Ilyich exactly as Ivan Ilyich treats the accused who come before him.

All this was exactly the same as what Ivan Ilyich had himself so brilliantly performed in front of the accused a thousand times. The summing-up of the doctor was just as brilliant and he looked as triumphantly, even cheerfully, at the accused over his spectacles . . . The doctor looked at him severely with one eye, over his spectacles, as if to say: "Prisoner, if you will not restrict yourself to answering the questions put to you, I shall be constrained to order your removal from this courtroom."

What is so horrible in the death of Ivan Ilyich is precisely that he is confronted with this sort of rigidity in every human contact, when in the face of approaching death he first becomes aware of an urge to establish human relationships with human beings and overcome the futile senselessness of his life.

The development of Russian society deepens the double hideousness, an autocracy combined with "Asiatic" capitalism. As this objective development drives inexorably on towards the revolution of 1905, Tolstoy's hatred and contempt of the dehumanized nature of such a society grows rapidly. In Karenin's figure this dehumanization is already put before us in completed form. Karenin and his wife are at a party when Karenin becomes aware of the nascent love between Anna and Vronski. He prepares to have it out with her.

. . . And everything that he would now say to his wife took clear shape in Alexey Andreyevich's head. Thinking over what he would say, he somewhat regretted that he should have to use his time and mental faculties for domestic consumption, with so little to show for it; but nevertheless the form and train of thought of the speech he would make shaped itself clearly and distinctly, like an official report.

In Tolstoy's later works, particularly in *Resurrection,* his hatred of this inhumanity has deepened. The main reason for this is that in his later years Tolstoy saw much more clearly the connection between the dehumanization of the state machine and the oppression and exploitation of the common people. In Karenin's bureaucratic careerism this tendency was present only implicitly, in the complete indifference with which Karenin, concerned only with his own career, decides the fate of millions of human beings as if it were a mere piece of paper. (From the point of view of Tolstoy's own development it is interesting to note that in some passages of *War and Peace,* e.g., in the figure of Bilibin, he still treats this inhumanity which manifests itself in a formal-bureaucratic attitude to all problems, with a certain good-natured irony.) But in *Resurrection* he already brings the whole inhuman machinery into relation with the sufferings of its victims and gives a comprehensive, many-sided and accurate picture of the machinery of oppression in the Tsarist form of capitalist state—a picture nothing comparable with which can be found in the *bourgeois* literature of any country. Here the ruling class is already shown as a gang of vicious imbeciles who carry out their functions either with unsuspecting stupidity or malicious careerism and who are by now nothing but cogs in a horrible machine of oppression. Perhaps never since Swift's *Gulliver's Travels* has capitalist society been depicted with such powerful irony. As Tolstoy grew older, his presentation of characters belonging to the upper classes increasingly took this satirical, ironical form. The representatives of the ruling class show an increasing resemblance, for all their polite and polished exterior, to the stinking Yahoos of Jonathan Swift.

The fact that Tolstoy depicts the specific Tsarist form of capitalist machinery detracts nothing from the universal validity of the picture—on the contrary the resultant concrete, full-blooded, lifelike quality enhances this universal validity, for both the hideous tyranny of the oppressors and the utter helplessness of the victims is deeply and universally true. The specific form in which this tyranny manifests itself at the hands of the Tsarist bureaucracy is merely a concrete aggravation of its universal qualities. For instance, Tolstoy's Prince Nekhlyudov intervenes in the interest of an imprisoned woman revolutionary and for this purpose goes to see one of the Yahoos who wears the uniform of a general. Because the general's wife would like to have an *affaire* with Nekhlyudov, the revolutionary is released.

> As they were starting, a footman met Nekhlyudov in the ante-room and handed him a note from Mariette: *"Pour vous faire plaisir, j'ai agi tout à fait contre mes principes et j'ai intercédé auprès de mon mari pour votre protégée. Il se trouve que cette personne peut être relâchée immédiatement. Mon mari a écrit au commandant. Venez donc* disinterestedly. *Je vous attends. M."* "Think of that," said Nekhlyudov to the lawyer. "Why, this is dreadful. A woman has been kept in solitary confinement for seven months and then turns out to be quite innocent and a word suffices to get her released." "That is what always happens."

This is of course no isolated instance in *Resurrection*. Tolstoy shows with an extraordinary fertility of imagination, how the fate of a great many people immediately depend entirely on such personal matters of chance, on such arbitrary personal interests of some member of the ruling class. But the sum of all these arbitrary happenings and actions constitutes a clear and coherent system; through all these chances and accidents the main purpose of the dehumanized machinery emerges—it is the protection, by any and every means, even the most brutal, of the private property owned by the ruling classes.

Thus Tolstoy in his later years created a hideous 'finished' world of increasing horror. The pores of society in which human beings could act with some measure of independence have been gradually stopped up. Nekhlyudov can no longer harbour any illusions regarding life on the land, regarding a compromise between the interests of the landowners and the interests of the peasants, such as Konstantin Levin could still harbour, even though in a tormenting, problematic form. Nor does the private safety-valve of family life, the possibility of an escape like that of Nikolai Rostov or Levin exist any longer for Tolstoy in his later years. From the *Kreutzer Sonata* onwards he sees love and marriage, too, in its modern form; he sees in them all the specific forms of lies, hypocrisy and dehumanization, which are brought about by capitalism. He once said to Gorki: "Man must suffer earthquakes, epidemics, dreadful diseases and all the torments of the soul, but the worst tragedy in life was at all times, is now and ever will be the tragedy of the bedroom." Here, as nearly everywhere else, Tolstoy expresses his thoughts in a timeless form; but when he gives such thoughts *artistic* expression he is incomparably more concrete and historical. His later *descriptions* of the "tragedy of the bedroom" may have been conceived as documents of his ascetic philosophy, but his earlier *artistic presentations* of the problem burst through this abstract-dogmatic frame and depict the specifically capitalist hideousness of modern *bourgeois* love, marriage, prostitution and two-fold exploitation of women.

Where is there in such a world any room for action? The world Tolstoy sees and depicts is to an increasing degree a world in which decent people can no longer find any opportunity for action. As capitalistically developing Russia, despite the "Asiatic" character of its capitalism, approaches ever closer to the normal forms of fully developed capitalism, the material of life on which Tolstoy draws must also approach ever closer to the material of life, the literary mirroring of which led to the naturalist disintegration of the great school of realism in western Europe. There was, of course, one objective possibility of action in the Russia depicted by Tolstoy: but only for democratic and socialist revolutionaries, and to depict such action was precluded for Tolstoy by his philosophy. When together with the strong and hopeful features of the approaching peasant revolt he also gives poetic expression to its half-heartedness, its backwardness, its hesitations and lack of courage, he leaves his characters no other possibility save the old dilemma of capitulation or flight. And we have seen that such a capitulation must of necessity take increasingly infamous and inhuman forms, and we have also seen that even the possibilities of flight are progressively narrowed for Tolstoy by the objective evolution of society and his own deepening poetical and philosophical insight into the structure of the society thus born.

It is true that Tolstoy also preached the need for good deeds, for individual non-participation in sin and the like and wrote many things in which reality, despite all the magnificent accuracy of detail, is manipulated in such a way as to provide evidence for the possibility and efficacity of such good deeds (*The Forged Coupon*, etc.). But the poetic greatness of the older Tolstoy manifests itself precisely in the fact that when he *writes*, he cannot help presenting the true circumstances of real life with inexorable fidelity, irrespective of whether they corroborate or refute his own favourite ideas. For instance, the impossibility of an active life in this world of which we have just spoken, is clearly expressed in *The Living Corpse* by Fedia into whose mouth Tolstoy, without mentioning his own favourite theory at all, even as a possibility, puts these words:

A man born in the sphere in which I was born has only three possibilities to choose from. Either he can be an official, earn money and increase the filth in which we live—that disgusted me, or perhaps I didn't know how to do it, but above all it disgusted me. Or else he can fight this filth, but for that he must be a hero and I have never been that. Or finally and thirdly he tries to forget, goes to the dogs, takes to drink and song—that is what I have done and this is to what it has brought me.

In Nekhlyudov's figure Tolstoy did of course attempt to present the individual good deed itself. But his inexorable truthfulness produces a quite different, bitterly ironical result. Only because Nekhlyudov himself belongs to the very ruling class he hates and despises, only because in his own social sphere he is regarded as a good-natured fool, as a harmless eccentric bitten by the bug of philanthropy, only because he can make use of old family and other connections, can he accomplish his "good deeds" at all. And objectively all these good deeds are mere insignificant trifles; they are as nothing in comparison with the horrible inexorability of the machine, and they fit easily into the amorous or ambitious intrigues of those who are parts of the machine. Subjectively Nekhlyudov himself is forced—often unwillingly, often full of self-contempt, but sometimes also yielding to a temptation—to wear the mask of the courtier in order to be able to accomplish at least a few of his "individual good deeds." And where Nekhlyudov draws the Tolstoyan conclusions from the earlier critical vacillations of Konstantin Levin, he is faced with the hatred and distrust of the peasants who regard every "generous" proposal of their landlord as a new cunning attempt to deceive them and take advantage of them.

Tolstoy thus pictures a world in which the relationships of human beings to each other and to society approach very closely the relationships depicted by western post-1848 realism. . . .

The Original of Tolstoy's *Natasha*

by Edmund Wilson

The principal model for Natasha in Tolstoy's *War and Peace* was his sister-in-law, Tatyana Andreyvna Behrs. She was sixteen when Tolstoy married, a gay, attractive and spirited girl, who was already a great favorite with him. She lived much in the Tolstoy household at Yasnaya Polyana in the country, and her brother-in-law used to tell her that she was paying her way by sitting as a model for him. Later, when she married a young magistrate, she continued to visit the Tolstoys, bringing her family to stay with them in the summer. Her husband died in 1917, and she went to Yasnaya Polyana to live with Tolstoy's daughter Alexandra, on a small pension from the Soviet government. Here, at seventy-five, she set out to write her memoirs, but did not live to bring her story much beyond her marriage in 1867, at the age of twenty-one.

This chronicle has just been translated and brought out for the first time in English under the title *Tolstoy as I Knew Him* and signed with the author's married name, Tatyana A. Kuzminskaya. The original Russian title, here retained as subtitle, *My Life at Home and at Yasnaya Polyana,* describes the contents better, for the book is by no means all about the Tolstoys; it is an autobiography of Tatyana. As such, it is a rewarding document, though not infrequently a boring book. Tatyana-Natasha was writing as a very old lady, on the basis of diaries and letters that date from her remote girlhood. Most of her comments on the literary figures whom she saw at close quarters in her youth—Ostrovsky, Turgenev, Fet and her brother-in-law Leo himself—show no respect for famous names. They are simply the reactions of a woman to various men she has met. At one point, after taking poison over a love affair that was going wrong, she quickly changed her mind about dying when another of her suitors called—received him politely and, going to her mother, begged to be given an antidote. Exercising no sense of selection, she merely writes down all the things that moved her at the moment of their occurrence, in the terms in which they interested her then. None of them seems to have acquired—it is perhaps what one would expect of Natasha—any sort of new significance in the light of her later experience. It is as if the child's passionate "crushes," her vanity in being admired, had been simply relived in memory. Though almost all Tatyana tells you fits perfectly the character created by Tolstoy and though the book is full of other people's testimony to her vivacity and her beauty, the excitement of Natasha is not there. What Tatyana had was evidently overflowing life, not literary ability. She was unable to dramatize herself and what she gives you is a long and slow record of sisters and brothers and parents, uncles and aunts and cousins, nurses and maids and coachmen, protracted visits to country houses and social calls in Moscow (where her father was Court Physician and the Behrses lived in a house at the Kremlin). All the incidents, the most serious and crucial, as well as the most trivial and frivolous, are noted down in the same casual proportions that they had for the young girl at the time. The marriage of a servant, the remodelling of a house, an accident on a dangerous road, a saddle that comes loose at a hunt, a cat that jumps out of the arms of one of the actors in amateur theatricals, are presented on about the same level as the volatile flirtations and engagements, the continual birth of children (in those days people had one a year), and the long illnesses and premature deaths that even the best city doctors could not seem to do much to prevent.

But the most important episode of Tatyana's youth affords a significant insight, much more so than she is aware, into the society to which she belonged and which her brother-in-law so brilliantly depicted. It is an episode typical of their world and yet one for which Tolstoy presents no equivalent in *War and Peace*—a drama that raises a problem which he was only much later to treat. The Natasha of real life had her Anatole Kuragin, as in *War and Peace*—his real name was even Anatole; and her eventual marriage with Kuzminsky seems to have had something in common with Natasha's final acceptance of Pierre. But, in between, had occurred the most serious love affair of her life: her tragically frustrated engagement to Leo Tolstoy's older brother Sergei.

Sergei Tolstoy had been living for years with a gypsy woman named Marya Mikhailovna, by whom he had two children. He had inherited an estate, which he farmed, not far from Yasnaya Polyana, and he lived there with his uncultivated mistress, shutting himself off from social intercourse with the neighbors of his own class. He fell in love with Tatyana and she with him, and he thought he could manage to marry her without telling Marya Mikhailovna. But the news of what was afoot soon reached her, and when her gypsy parents were told, they threatened to sue Sergei and create a public scandal. She was having another baby, which made things very difficult for him. And there was also another difficulty. Two brothers, in Tsarist Russia, were forbidden to marry two sisters unless both ceremonies were performed at the same time—since as soon as one of the marriages had taken place, the in-laws of both the bride and the groom became technically their blood relations. This in itself made the match between Sergei Tolstoy and Tatyana rather a shady transaction: a compliant priest had to be found. (This point is not explained by the editors, with the result that the situation is partly unintelligible to the non-Russian reader.) Sergei began to stay away from Yasnaya Polyana, and when Tatyana grasped the situation, she broke the engagement off, though her disappointment was bitter and the shock had a serious effect on her health. The rest of Sergei's story is not told by Tatyana, but one can find it in *The Tragedy of Tolstoy,* by Tolstoy's daughter Alexandra. Sergei married Marya Mikhailovna and became more and more unsocial. His wife and daughters did all the housework and lived in terror of him. He made it impossible for one of these daughters to see a young man of the local gentry who was in love with her and wanted to marry her, on the ground that he was not well enough educated; and presently another of the daughters, "homely, small, almost a dwarf," ran away with a good-looking cook, who opened a shop with her money, treated her brutally and finally deserted her, leaving her with several children. She died during the Revolution, "alone and unhappy in a faraway village." The third daughter eloped with a Bashkir, who had been brought from the steppes to make kumiss, a fermentation of mare's milk which had been prescribed for her health. She returned the next year, with an undergrown little boy, who had yellow Oriental skin and slanting Oriental eyes. Her father let her live in the house, in a back room as far as possible from his study, but would not see the child. They and Marya Mikhailovna, left alone by Sergei's death, died miserably after the Revolution, when their house, from which they had fled, was burned down and the estate sacked. After the elopement of the second daughter, Sergei had made haste to agree to the marriage of his only remaining child to her insufficiently educated nobleman.

Now, Tatyana could hardly have known at the time that her brother-in-law Leo, who had first accepted her match with Sergei, than applauded her breaking it off, had himself had a serf-girl for a mistress not long before he married her sister. His diaries show how much he had cared for this girl: "I am in love," he declares in one entry, "as I never was before in my life. I have no other thought. I suffer." He has moments of indifference, of revulsion even, but his affection for her seems steadily to grow stronger, "It is getting to be even frightening," he later writes, "how close to me she is. . . . It is not merely the feeling now of a rutting stag, but that of a husband and a wife." He had a son by her, who afterward became coachman for one of his legitimate sons. And in the meantime, by one of those gestures of what he liked to regard as uncompromising honesty that were often so admirably calculated to give pain to other people, he had shown his young wife this diary at a time when his former mistress still sometimes came to the house—with the result that the poor Countess, already of a jealous disposition, was visited by homicidal impulses when she found the woman scrubbing the floors, and even took to disguising herself as a peasant and waylaying her husband about the estate to see whether he were still susceptible to the blandishments of pretty serf-girls. Twenty-seven years after his marriage, Tolstoy tried to write about this love affair, combining it with the story of a similar complication, in which a neighbor, after marrying a jealous wife, had shot his peasant mistress. Tolstoy, in one of his versions of this story, follows the real tragedy; in another, he has the landowner shoot himself. He could not bring himself to publish the piece—to which he gave the title *The Devil*—presumably because, when he showed it to his wife as late as 1909, she was upset by it and made a scene; and it did not appear until after his death.

This situation was evidently a common one. Tolstoy's father, at the age of sixteen, had had an affair with a peasant girl, an affair arranged by his parents themselves; and a son, who was the product of this union, had turned up from time to time to plague the legitimate children. Tolstoy tells of his "strange feeling of consternation when in after years this brother of mine, fallen into destitution and bearing a greater resemblance to my father than any of us, used to beg help of us and was thankful for the ten or fifteen rubles we used to give him." The memory of his own illegitimate family recurred to torment Leo. "I looked at my bare feet," he wrote in his diary of 1909, "and remembered Aksinya [his mistress]—that she is still alive and that they say Ermil is my son, and that I do not beg her forgiveness, have never done penitence, do not repent every hour, and dare to judge others."

D. S. Mirsky, in his *History of Russian Literature,* has truly described *War and Peace* as an "heroic idyll of the Russian nobility," and pointed out that, in spite of the horrors of war and the ineptitudes of civilization, "the general message . . . is one of beauty and satisfaction that the world should be so beautiful." He suggests, I believe correctly, that

Tolstoy's penchant for the idyllic is "the opposite pole to his unceasing moral uneasiness." Certainly *War and Peace* is one of the greatest of novels as it is one of the most enchanting. If it is not, as I do not think it is, quite one of the very summits of literature, it is because this idyllic tendency does here get the better of the author at the expense of the conditions of life as he actually knew and lived it. There is in the book, for all its realism, a certain element of the idealization in which we are all disposed to indulge in imagining the lives of our ancestors. In the case of Tolstoy, who had hardly known either his grandparents or his parents, this temptation must have been very strong. In the novel, Prince André and Pierre have their struggles with the problem of the peasantry, but the main problem is expelling the invader, and neither Natasha nor any of the men has to face any human relationship as painful as those in which the real Tatyana and the real Sergei and Leo Tolstoy found themselves involved. The Levin of *Anna Karenina,* which followed *War and Peace,* has to deal in a more direct and drastic way with his relation to the estate he has inherited and with the humans who are part of the estate, as Tolstoy did with Yasnaya Polyana; and immediately after *Anna Karenina,* Tolstoy himself appears in the character of Levin, writing the eloquent *Confession* in which he declares the insufficiency, for the moral life of a man, of property, social position and a comfortable family life, as well as of philosophy and science and the enjoyment and practice of literature. And he later tries to satisfy his moral needs by bringing himself closer to the peasants, on whose work he has always lived and who have given him the leisure to write—eating the same food as they and wearing the same clothes, working the same hours in the fields and mastering their manual skills. It was disturbing, no doubt, to a sensitive man, even after the liberation of the serfs in 1861—which Tatyana, by the way, hardly mentions, so little was it evidently noticeable in the relations of her people with their laborers and servants—to feel that one owed one's education and one's chance to pursue serious interests, as well as one's luxuries and pleasures, to the maintenance of a breed of inferior beings. But to know that one's own blood was mixed with the blood of this breed and to have to watch, in one form or another, the humiliation of one's own children must have been even harder to bear, a constant source of helpless anguish. (A gypsy singer, of course, might represent a higher stratum than that of a simple serf, but the consequences of marrying one, in Sergei's case, turned out to be just about as disastrous as if she had been a serf. When his daughter who eloped with the cook went to her Uncle Leo and asked him to approve this union, on the ground that she was following his doctrine by trying to put herself on a plane with the peasant, he lectured the girl severely, telling her that "no marriage could be happy between people who stood on different levels of development and had no interests in common.")

The emotional effects of this dilemma are not anywhere presented directly either in *War and Peace* or in *Anna Karenina,* though the situation appears in both. In the former, it is idyllic, like everything else. The uncle at whose house the Rostovs spend the night after the hunt has a housekeeper who is also his mistress, but the whole thing is most amiable and comfortable, and when Natasha has done her peasant dance—Tatyana tells us that this incident was derived from a performance of her own—the rosy and plump and good-looking woman sheds a tear or two through her laughter as she perceives that "this slim graceful countess, brought up in velvet and silk, this being so alien to her . . . was able to understand everything about Anisya and Anisya's father and her aunt and her mother, and every Russian in the world." In *Anna Karenina,* a similar situation is presented in a more embarrassing light. When Levin goes with his wife to visit his dying brother, he winces at having her meet the latter's ex-prostitute mistress, with whom he has been living in misery, and he notes, for a fleeting moment, her "expression of eager curiosity" at encountering "that dreadful woman, so incomprehensible to her." It is only later, with *Resurrection,* begun in 1889 and not finished and published till 1899, that Tolstoy comes to grips with this situation. In his youth, he had had an affair with one of his aunt's maids, who had been dismissed for this reason and had come later to a bad end. In the novel, Prince Nekhlyudov finds himself sitting on a jury which has to pass judgment on a girl whom he recognizes as a maid of his aunt's whom he had seduced under similar circumstances and deserted when she was pregnant. She has since become a prostitute and is now implicated in a sordid murder, of which she is completely innocent. At the trial, there is a miscarriage of justice, due partly to the carelessness of the Court but partly to Nekhlyudov's own cowardice, and the girl is condemned to Siberia. Nekhlyudov now brings all his influence to have the decision reversed and makes a vow to expiate his guilt by following her into exile and marrying her. He does get her sentence commuted, and he accompanies the convicts on their journey; but Maslova spares him the final test, for, understanding the undesirability of his spending the rest of his life with her, she marries one of her fellow-prisoners. Nekhlyudov, on the very last pages, happens to pick up a copy of the *New Testament* which has been given him by a travelling evangelist, and is converted to a creed like Tolstoy's own. From that day, for Nekhlyudov, says the author, a new life begins, and "what the new period will come to, time alone will show."

So we never know what happened to Nekhlyudov. It is impossible, from what we have been told of him, to imagine him turning saint or even finding employment that would satisfy his hunger for righteousness. Yet *Resurrection,* though it ends in the air, is not unworthy of its predecessors, and certainly does not deserve the disparagement that it usually gets. It is the novel in which Tolstoy comes closest to the problems of his own life, the only one in which he really grapples with the tragedies of a class-society, as he had seen them at first hand, as he had helped to produce them himself—the only one that gets out into the open such episodes as Tatyana had locked away in her diary. We do know what happened to Tolstoy when he tried to lead a new life: his fanaticisms and his worldly relapses, his absurdities and his desperate death. The story he himself had been living could no more come out satisfactorily than Nekhlyudov's story could. After the period of his first gratification at re-creating his lost parents and in restoring at Yasnaya Polyana the patriarchal family life of which in the preceding generation the continuity had been broken, a malaise which had survived these distractions inescapably asserted itself and came to ache through the whole of his work.

We have seen a somewhat similar preoccupation in the literature of our own South, from the days when George W. Cable was forced to come to live in the North for his boldness in describing the half-colored branches of the prominent white families of New Orleans to the days when the continued anguish of Negro and white relations has inspired those stories of Faulkner's in which neither reader nor author is ever allowed a moment's relief or repose, because the subject admits of no resolution. In Russia, the black-and-white issue was not present to deepen the class distinctions, and it was possible for the landowners in Tolstoy's fiction to contemplate marrying their mistresses, as it was possible for Sergei Tolstoy to remain in serious doubt as to whether it was right for him to put away his gypsy and marry Tatyana. But the strains and the mutilations incurred through these social differences periodically made themselves felt among all those gay parties in country houses, all those balls in St. Petersburg and Moscow, all those jolly affectionate family scenes, all those gallantries of handsome cousins.

Style in *War and Peace*

by *R. F. Christian*

A person who has read only one or two books by Tolstoy will have no difficulty in assigning passages from other books of his to their correct author. He will not confuse the language with that of Dostoevsky or Turgenev, Gogol, or Leskov. There is no mistaking, even in English translation, the simplicity and lucidity of Tolstoy's writing. But the English reader may not be so aware of that other distinguishing feature of Tolstoy's style which is everywhere apparent in the Russian text of *War and Peace*—namely, repetition.

Many varieties of repetition are encountered in prose fiction. A novelist who writes at such length as Tolstoy cannot afford to say a thing once only. He is more or less obliged to repeat a piece of information at least once if it has any significance. But Tolstoy is not content with merely saying a thing twice. How often are we told that Julie Karagina became a wealthy heiress on her brother's death? That Kutuzov occupied his leisure time writing to Madame de Stael and reading French novels? That there was straw beneath the windows of the dying Bezukhov's house? That the French envoy Michaud knew no Russian? These facts are repeated two, three and four times even. Their repetition aids the memory. It facilitates reading. It is the novelist's concession to his reader. But there is no doubt that in this respect Tolstoy was much more considerate than he need have been.

Another variety of repetition, and one which is characteristically Tolstoyan, is the constant reiteration of some external detail designed to characterize an individual: a repetition which has nothing to do with the fact that the novel is long and the reader's memory is short. No one can fail to notice how the essence of a Tolstoyan character is distilled into a mannerism, a gesture, a physical feature, an outward and visible sign which recurs continually and is the permanent property of that character.

Such attributes are not repeated to remind us of something we may have forgotten. Nor are they generalizations like the epithets *pius* or πολύμητις which qualify Aeneas and Odysseus, whether or not their behaviour happens to be dutiful or resourceful. They resemble rather musical *leit-motivs*. They identify the person by something more meaningful than a name, and something less ossified than a stock epithet. The repeated reference to Napoleon's small white hands, Hélène's bare white shoulders, Princess Marya's radiant eyes is not a conscious epic device. It is a combination of the assertion of a permanent, individualizing feature with the expression of a moral judgement. As well as suggesting what is most significant about his heroes, Tolstoy tries to evoke in the reader at the same time a positive or negative response to them. Napoleon's small hands suggest effeminacy and the absence of work; Hélène's inadequate clothing is a sign of her brazenness; the light in Princess Marya's eyes reflects the inner light within her soul. We are intended to disapprove of Hélène and Napoleon, and to approve of Princess Marya. This type of repetition of external detail, involving as it does the frequent recurrence of identical words, is an example of how closely related a novelist's language and characterization are. Words are repeated because aspects of character have to be repeated, and once the words chosen to convey those aspects are altered, the characterization itself is altered, however slightly.

Another type of repetition to which Tolstoy was prone also demonstrates how difficult it is to divorce words from the ideas they express. Nobody who has read *War and Peace* carefully could fail to notice the frequency of such words or phrases as, for example, "peculiar to" (*svoistvenny*), "simple" (*prostoy*), "natural" (*estestvenny*), "as is always the case" (*kak vsegda byvaet*), or "all this must be so" (*eto dolzhno byt' tak*). Sometimes one can regard a frequently-recurring expression as nothing more than a linguistic mannerism, characteristic of one author and not another. Such phrases as "to experience a feeling similar to that experienced by . . ." (*ispytyvat' chuvstvo podobnoe tomu, kotoroe ispyty-vaet . . .*) or "as as a sign of" something or other (*v znak chego . . .*)—are good examples of obtrusive verbal idiosyncrasies characteristic of Tolstoy's style of writing, but having no real significance in themselves. But the phrases quoted earlier in this paragraph belong to a different category. The crux of Tolstoy's thought is that every human being has features which mark him off from every other human being—hence the frequency of the word "peculiar to"—while at the same time human beings in the mass exhibit a sameness, a uniformity, a predictability, an inevitability which is conveyed in Tolstoy's language by the repetition of "as is always the case," "as all people do," or "all this must be so." The insoluble problem of the individual personality and mass uniformity, of free will and determinism, is reflected on the linguistic plane by the insistent use of identical words to express identical content.

✔ What has been said so far concerns the tenuous distinction between form and content. Tolstoy repeats the same words because he wants to repeat the same ideas, which can only be repeated exactly by using again the form in which they originally occurred. This is a justification for some repetition, but not for all/There are certain limits within which a writer can express his meaning in more ways than one, and within these limits, meaning is not affected by style. Tolstoy, in his old age, remarked that "the basic content of a work of art in all its fullness can be expressed only by itself" [1]—that is to say that you cannot describe it without reproducing it word for word, and that the change of a single word means a change, however minute, in the content of the whole. But this is only true if we understand content as the sum total of everything in the work of art. It is possible to make stylistic alterations, without affecting the meaning to the slightest extent. And this brings us to another aspect of Tolstoy's repetition, which is not inevitable. Let us examine the following typically Tolstoyan sequences. The subject of the first one is Pierre, and he is scrutinizing his feelings for his first wife Hélène (the italics here and in the passages which follow are mine):

> "But how often have I *felt proud of* her, *felt proud of* her majestic beauty, her social tact', he thought, *'felt proud of* my house in which she received all Petersburg, *felt proud of* her unapproachability and beauty. So this is what I *felt proud of*! I thought that I did not *understand* her. How often when considering her character have I told myself that I was to blame for not *understanding* her, for not *understanding* that constant composure. . . ." [2]

In Russian the single word *gordilsya* ("I felt proud") occurs five times and the word *ponimayu* ("I understand") three times.

The next passage is self-explanatory:

> . . . thought Prince Andrei, as he waited among a number of important and unimportant people in Count Arakcheev's *reception-room*.
>
> During his service, chiefly as an adjutant, Prince Andrei had seen the *reception-rooms* of many important men, and the different types of these *reception-rooms* were well known to him. Count Arakcheev's *reception-room*

---

[1] Goldenweiser, *Vblizi Tolstogo,* Moscow, 1959, p. 68.
[2] *War and Peace,* II. 1. 6.

had quite a special character. The faces of the unimportant people waiting their turn for an audience in Count Arakcheev's *reception room*. . . .[3]

Here the Russian *priemnaya* recurs five times in as many lines—a fact which is glossed over in the Maudes' English translation by omitting it once, calling it a "waiting room" once, an "ante-room" twice and simply a "room" once.

When Prince Andrei died

. . . everyone came to take leave of him and everyone *wept*.

Little Nikolai *wept* because of the painful perplexity which rent his heart. The Countess and Sonya *wept* from pity for Natasha, and because he was no more. The old count *wept* because he felt that he would soon have to take the same terrible step.

Natasha and Princess Marya also *wept* now, but they *wept* because of their own personal grief; they *wept* because. . . .[4]

To translate these seven past tenses of *plakat'* ("to weep") the Maudes say "wept" three times, "cried" three times, and omit one altogether. Finally one might add the second half of a sentence which occurs when the Russian prisoners, Pierre included, are waiting their turn to be shot by their French captors, who are the subject of the sentence: ". . . and it was noticeable that they were all *hurrying,* and were *hurrying* not as people *hurry* in order to perform a comprehensible task, but as people *hurry* to complete a necessary, but unpleasant and incomprehensible task." [5] These few examples out of many hundreds (one is tempted to add that in describing Platon Karataev, Tolstoy uses the word *krugly* ["round"] five times in a single sentence!) are more than enough to make the point. It will be noticed, incidentally, that very commonly a basic verb is met at the beginning of a sentence and is then repeated at the beginning of several successive sentences or clauses. One example will suffice, in literal and abbreviated form, from the opening scene in *War and Peace*: "*There arrived* the highest Petersburg society . . . ; *there arrived* the daughter of Prince Vasily . . . *There arrived* too the youthful little Princess Bolkonskaya . . . *There arrived* Prince Hippolyte . . . ; *there arrived* too the Abbé Morio and many others." [6] The monotony of the reiterated past tense of the verb is quite unjustifiably disguised by the Maudes, who translate it in five different ways:

[3] *Ibid.,* II. 3. 4.
[4] *Ibid.,* IV. 1. 16.
[5] *Ibid.,* IV. 1. 11.
[6] *War and Peace,* I. 1. 2.

"was assembled," "came," "was also there," "had come," "had also come."
Consequently English readers do not notice as readily as Russians these
sledge-hammer blows: "She could not understand. . . . She did not
understand. . . . She did not understand. . . . Still less could she understand. . . ." Or: "Pierre did not know that. . . . He did not know
that. . . . Pierre did not know that. . . . He did not know that. . . .
And therefore Pierre. . . ."

This recurring pattern for introducing sentences and clauses, a variant
of the pattern of single word repetition which we meet so commonly in
Tolstoy, is a characteristic device for achieving balance and rhythm. In
this matter of balance, furthermore, Tolstoy was particularly addicted to
a classical, rhetorical arrangement of his material in groups of three—
three adjectives, three nouns, three verbs, three prepositions. Take for
example the following sentence, in which I have inserted letters and
numbers:

> On his return to Moscow from the army, Nikolai Rostov was welcomed
> (A) by his home circle as (1) the best of sons, (2) a hero and (3) their
> darling Nikolenka; (B) by his relations as (1) a charming, (2) agreeable and
> (3) polite young man; (C) by his acquaintances as (1) a handsome lieutenant
> of hussars, (2) a good dancer and (3) one of the best matches in Moscow.[7]

Or the description of the preparations for the Olmütz review:

> Now thousands of feet and bayonets, with colours flying and at the officers'
> command, (1) halted, (2) turned and (3) formed up at intervals, wheeling
> round *other* similar masses of infantry in *other* uniforms; *now* could be
> heard the rhythmic hoof-beats and jingling of the smart cavalry in (1) blue,
> (2) red and (3) green braided uniforms with smartly dressed bandsmen in
> front on (1) black, (2) roan or (3) grey horses; *now,* deploying itself *with
> its* brazen clatter of cannons, (1) polished, (2) shining and (3) swaying on
> their gun-carriages and *with its* smell of linstocks, the artillery crawled up
> between the infantry and the cavalry and took up its appointed positions.
> *Not only* the generals *wearing* full parade uniforms with their thin and
> thick waists drawn in to the utmost, their red necks propped up by their
> collars and *wearing* scarves and all decorations; *not only* the elegant,
> pomaded officers, *but every* soldier with his (1) fresh, (2) washed and (3)
> shaven face, and his weapons polished and shining to the last degree, every
> horse, groomed till its coat shone like satin and every hair of its wetted
> mane lay smooth—all felt that something (1) serious, (2) important and (3)
> solemn was happening.[8]

[7] *Ibid.,* II. 1. 2.
[8] *Ibid.,* I. 3. 8.

Running through the syntax of Tolstoy's narrative passages is every device of arrangement and balance known to Cicero and Demosthenes (excluding the rhetorical question). There are the "threes," the "not only . . . but also," the "either . . . or, neither . . . nor"; there is the fondness for "in the first place," "in the second place," "in the third place"; there is the frequency of "some said," "others said," "yet others said" (in one passage the pronominal sequence "some" . . . "others" . . . "others" . . . (*kto . . . kto . . . kto . . .*) is carried to the length of ten successive repetitions); there is the love of "now" . . . "now" . . . "now" . . . (*to . . . to . . . to . . .*); and there are the divisions of people and opinions into parties, groups and categories. We saw in the first chapter, in examining the draft versions of *War and Peace,* how some of Tolstoy's alterations were conditioned by the need to achieve greater balance and symmetry. It is this same objective which Tolstoy is continually pursuing through his use and abuse of the repeated word. There is no subtlety here, no attempt to disguise his method. But there is a blunt, simple, overwhelmingly direct attack which is characteristically and unmistakably Tolstoyan. Perhaps the following few sentences contain the quintessence of his unashamed repetitiveness:

> It *seemed* to Pierre so *natural* that everyone should *like* him, and it would have *seemed* so *unnatural* if anyone had not *liked* him, that he could not help believing in the *sincerity* of the *people* around him. Besides he had no *time* to ask himself about the *sincerity* or *lack of sincerity* of these *people*. He was *constantly* short of *time,* he *constantly felt himself* in a state of mild and cheerful intoxication. He *felt himself* the centre of some important and general movement; he *felt* that something was *constantly* expected of him. . . .[9]

The principle, broadly speaking, is to introduce a word and then repeat it in the next sentence; introduce a new word in that sentence and repeat this new word in the following one. It is not a consistent principle, of course, but the pattern is clear, and there is often an easily discernible system of links between consecutive sentences, and even, on occasions, between consecutive paragraphs.

Before we leave the subject of repetition we may mention those sequences, common in Tolstoy's writings generally and not merely in *War and Peace,* in which a person's thoughts which have been expressed in narrative are repeated in direct or indirect speech. When Prince Bolkonsky is reflecting on the possible betrothal of his daughter to Anatole

[9] *Ibid.,* I. 3. 1.

Kuragin the thoughts attributed to him by Tolstoy are immediately repeated in his own words:

> "Well, I've nothing against it," the prince said to himself, "but he must be worthy of her. And that is what we shall see."
> "That is what we shall see, he added aloud. "That is what we shall see." [10]

One recalls the passage in *Anna Karenina* where Anna and Vronsky meet on the train in the snowstorm on Anna's return from Moscow to Petersburg. "She had no need to ask," writes Tolstoy, "why he was there. She knew as surely as if he had told her that he was there in order to be where she was." At once Anna asks why he is there and Vronsky replies that he is there in order to be where she is. When Princess Marya imagines herself setting off from home as a pilgrim, her thoughts are described initially in narrative form and then voiced in the first person:

> She pictured herself walking by Theodosia's side, dressed in coarse rags, walking with a staff . . . and reaching at last the place where there is neither sorrow nor sighing, but eternal joy and bliss.
> 'I shall come to a place and pray there. I will go on until my legs fail . . . and I shall at last reach that eternal quiet haven where there is neither sorrow nor sighing,' thought Princess Marya.[11]

Repetition, then, of one type or another, is the most characteristic single feature of Tolstoy's style. Perhaps next to it one might place a certain unorthodox "incorrectness" of grammar and syntax. For all his preoccupation with balance and symmetry, Tolstoy was very far removed from academic fastidiousness or pedantry. Rules irked him and the student will not find his prose a model of grammatical conformity. One is surprised at times by his inability to distinguish the gerund from the participle, a confusion which is, of course, concealed in English translations. Again, one meets such examples of syntactical clumsiness as "Today, having caught a glimpse of her, she seemed to him still more lovely." [12] On several occasions, too, one notices the redundant pronoun "he," acting as the subject in a sentence in which the same subject has already been denoted by a noun: "Trembling and panting, the old man, flying into a state of fury . . . *he* fell upon Eykhen. . . ." [13]

These un-Russian turns of speech can in some cases be ascribed to the influence of French syntax on the Russian language—as also can the peculiar use of prepositions which astonish one from time to time in

---

[10] *War and Peace*, I. 3. 4.
[11] *Ibid.*, II. 3. 26.
[12] *Ibid.*, II. 1. 1.
[13] *Ibid.*, IV. 2. 5.

reading *War and Peace,* or lexical combinations such as *delat' vpechat-lenie* for the normal Russian *proizvodit' vpechatlenie (faire impression).* There are at least three ways of looking at these "mistakes." It can be argued that Tolstoy was deliberately using an archaic, gallicized syntax as a period detail in order to recapture the flavour of the language spoken in the days of his characters. But this is far too clever to be true; and in any case the gallicisms are mostly confined to the author's narrative and are comparatively rare in the speech of the characters themselves. Secondly, one can say that Tolstoy's gallicized syntax is not untypical of the Russian language as spoken in his own day, when the influence of French constructions was still strong and when the French language was known at least as well as Russian by most educated men. This fact undoubtedly explains some "mistakes" in *War and Peace,* but does not explain their absence in other contemporary novels. Thirdly, one can give credence to Tolstoy's own statement on the subject of language: "I like what is called incorrectness, that is to say what is characteristic." [14] His words could be taken to strengthen the suggestion that he deliberately tried to capture the inaccuracies of the living spoken word, the looseness of syntax, the unfinished sentences of the average speaker. And there is certainly some truth in this, at least in so far as it concerns the dialogue of *War and Peace* or the author's reproduction of the thoughts of his characters. But the fact still remains that Tolstoy neither knew nor cared much about formal grammar and was a good deal more careless than, say, his sophisticated contemporary Turgenev. He thought aloud, transferred his thoughts to paper and sometimes forgot that he was writing, not talking.

If we continue to look for distinguishing features of Tolstoy's language, we will not find, as we do with many other Russian authors, that he has a marked preference for any one particular part of speech. Vinogradov has observed the frequency of the verb in Pushkin's prose, Turgenev's love of adjectives and adverbs; Goncharov's fondness for the noun. We find no obvious partiality in Tolstoy. But one cannot help observing a particular type of *sentence* structure which, while not confined to Tolstoy, is a stylistic feature which is certainly associated with him. This can only be conveyed in English by a translation which exactly follows the word order of the original: "And a joyful, and at the same time pathetic, asking forgiveness for her joy, expression, settled on Natasha's face." [15] This is a fairly typical example of his marked tendency to insert between adjective and noun a complex adjectival or participial expression in paren-

---

[14] Letter to Tishchenko, 1886, quoted by Vinogradov, *Literaturnoe Nasledstvo,* 35/36, Moscow, 1939, p. 141.
[15] *War and Peace,* IV. 4. 20.

thesis as it were. Although economical of words it creates an impression of overcrowding. It has been remarked that not only individual sentences, but whole periods in Tolstoy's narrative are weighted down and unwieldy. Chekhov noticed this fact and saw in it a virtue: "Have you noticed Tolstoy's language? Enormous periods, sentences piled one on top of another. Don't think that it happens by chance or that it's a shortcoming. It's art, and it only comes after hard work. These periods create an impression of power." [16] . . .

[16] S. Shchukin, *Iz vospominanii o Chekhove, Russkaya Mysl'*, No. 10, 1911, p. 45. Quoted by Bychkov, *L. N. Tolstoy*, Moscow, 1954, p. 220.

The Moral Vision: Tolstoy

by Albert Cook

If fiction is essentially concerned with the commitment of its characters to moral ideas, its main stream is more to be traced in moral observation than in the tributary of figurative implication. As the instinct of Leavis has shown us, the great tradition of English—as of any—fiction is a moral tradition.

Each original novelist, by virtue of the uniqueness of the world he creates, has a distinct kind of moral observation. We find that Hemingway analyzes the moral gestures of courage, Trollope of sincerity, Jane Austen of altruistic social insight, Defoe of economic and sexual scruple, Stendhal of crassness or fineness.

Tolstoy's world, for all its breadth, is no less single in its moral outlook. It is a truism that the greater the novelist the more sweeping his vision. We tend to combine the persuasive universality of the moral abstraction with the wide scope of the major novelist and attribute to Tolstoy a representation of all life. This ascription, praiseworthy as a tribute to the commanding imagination of a superb writer, has the pernicious critical result of disarming in advance the attempt to define the theme of *War and Peace*. Even so responsible a critic as Forster (in *Aspects of the Novel*) seems almost captiously, and at the same time indolently, content merely to gape at the masterpiece, leaving unchallenged Lubbock's equally imperceptive assertion of thematic disunity in the novel.

The meaning of *War and Peace* is, however large, single and coherent. It creates its characters and builds its panoramic universe of moral meaning out of a sequence of observed and analyzed moral gestures:

> Prince Vassily always spoke languidly, like an actor repeating his part in an old play. Anna Pavlovna Scherer, in spite of her forty years, was on the contrary brimming over with excitement and impulsiveness. To be enthusiastic had become her pose in society, and at times even when she had,

"The Moral Vision: Tolstoy" by Albert Cook. From *The Meaning of Fiction* (Detroit: Wayne State University Press, 1960). Copyright © 1960 by The Wayne State University Press. First published as "The Unity of *War and Peace*" in *Western Review* (1958). Reprinted by permission of The Wayne State University Press and the author.

indeed, no inclination to be so, she was enthusiastic so as not to disappoint the expectations of those who knew her. The affected smile which played continually about Anna Pavlovna's face, out of keeping as it was with her faded looks, expressed a spoilt child's continual consciousness of a charming failing of which she had neither the wish nor the power to correct herself, which, indeed, she saw no need to correct.

The surface of social life in the *soirée* of this chapter is presented as a kind of play. Most prominent are the most acting, the most hypocritical (Greek, actors); there are moving at the same time shyly and clumsily in the background, of this scene as throughout Book One, those dedicated beings we will come to know as the agents of a real moral life. Not that they yet know to what they are dedicated. Prince Vassily and Anna Pavlovna know; but their knowledge is not a true superiority; as here rendered, it is only the superficial skill of the actor. Their limit is that they know all they are to do; so they have chosen it.

In the keen individuation of Tolstoy's moral analysis, these two hypocrites are distinguished from one another: Prince Vassily is languid, Anna Pavlovna "brimming over with excitement and impulsiveness." These traits in turn are subjected to analysis. Every nuance of behavior undergoes a moral scrutiny.

What is the domain of Tolstoy's analysis? It is so perfectly fused with the theme of the novel that a short definition is not possible, but, roughly, he is always analyzing a character's attitude toward his own destiny, his own tempo, his own potentialities. Gesture always has become or is becoming moral habit in Tolstoy. He analyzes the certitude of the become, the hesitance of the becoming. Habit is subjected to time, transmuted and retransmuted, in a number of ways whose diversity his moral analysis renders, whose underlying interdependence the plot coordinates. The plot's grand scale of social process changes each phase's moral appearance into a new reality. To keep up with the times, with Time, to be morally real, a character must meet a challenge which faces everyone equally as it faces each at his own individual angle. What makes Anna Pavlovna Scherer and Prince Vassily superficial is their dedication to surface, implied in the meaning Tolstoy analyzes into their almost ritual gestures. Oriented toward mere appearance, they commit themselves toward their temporary social masks. This commitment affords them a certain adroitness, but it cuts them out of all the profounder resurrections of the years to come. Nine years and a thousand pages later the bumbling Pierre of the first scene of the novel will have become spiritually baptized and rebaptized into a moral giant. But Anna Pavlovna, withdrawn from the horribly contrasting background of devastated Moscow, will be giving the identical Petersburg *soirée*, politely and coldly ignoring the cataclysm that is to be the death through which the best will be reborn. And who is her honored guest but the same Prince Vassily, unchanged in his diabolical superficiality.

In *War and Peace*, the analyzed gestures of the characters find their stated meaning in what will become their final destiny. The appearance of detail is being compounded with the reality of the whole. The constant relevance of these analyzed components to the reflected whole lends, to detail and overall canvas alike, a uniformity and proportionateness which recalls the realism of Vermeer or Caravaggio or better, Velasquez: what Blackmur has called the "buoyancy and sanity of Tolstoy's novels."

The fifteen books and epilog of the novel are orchestrated into an almost contrapuntal order, war and peace being not, as Lubbock thought, disorganized strands, but the basic alternation, each defining the other, of the plot's form and the characters' evolution. War is repeated, and peace. A new stage of peace varies the war epoch immediately preceding it, and vice versa. Each book has a prevailing mood, a phase of the common life to which every character responds in the very act of contributing to create it. The mood of one person is, with the variation of destined personality, the temporary mood of all, a mood to be resmelted from phase to phase till the final temper of the whole novel's vision has been enunciated.

There is a dominance of superficies in the peaceful Book One. Anna Pavlovna's ostentatious *soirée* sets the tone for the preliminary interests of all the characters. Pierre—first shy, then tactlessly professing Bonapartism, finally deferring abashedly as he parts from Anna Pavlovna—goes on to assert his mere surface in the very frankness of his subsequent talk with Prince Andrey, in the sociable inconsequence of his early morning tomfoolery. Prince Andrey on the surface of his mind can express no more probing reason for his military departure than that peacetime life is not to his taste. His unconscious reason is that so far life is as superficial as his first marriage seems to him here. Natasha is likewise enmeshed in surface. At her name day she impulsively wakens to the world of the opposite sex in Boris Drubetskoi, the very puppet-like incarnation of surface, though her keen insight leads her to ask him, symbolically, to kiss her doll before kissing her. Boris' mother makes an abrupt shift of allegiance from the superficial service rendered by Prince Vassily to the superficial hope that Pierre's naïveté can be prevailed on to assume the burdens of a merely external patronage. The death of Count Bezuhov entails not the soul searching of the novel's subsequent deaths but a mere squabble over an inheritance, a manipulation of surfaces about money. Marya's devoutness, as yet a mere form, presses on her departing brother an ikon to which he is indifferent. She has been corresponding with the stultified, pretentious Julie Karagina, not yet sufficiently awakened to cast off this mere husk of a friendship. Dolokhov's bravado is confined to mere surface acting in this book. Marya Dmitrievna's "terrible dragon" frankness is merely another social form, here analyzed in terms of its effect on polite society; its real effectiveness will come into its own only when it saves Natasha in the deeper Book Eight.

Yet Tolstoy is all the while individuating these people, analyzing attitudes of a specific bent and tempo which will recombine for deeper and deeper meaning. Even in the superficiality of Book One, sudden insight into destiny can pierce through the decorum of such shallow characters as the crudely, shamelessly driving Anna Mihalovna, and the bewildered Countess Rostov, friends from girlhood who "wept because they were friends, and because they were soft-hearted, and that they, who had been friends in youth, should have to think of anything so base as money, and that their youth was over. . . . But the tears of both were sweet to them."

In these tears, and throughout Book One, there is a meaning portentously present. People are brought mysteriously into each other's orbits; as Prince Vassily carries on the conversation which will culminate in Anatole's unsuccessful overture for Marya, the stupid Julie Karagina writes portentously of Nikolai Rostov, a man unknown to her correspondent, who will at last, through the transformations of war, become Marya's fitting husband. The circumstances of the Duc d'Enghien's death discussed in the very first chapter's *soirée*—what do they foreshadow but La Belle Hélène's death in Book Twelve as the outcome of a parallel adulterous triangle? Pierre will then be liberated to marry the girl he will love from Book Eight on, though here, in Book One, he scarcely dreams, sitting across from her at a dinner party, that the thin thirteen year old is to become of such absorbing interest. Yet he must have some intimation of this future, or why at her look has he "felt an impulse to laugh himself without knowing why"? Why does her look keep straying from Boris to him; why does she feel so amused in his presence and go up to ask him for a dance (at her mother's prompting, to be sure) "laughing and blushing"?

The peaceful surface of Book One can give us only such hints as these. The foreboding grows and the breach between people widens in Book Two, where war displays its surface. In Book One we approached society from the outside in, at a *soirée*. Here we approach panoramically, from above, the campaign of 1805, which will turn out to have been war's mere surface in the later light of 1812. Parade, strategy, honor: surfaces and abstractions crowd the stage; the wretchedness of the ill-shod soldiers is only an uncomfortable logistic detail, and a death at the Enns bridge will occasion a joke more brutal but of the same kind that Bilibin regales his comrades with at staff headquarters. Here superficial discipline, finding in Dolokhov a lack of punctilio, demotes him to the ranks, when in the total upheaval of Book Fourteen he will be elevated to guerrilla command.

Peacetime superficiality is replaced in Book Two by the wartime superficiality of mere military reputation: Bagration, Zherkov, the jocular but impassive Nesvitski sweeping his field glasses across the walled nunnery, the nameless regimental commander whose "quivering strut seemed to say that, apart from his military interest, he had plenty of warmth in his heart for the attractions of social life and the fair sex." Kutuzov turns away sadly from this show to avoid having his deep disillusionment, here incongruous, bewilder his subordinates. Nikolai, dreamily content or dreamily fearful, eats up surface, proud of his initiation into what his shallow mind takes for the reality of military life (the Telyanin incident), of battle (Schoen Grabern). We know no more here of Denisov but his function, that he is an honorable captain. And Andrey is here superficially disillusioned by war, just as he had been by marriage and social life in Book One. A slight wound sends him to the manipulators of this surface, the headquarters staff at Bruenn, where Bilibin's interpretations of diplomacy and strategy will invest these battles with all the meaning they can yet have. Significances are more portentous here; such is the nature of war. But no one can guess why. Tushin parts from Andrey at Schoen Grabern "with tears, which for some unknown reason started suddenly into his eyes." Seeing the unjust and uncomprehending disgrace of the hero Tushin "Prince Andrey felt bitter and melancholy. It was all so strange, so unlike what he had been hoping for." Nikolai's sorrowful dreaminess confuses the meaninglessness of the many wounded with disjunct recollections of peace, bringing the book to a close.

The surface of war in Book Two looks back to Book One; its note of frustration is the first of a chord which looks ahead to the frustrated life of Book Three. Nikolai's family misses him all the more for his wound. Natasha refrains from writing Boris, to whom her brother is telling falsehoods about heroism. Pierre frustrates himself for seven years by yoking himself to the voluptuous, heartless Hélène.

Here mere surface, as a frustrating influence, asserts its fullest power. The sheer spell of Hélène's body shakes Pierre. Nikolai huzzahs the Czar and evaporates into dreams more confused than those of Book Two ("Natache . . . sabretache.") Boris' God, surface, empowers him with an understanding of that unwritten code of confident tact which makes a lieutenant superior to a general. Andrey abandons all his illusions as he lies wounded under the sky at Austerlitz, his hero Napoleon dwindled to insignificance. He will await no longer his own Toulon; his depression more than his physical condition has classified him as a hopeless case. But Austerlitz, in all its dominance, is a mere surface beside the Moscow of Book Twelve; it is meaninglessness that Andrey feels under this sky. His frustration with surface is his own special descant to the mood of this book.

Book One: peace; Book Two: war; Book Three: war and peace. These three books state the thesis, antithesis, and synthesis which the rest of the novel works out. The frustration of war in Book Three breaks up after the truce of Austerlitz; in Book Four it invades peace with all the back-washing sterility of war ill concluded. There come from the battle-front a searing fusion of wastes, a series of false notes.

"All Moscow was repeating the words of Prince Dolgorukov: 'Chop down trees enough and you're bound to cut your finger.'" Berg is falsely supposed a hero, Andrey falsely thought dead, till he returns in time to witness the puzzling waste of his wife's death. Hélène takes the abrupt, brutal Dolokhov as a lover, and Pierre challenges him to a duel that drains both men. Denisov proposes to Natasha, who has burned her arm as a proof of love to Sonya. And when Sonya rejects Dolokhov's absurd proposal, his desperate, wasteful revenge is to entice Nikolai into the waste of heavy losses at cards.

The waste of Book Four plays itself out into the mechanism and flatness of Book Five. After Pierre's duel, "Everything within himself and around him struck him as confused, meaningless, and loathsome." "It was as though the chief screw in his brain upon which his whole life rested were loose. The screw moved no forwarder, no backwarder, but still it turned, catching on nothing, always in the same groove, and there was no making it cease turning." The mechanical image of stagnation receives a mechanical answer, the rational religion of Masonry. This book introduces the novel's flattest character, the Mason Bazdeev, who converts Pierre. The crotchety, obsessively mechanical old Prince Bolkonsky moves to the fore as director of conscription. Colorless Boris Drubetskoi dominates Anna Pavlovna's salon to become the lover of a "misunderstood" Hélène. Nikolai candidly recognizes the place of his military profession and returns to find the hospitalized Denisov strangely stagnating at his calamity. Denisov presses a petition on him; he abandons it in order to join a crowd cheering the emperor, and he gets drunk in the last scene of the book. Prince Andrey likewise stagnates, unmoved by Pierre's convert enthusiasm. Still the sight of the sky over the flat ferry raft where they have been talking reminds him of Austerlitz and awakens intimations of "new life in his inner world," the mood of Book Six beginning to gather force.

Against Book Five's stagnated winter rises the burgeoning spring of Book Six. As the flatness of Book Five brought dull Prince Bolkonsky to the political fore, the vitality of Book Six marks the sudden rise of the charismatic Speranski. Andrey, with the rest of society, is to be renewed like the apparently dead oak—"seared with old scars," on his ride out, throwing out a profusion of green shoots on his ride back. Natasha does not burn her arm for love here, as in Book Four; instead she dresses in a yellow gown to set off her black eyes and stays awake ecstatic at the moon through the open window, where Andrey hears her. All draw to her vitality; even Boris gives up Hélène to court her. Happily immersed in his Masonry, Pierre takes a joyfully melancholy consolation in urging Andrey to press his own suit, and the engagement is brought about in the general matchmaking spirit which also unites Vera and Berg. Out at Bogutchorovo Princess Marya, weeping in an excess of love, "felt that she was a sinner, that she loved her father and her nephew more than God," losing herself in the joy of raising Nikolushka and entertaining "God's folk," the vital itinerant pilgrims.

Books Four and Five, waste and flatness, form a pair; so do Books Six and Seven: vitality and unearthly joy. In Book Seven Natasha is riding too high even for her earlier moon ecstasy. The incredible joy, the magically perfect success of a day's hunt, evokes from her a prolonged unearthly shriek:

> At the same moment Natasha, without drawing breath, screamed joyously, ecstatically, and so piercingly that it set everyone's ear tingling. By that shriek she expressed what the others expressed by all talking at once, and it was so strange that she must herself have been ashamed of so wild a cry and everyone else would have been amazed at any other time.

Hunting, dancing, food, moonlight—all of an unearthly perfection. The general elation has roused Nikolai home from the army where he has previously felt willing to vegetate.

This joy is too intense to be more than a phase. "It would be too happy," Natasha feels, if her engagement to Prince Andrey concluded in marriage. The unreality of this momentary joy is exemplified in the falseness of Nikolai's engagement to Sonya. It had been set off by a mere play, the moonlight masquerade ride with burnt cork moustaches and transvestite costumes. "Madagascar, Madagascar," Natasha surrealistically

mulls to herself after a transvestite buffoon has told her that her children
will be "fleas, and dragonflies, and grasshoppers."

The unearthly joy, at its moment, brings clairvoyant powers that forecast the final reality. In the crystal ball of her looking glasses Sonya sees
the real future mirrored:

> "No, I saw. . . . At first there was nothing; then I saw him lying down."
> "Andrey lying down? Is he ill?" Natasha asked, fixing her eyes of terror
> on her friend.
> "No, on the contrary,—on the contrary, his face was cheerful, and he
> turned to me"; and at the moment she was saying this, it seemed to herself
> that she really had seen what she described.
> "Well, and then, Sonya? . . ."
> "Then I could make out more; something blue and red. . . ."

Not only Prince Andrey's ultimate deathbed vision is foretold here, but
also Natasha's marriage to Pierre. For when the joy of Book Six sent her
in curl papers and pyjamas to her mother's bedroom, Natasha said surrealistically of Pierre: "Bezuhov now—he's blue, dark blue and red, and
he's quadrangular. . . . He's jolly, dark blue and red; how am I to explain to you? . . ." But her fear and her poise on the crest of the moment make Natasha here pass by the real significance of "blue and red,"
and she goes on to query Sonya about Prince Andrey's future calamity.

Unearthly joy, having forecast the future at its zenith of vision, gives
way to the next stage. Peace is spent, and Book Eight is dominated by the
crass pain of coming war, searing and wasteful in the manner of Book
Four. Everyone is involved more deeply than he had been in Book Four,
and consequently loss is more durable. Natasha quarrels with her future
sister-in-law. Old Prince Bolkonsky flouts his devoted daughter and fanatically flirts with the heartless Mlle. Bourienne, who had drawn Anatole
away from Marya in Book Three. Boris Drubetskoi contracts a loveless
marriage with Julie Karagina. But the coldest horror comes when Natasha
is nearly seduced by Anatole, at the perhaps jealous instigation of his
sister Hélène. Natasha's attunement to the mood of this book brings her
into spellbound fascination with this unholy pair. Prince Andrey breaks
off their engagement, and the coming war will permanently widen the
breach till the presence of death unites them. Pierre, leaving Natasha in
consternation at the end of the book, sees the comet of 1812.

Book Five's flatness follows the searing waste of Book Four; so after
the crass pain of Book Eight comes the abstract mechanism of war in
Book Nine. German strategy, formidably competent and colossally stupid,
dominates the war planning of this book. Even Pierre supplies soldiers
and contrives a Masonic abstraction to explain Napoleon as the 666 of

the Apocalypse. The profoundly intuitive Andrey can only turn from the abstractions of this phase to find life again meaningless, while Natasha, on the heels of illness, embraces religion, for her an almost mechanical ritual (her true religious life going on through the high rightness of her acts earlier in Book Six, later when she is a wife and mother).

In Book Six, vitality followed a phase of mechanism; so Book Nine's abstract mechanism leads to creative destruction, the keynote of Book Ten. Pierre weeps with forgiveness for the badly wounded Dolokhov at Borodino. Andrey, wounded, sees the creatively swarming white bodies of soldiers as cannon fodder; he contemplates the creativity inherent in children who run for green plums through the threatened orchard. The death of her father is a creative release for Princess Marya. Into threatened Bogucharovo rides the gallantly rescuing Nikolai, led by the emotions this role arouses to become Princess Marya's only possible husband. The destruction of Borodino brings Anatole to creative atonement, Andrey to creative forgiveness. And the physical destruction of defeat, at the end of the book, is declared to have been a creative moral victory for the Russians.

In Book Eleven the destructiveness of Book Ten descends to an empty horror, as not Smolensk but now Moscow itself is under siege. Toward the end of this book the counterbalancing creation in Book Ten is transmuted to a growing joy. Horror holds sway as Princess Hélène takes two lovers at once, as the innocent Vereschagin is torn to pieces by the crowd, as Moscow is captured and bursts into blaze. Pierre wanders dazed in the empty house of his dead master Bazdeev, Andrey lies wounded on a cart. But growth predominates: Andrey's cart is moved into the procession of the evacuating Rostovs; Natasha comes to him, and they forgive each other in a new, deepened devotion. At the end of the book Pierre saves a child from the fire.

In Books Ten and Eleven destruction and creation counterbalance each other. In Book Eleven they have already been separated as well as transmuted: the horror of the beginning had to wait till the end for a growing gladness. Book Twelve transmutes only the horror into a rigor under which Hélène dies from physical exhaustion of her simultaneous lovers. Andrey dies. Natasha is speechless, Pierre a prisoner, Nikolai perplexed, Marya misunderstood in the train of the Rostovs.

Book Thirteen, however, transforms the gladness of Book Eleven into a philosophical joy, as Napoleon's army moves out of Moscow and Pierre learns the meaning of Russian folk life from Platon Karataev's total reconciliation to process.

In Book Fourteen, recalling the mood of Books Four and Eight, a surreal cruelty emerges as the back thrust of war. Dolokhov in his wierdly correct garb leads guerrillas against the ragged retreating French. The saturnine Denisov, too, comes into his own as a guerrilla commander. And Petya, induced to enlist in the general surface dedication of Book Nine, is grotesquely seduced (Tolstoy develops the notion through a horrible kiss Dolokhov gives him) toward his death.

Book Fifteen establishes for good a calm reconciling joy. Marya marries Nikolai, Pierre, a Natasha so transformed he does not at first recognize her.

In the epilog, process evens off. A retransmuting[1] is hinted in Nikolinka, hiding in the shadow as his elders reveal their fixity in the lax rambling of their manners and conversation. He combines the nobility of his real father with the strength of his adopted father and the sensitivity of his adopted mother. Existence can only remain substantially the same, appearance and reality one, for the middle life of our major characters.

I have deliberately exaggerated the unity of each book to bring out its dominant mood. There are in every book, in every episode, many strands which lead back or ahead. The more stultified characters—Anna Pavlovna, Prince Vassily, Berg, Boris—are out of tune entirely with the later developments of the novel and often act in contrast to the prevailing mood. Yet the over-all pattern of the plot is one of successive dominances orchestrated into unity.

Into this structured time, this process of phases, grow the individual rhythms of the various characters. Each phase subjects to itself the destinies of all. What separates Andrey from Natasha is as much 1812 as the baseness of Anatole; and the titanic force of national events, into which the individual destinies flow, parts Andrey from the Anatole he has desperately been seeking till the moment when, as destiny exacts, he will feel deeply enough to forgive him. Without the siege of Moscow he could never have plumbed the marvel of Natasha's love: but death follows reunion.

Through the phases, the individual destinies realize the tempo of their own development. Present is appearance, future is reality, till the time when there will be no real future. Neither society nor self get beyond appearances until their reality can be embodied in time. Pierre's gradual maturation takes him through no fewer than nine stages: first, the flouted bastard, then the wealthy cuckold, then the stern, confused victor over

---

[1] That Tolstoy might have carried this transfiguration into another large novel is suggested by his original plans for a vast epic about the Decembrist Revolt of 1825. Nikolinka would have been just of age to take part in that.

Dolokhov, then the dedicated Mason; then the hopeless lover of Natasha, followed by the courageous dreamer at the siege of Moscow. Already he has worked up to such stamina that he can pull out of the dream and save his own life by looking Davoust square in the eye, but he has still to have a philosophical revelation of life from Platon Karataev, and thereafter a final calm happiness, distinct from that of his revelation. To Natasha, at last, he looks "exactly as though he had come . . . out of a moral bath."

The tempo of each character is peculiar to each. To Pierre's gradual, unaware changes, Andrey counterposes the abrupt, somewhat repetitive, self-torturing resurgences of his vast spiritual capacities. First one disillusionment with social life; then another under the sky of Austerlitz. Then the strange joy at the blossoming oak tree, the engagement. Then another bout of disgust, leading to the post-Borodino feeling where, at his death, all is subdued under the light of the Gospels, a light so faint, though intense, that Andrey cannot get the full word out.

Natasha is so sympathetic to phases that she develops only at the innermost heart of her spirit. In the superficies of the beginning she is frivolous, a would-be dancer. Hers is the psyche delicate enough to suffer each prevailing mood into symbolic expression: a burned arm in Book Four, moon-gazing in Book Six, a prolonged unearthly shriek in Book Seven, in Book Nine a rote religion. But her sacrifice to the spiritual demands of war is to submerge this real sensitivity into the appearance of a most ordinary woman—for her the halo of an even more extreme phase than any of the others, one so absolute that Pierre does not recognize her. "No one would have recognized her at the moment when he entered, because when he first glanced at her there was no trace of a smile in the eyes that in old days had always beamed with a suppressed smile of the joy of life. They were intent, kindly eyes, full of mournful inquiry, and nothing more." Yet "Pierre's embarrassment was not reflected in a corresponding embarrassment in Natasha, but only in a look of pleasure that faintly lighted up her whole face." The light has gone out of her eyes for the radiance of a wholly inner light.

Nikolai combines the Rostov dreaminess with the Rostov practicality. He drifts with the tide, and the depth of its currents more than his own blind will conveys him at last to his true destiny, gentleman farming. Marya is enough like him to be his true wife; her religious passivity merely undergoes—though willingly—the ennobling phases. She seems to derive consolation from misunderstanding, first with her father, then with her husband. And at the end, "she felt a submissive, tender love for this man, who could never understand all that she understood; and she seemed, for that very reason, to love him the more, with a shade of passionate tenderness."

The real life of the novel transcends what it must grow out of, the harrowing appearances of war. What marks the stupidity of a public character like Napoleon is his failure to understand these deeper currents. Kutuzov's signal heroism is the sad realization of his own submission to process, of his underlings' opportunistic blindness to it. The national destiny is expressed by Tolstoy not only through the plot but through these historical characters on the top; on the bottom by the anonymous masses, or by characters who, like Platon Karataev or Lavrushka, are too low for responsive will. Top meets bottom only once, in Napoleon's brief conversation with Lavrushka; this is a mutual deception, though on the whole Lavrushka prevails.

The meaning of this novel, for all its vastness and variety, is so articulately single that it is hard to see how critics could see in it either thematic disjunction or vague grandeur. As Hugh Walpole says, "Its final effect is as concrete and symbolic as a sonnet by Keats; its theme is as simple and singlehearted as the theme of a story by Chekhov."

A world grounded in the moral life of national destiny had exhausted its implications for Tolstoy, or he would not have turned from his planned trilogy first for an abortive historical novel on Peter the Great, then for the changed emphases of *Anna Karenina*. This novel's moral reality lies in the appearances that indicate, as they conceal, sexual involvements which the narrative is constantly analyzing. The rhythm of everyone's gestures toward the whole of life is crucially embodied here in some mysteriously appropriate member of the opposite sex. Nikolai's death is foreshadowed in the almost catatonic cruelty of his attitude toward the rescued prostitute who shares his life. Stiva's callousness, his utter lack of the honesty on which he prides himself, is embodied in his successive, purely physical affairs. Sergey Ivanovitch's hollow intellectuality emerges strikingly in his nervous failure, tantamount to a refusal of life itself, to propose to the equally timid pietist Varenka.

Sex is the cause and effect of brightness or darkness, harmony or discord; and Levin's soul-searching is shown as depending on his real search for a harmonious fruitful marriage with Kitty. Sex is the point at which body meets spirit, a fitting point, then, for "the dialectic of incarnation" as Blackmur[2] calls the action of this novel (and Blackmur's analysis of

[2] "*Anna Karenina*: The Dialectic of Incarnation," *Kenyon Review*, XII, Summer 1950.

it is so final as to forestall any duplicating attempt here): "The bodying forth in aesthetic form by contrasted human spirits of 'the terrible ambiguity of an immediate experience.' "

Deeply needing reality, Anna finds Karenin most intolerable because he is a sham, and he loses her at first by insisting on keeping up appearances, his voice rising habitually to a histrionic shrillness as he cuts off contact with a reality he finds hideous. Vronsky's presence is excruciating from the beginning, but real, for Kitty as for Anna. Sham too is the piety of Madame Stahl and Varenka; under the appearance of charity lies the reality of sexual estrangement—Madame Stahl's old marital trouble and invalidism, Varenka's sterile impatience with the vulnerability of love. The hesitant reality of the sick artist Petrov's love for Kitty cuts through these shams, sending her home cured as she refuses to maintain that connection on a false basis of pity. False, because sexless, is the overindulgent mutual adulation of the separated Lidia Ivanovna and the abandoned Karenin, and she sears with all her own falsity the unbearable, if sinful, reality of Anna's attachment.

The reality observed in the statements of the novel's narrative is appropriately moral, and, as always in Tolstoy, redolent of destiny; he delineates reactions to the whole complex of what always amounts to a sexual situation, whatever disguise it may wear:

> Left alone, Darya Alexandrovna said her prayers and went to bed. She had felt for Anna with all her heart while she was speaking to her, but now she could not force herself to think of her. The memories of home and of her children rose up in her imagination with a peculiar charm quite new to her, with a sort of new brilliance. That world of her own seemed to her now so sweet and precious that she would not on any account spend an extra day outside it, and she made up her mind that she would certainly go back next day.

The agony concealed under the strained elegance and pretended frankness of Anna's sexual situation has caused this reaction in Dolly. Before her visit she had thought of taking a lover; now, faced with the reality of a suitor, she rejects what was the mere transient appearance of a desire and refuses Veslovsky as definitely as Kitty had, though less summarily. Her home situation previously wore the aspect of intolerable frustration. Now it seems "sweet and precious," a fruitful reality in contrast to the willed sterility (they have been discussing birth control) of Anna's. Anna leads Dolly to redefine her sense of her own (sexual) destiny. The heart of the home now "sweet and precious" is the husband whose sexual conduct previously exasperated her. Tolstoy here tells us she said her prayers, and the prayers are, we may imagine, a protection against the forces of sex that are rending Anna and Vronsky. Anna, so frank before, is lowering her eyelids "just when the deeper questions of life were touched upon." So Dolly's confrontation of Anna. Anna, too, confronts Dolly, and the departure of her friend saddens her:

> She knew that now, from Dolly's departure, no one again would stir up within her soul the feelings that had been roused by their conversation. It hurt her to stir up these feelings, but yet she knew that that was the best part of her soul, and that that part of her soul would quickly be smothered by the life she was leading.

Anna's tragic flaw is a kind of impatience with the subjecting appearances of the moment, as well as an obscure desire for a life only precariously whole. She at once faces and averts her crises; so she at once wills and resists unbearable pretense; she shortly commits suicide out of despair at holding Vronsky to the situation he chafes in. Analogically, as Blackmur points out, Vronsky has earlier broken the back of his mare Froufrou by not shifting position fast enough to balance her course; and he does not shift fast enough for Anna, who runs to her suicide because he has delayed writing in reconciliation. There is an unconscious will to murder in his sexual involvement, as Tolstoy shows in the images of sadism by which he describes their first love scene. And Anna is a preconsciously willing victim.

Society has an inertia of health, and Anna is miraculously restored to the life of her home by her almost fatal puerperal fever at the birth of her illegitimate daughter. That upheaval would have cut the Gordian knot of cross purposes in the triangle; in accordance with her earlier dream, the two Alexeys, husband and lover, close in forgiveness. But as well as its health society has the germ of original sin. Anna's brother Stiva interrupts to assert the lover's claims; and Vronsky, recovering from his own suicide attempt, would have gone off to leave Anna and Karenin in peace had not Stiva harried Karenin into the fatal interview that determined the unexpected situation; at a stroke the reversal was undone, and there resulted a deeper and wholly inextricable version of the previous tangle. No Stiva, no more Vronsky; but Stiva is present, Anna's demon and brother. And since it was to extricate Stiva from his own adulterous guilt that Anna travelled to Moscow in the first place, she owes her meeting, as her fatal reconciliation, to the offices of her brother.

A single sin is not the same for two different people. Around the basic sexual situation crystallizes a circumstance unique for everyone. We measure the depth of Anna's degradation by the shallowness of her brother's.

And we measure the spiritual majesty of Anna, petrified in sin, by Levin's response toward the very end:

> Besides wit, grace, and beauty, she had truth. She had no wish to hide from him all the bitterness of her position. As she said that she sighed, and her face suddenly taking a hard expression, looked as if it were turned to stone. With that expression on her face she was more beautiful than ever; but the expression was new; it was utterly unlike that expression, radiant with happiness and creating happiness, which had been caught by the painter in her portrait.

Levin is a spiritual barometer, like Anna. And he is contrasted to her in the lawful health of his relationship, typified as hers is individualized according to the pattern set down by the novel's first sentence: "Happy families are all alike; every unhappy family is unhappy in its own way." His destiny rises out of her disaster; God creates good out of evil; if Vronsky at the beginning had not abandoned Kitty for Anna, Levin could never have married the woman who initially refused him for Vronsky. And at the end it is confronting Anna that brings home to him the rooted spiritual sense he has been striving to achieve. For her, though, the "light was quenched forever." For him: "my life now," he says at the novel's conclusion, "my whole life apart from anything that can happen to me, every minute of it is no more meaningless, as it was before, but it has the positive meaning of goodness, which I have the power to put into it."

So Levin at last comes into his destiny in the unity of all his acts, here perceived as religious. For everyone destiny is unified or perilously not; sex is the index of the unity, in living and in career. At the ascendancy of sham and cuckoldry Karenin's career arrests and begins declining. Levin's farming has meaning which it finds, and funds, in his relationship with Kitty. Vronsky's agricultural methods, as he advocates them in his council dialog with Levin, are harshly mechanized, lacking the intuitive sense of land and peasantry which signalizes Levin's health: Vronsky's career is his sexual displacement; he realizes at the outset that to take up Anna is to forego the opportunities exemplified in the career of his friend and advocate Serpuhovsky; and after her suicide he departs for the Servian campaign with all the riffraff of Russia, a man stalled in career as in sex. His rather plodding selfishness has become the downfall of his sound capacity.

Levin is all the time working toward spiritual perception; Vronsky, like Karenin, toward special failure. The unity of destiny, objectified in the sexual action, is present at every moment in the feelings of the characters. Anna and Vronsky know, when the peasant throws himself under the train in the portentous scene of their meeting, that she will thus commit suicide; that is why she is so profoundly disturbed, why Vronsky sends two hundred rubles to the nameless widow out of apparent generosity and real self-protection. Both dream at particular moments throughout of the strange unkempt peasant, bearded and nasty, who suddenly materializes into reality on the train platform where Anna does commit suicide. Spiritual insight at moments of tension, as in *War and Peace*, materializes into clairvoyance. But all know in their perceptions, and act with the loaded unity of their sexual destiny; this they are constantly creating and responding to.

There is no deep change from part to part of *Anna Karenina*. The unity of Tolstoy's insight in this novel is at once more polished, simpler, and less breathtakingly concrete than in *War and Peace*. Still it is grounded in the unity of a moral plot, of sequenced moral statements which analyze, point by point of the narrative, the moral destinies of the characters.

Reality in some strange way seems to have broken Tolstoy as he turns from moral insight to moral program in his insane last years. His penchant to substitute shallow abstraction for deep perception is prefigured by *War and Peace*'s disjunct disquisitions on a meaning already commandingly present in the analyses of the narrative itself. This tendency to disrupt fiction for tendentious theorizing is held in abeyance by the formal finish of *Anna Karenina*. But it breaks out shortly in Tolstoy's abandonment of art for the half-lights of nightmare abstraction. Sex, mastered in the vision of *Anna Karenina*, has become an obsession in those conversations Gorky records; in his writing it becomes either a platitude in *Resurrection* or an obsession with the extreme and narrow force of *The Kreutzer Sonata*, itself a gargoyle on the cathedral of *Anna Karenina*.

A novel must fully realize its center of moral insight in order to characterize its people fully and consistently, as Tolstoy does. His people are inward, and they grow in process, lucidly enunciated, into whole selves. But they exist in society, and their psychology, however, inward, is defined through the consistent social insight which a moral idea implies, into a world widely coordinated in its relations and its temporal process.

The novel, perforce implying moral ideas, demands the social life for the existence of its characters. Even Robinson Crusoe is not so much an isolated individual as a society of one.

The Dialectic of Incarnation:
Tolstoy's *Anna Karenina*

by R. P. Blackmur

If there is one notion which represents what Tolstoy is up to in his novels—emphatically in *Anna Karenina* and *War and Peace*—it is this: He exposes his created men and women to the "terrible ambiguity of an immediate experience" (Jung's phrase in his *Psychology and Religion*), and then, by the mimetic power of his imagination, expresses their reactions and responses to that experience. Some reactions are merely protective and make false responses; some reactions are so deep as to amount to a change in the phase of being and make honest responses. The reactions are mechanical or instinctive, the responses personal or spiritual. But both the reactions and the responses have to do with that force greater than ourselves, outside ourselves, and working on ourselves, which whether we call it God or Nature is the force of life, what is shaped or misshaped, construed or misconstrued, in the process of living. Both each individual life and also that life in fellowship which we call society are so to speak partial incarnations of that force; but neither is ever complete; thus the great human struggle, for the individual or for the society, is so to react and so to respond to "the terrible ambiguity of an immediate experience" as to approach the conditions of rebirth, the change of heart, or even the fresh start. Tragedy comes about from the failure to apprehend the character or the direction of that force, either by an exaggeration of the self alone or of the self in society. That is why in Tolstoy the peasants, the simple family people, and the good-natured wastrels furnish the background and the foils for the tragedy, for these move according to the momentum of things, and although they are by no means complete incarnations of the force behind the momentum are yet in an equal, rough relation to it. The others, the tragic figures, move rather, by their own mighty effort, in relation, reaction, response to that force, some with its momentum, some against it; some falsifying it in themselves, some falsifying it in society, but each a special incarnation of it; some cutting their losses; some consolidating their gains; some balancing, some teetering, in a permanent labor of rebirth. There is thus at work in the novels of Tolstoy a kind of dialectic of incarnation: the bodying forth in aesthetic form by contrasted human spirits of "the terrible ambiguity of an immediate experience" through their reactions and responses to it. It is this dialectic which gives buoyancy and sanity to Tolstoy's novels.

Let us see how this happens in *Anna Karenina*—how it happens not only in the name and tale of the heroine but also and in relation to the tale of Levin; and how these gain some of their significance through being told against the background of Stiva and Dolly Oblonsky's unhappy marriage. That unhappy marriage is the image of society in momentum, that momentum which only requires the right face to be put upon it to be tolerable, which is true neither for the illicit affair of Anna and Vronsky nor for the profoundly lawful affair of Levin and Kitty. Stiva and Dolly are too near the actual manner of things, are too wholly undifferentiated from the course of society and of individuals, ever to feel the need or the pang of rebirth. All they want is for things to be as they are. Stiva, as the old nurse tells him when Dolly has caught him in an affair with a governess, Stiva has only to do his part; and Dolly has only, now and always, to return to her part. Anna and Levin are very different. Each, in a separate and opposed way, can be satisfied with nothing less than a full incarnation, a rebirth into the force which at crisis they feel moves them. Anna craves to transmute what moves her from underneath —*all* that can be meant by libido, not sex alone—into personal, individual, independent love; she will be stronger than society because she is the strength of society, but only so in her death at the hands of society. Levin craves to transmute himself upwards, through society, into an individual example of the love of God; he, too, will be stronger than society because he finds the will of God enacted in the natural order of things of which society is a part, but he will only do so as long as God is with him in his life. What separates both Anna and Levin from the ruck of rebels is that they make their rebellions, and construct their idylls, through a direct confrontation and apprehension of immediate experience. There is nothing arbitrary about their intentions, only their decisions; there is nothing exclusive or obsessed about their perceptions, only their actions. They think and know in the same world as Stiva and Dolly, and indeed they had to or they could never have been in love with such eminently natural creatures as Vronsky and Kitty. They live in the going concern of society, and they are aside from it only to represent it the better.

This is the world, the society, which is for the most part understood through its manners; and that is how Tolstoy begins his novel, by showing his people through the motion of their manners, first those of Stiva and Dolly, then those of the others. By the end of the first Part of the novel, we know very well the manner of life of each person and could extend it to suit any further accident of life: we know the probable critical point in the temperament of each which rises or descends to some old or new form of action or inaction, and we know it by the kind of manners each exhibits and by how far into the being of each the manners seem to penetrate: into all that is on the surface of Stiva, into all there is anywhere for Dolly, into a layer of permanent irritation for Levin, into a layer of perpetual possibility for Anna, into the radiant sweep of things not yet her own for Kitty, and into the animal vitality of things for Vronsky (who is at the beginning, and always, less a man than a sensual force inhabiting a man). For all this the comedy of Stiva's manners and Dolly's manners coming to terms with each other, not *they* but their manners, stands. Stiva deals with the ambiguities, Dolly with the intolerable things of marriage by manners. Stiva brings the huge pear of his own zest, but he can also weep. Dolly has a temper, but she can also weep. For both, tears are a kind of manners; and thus a reconciliation is effected. We see in this couple how it is that manners dictate the roles by which we escape acknowledging reality.

We begin with the same *kind* of manners Jane Austen mastered, the manners that pass for things otherwise only potentially present. But in Tolstoy we know at once that the manners are *of* something whose potency is pressing into the actual situation, something yet to be revealed in the words of the book, or at any rate to be carried into the open of our consciousness by them. Manners are a flowing stream; they are on the surface of what is swept along, hardly more by themselves but a wayward intimation of what is swept. In Jane Austen, even in *Emma,* the shape— the very water-shapes—of the stream of manners is itself pretty much the subject. In Tolstoy the stream will gradually take on the subject, will become united with it, as a brook takes on the brown of wood-earth and peat: as the Mississippi pushes its mud-color burden twenty miles to sea. Indeed the process begins, in *Anna Karenina,* in the first half-dozen pages, with the old nurse's remark to Stiva: Go, do your part. She tells us real things are at stake in this play of manners, things to be dealt with even the more because they are not acknowledged. And so it is with each personage as he turns up, except perhaps for Vronsky. There are hints of something pushing through.

For Dolly, there are the children, a noise in the hall and a clatter in the nursery, the *unattended* children; and they hint that Dolly's manners, temper and all, are only a part—of what? For Stiva, there is the moment of extreme aloofness after dinner in the restaurant, that aloofness among intimates for which he knew what to do: to make conversation with some *aide-de-camp*, or some actress, with someone not at the center but approaching the center; and so we are aware that the aloofness is from something. For Anna, there is, as an exercise in manners, her *first taking note* of her hypocrisy in dealing with her husband. For Kitty there are such things, still in the play of manners, as her recognition in Anna of something uncanny and her excitement at the utterance, not the substance, of Levin's declaration of love for her. Only for Vronsky there is nothing, as if his manners were so vital or his life so lacking that they were equal to his need.

But for Levin, the other half of Vronsky, there is enough to make up for all the rest. He is, in his unmannerliness, in his steady breach of the expected manner, an effort at declaring what the manners are about; but he is only one effort, one declaration, which can by no means minimize or defeat the others should they come to make their declarations. Levin's very breaches of manners are organized into manners themselves, as organized as the fools and the plain-spoken men in Shakespeare. He is a foil, a contrast, a light to Anna, Stiva, Karenin, Kitty, and Vronsky; and he is a successful foil by the accident of the condition of his temperament, by what he misses or ignores of what they all see. Stiva was right: Levin had no idea of girls as girls; he had no idea how good a fresh roll might smell and taste even after dinner—and indeed there is something vulgar in Levin when he sees a wife as a dinner, vulgar in the bad sense. But he is vulgar in the good sense when, thinking of Kitty, he tells Stiva it is not love but the force outside him which has taken possession of him. It is as if he had found a concrete parallel to the perception which had come to him in reading a sentence from Tyndall: "The connection between all the forces of nature is felt instinctively." Better still is his deep human illumination of the relativity of morals when under the impact of his rejection by Kitty in presumed favor of Vronsky, he comes to a new and compassionate judgment of that intellectual wastrel and revolutionary libertine his brother Nikolay. He thinks of him, and sees how the good force is corrupted. No doubt it is in this passage that we see through Levin's vision of his brother the death and life that are to come in the book. The shift from scorn to compassion, under the pressure of his own brooked love, seems a true act of imitation—of mimesis—which Aristotle tells us is a fundamental delight to man's mind, no matter whether the object of imitation is ugly or beautiful or monstrous.

But this is perhaps to get ahead of the story, when what we want is to become part of the momentum of the story to which the manners of the characters point. The instances of perception isolated above are all pretty mechanical; they do not yet occur organically, by the psychic drive of what has already been formed; they merely illustrate how the characters are being gotten hold of by the story: by the little or big things manners cannot quite either cover up or handle. Mainly, so far, it is a story told of how the people do cover up and do handle. We are on our most familiar living ground. For manners are the medium in which the struggle between the institutions of society and the needs of individuals is conducted. Viable dramatic manners exist so long as the struggle has not become too one-sided, so long as no total credit is given either to one side or the other. When in imagination or dogma the institutions are seen to triumph the manners become hollow, cold, and cruel. When the needs of the individual triumph the manners tend to disappear, so that life *together* becomes impossible. In either case we get a monstrous egoism, incapable either of choice or comparison, an exercise in moral suicide and sterile fancy.

No such case is reached in this novel. Far from breaking down in either direction, we find, even at the worst, at Anna's death or at Levin's access of life, everywhere but at the last retreat of Vronsky to a death in which he does not believe, that the great part of human behavior is viable in manners. It is through manners that the needs and possibilities of each person are seen in shifting conflict with the available or relevant institutions, including the twilight institutions—the illicit, amorphous institutions—which stand at the edges of the institutions of broad day. Stiva, Anna, and Vronsky depend on the twilight institutions of marriage and general social conduct which encroach on the edges of the broad day institutions upon which Dolly, Kitty, and Levin depend. Karenin, at Petersburg, belongs to something else again; he has composed his dissatisfactions in a manner which contains its own rebelliousness: his jeering, desiccated conformity. But it is only the public aspect of the struggle which is between the broad day and the twilight. In actuality the struggle is conducted in the medium of manners between individuals trying from their different needs to shape institutions into some tolerable relation to their own partial apprehensions of reality. Here again it is Levin who has the first illumination; he knows there can be no victory and that there must be a balance. Himself a disbeliever in institutions, and therefore the more apprehensive of their force, he resents the maimed and maiming complaints of his brother Nicolay against the need of institutions: the forever need of make-shift. But best of all are the brother and sister Oblonsky, Stiva and Anna of the voided marriages: the one whose manners will last him forever, the other whose manners will be less and less good to her where they lead her, until at last she creates a fatal manner of her own. Stiva rises always into good nature. Anna is herself a form of nature. Both have something more than sincerity and both, because of the twilight of their actions, have something less than honesty. Think of Stiva at waking reaching for his dressing gown and finding, because he is not in his wife's bedroom, uncertainty instead. Think of Anna, away from home and because of that looking down the stairs at Vronsky and seeing possibility.

What Stiva finds, what Anna sees, is the momentum their manners had been about; and if we look at the gap between Part One and Part Two we see that the momentum is what carries us across the gap. Everybody has been left in an unfinished situation (Anna, Vronsky, Levin, the Oblonskys) or in a "finished" situation (Kitty) which must change. Thus there is both anticipation (uncertain but selected) and expectation (certain but unknown) but we cannot know which is which and cannot determine what is authentic until it has transpired. The business of the novel is how to find out and body forth what has already happened. We know only that for each of these people and for all of them together there must be more of the same thing, with the difference that they will know it better.

The emergence of this sort of knowledge depends on plot, but not upon the mechanical plot, not upon the plot of the "well-made" novel, or at least not primarily, but upon the organic, self-perpetuating, self-reproducing plot (reproducing whether by cycle, by scission, by parallel) which, as Aristotle says, is the soul of action. Surely it is not too much to say that the soul of action is momentum, and that, therefore, plot is the articulation of momentum. Only, in our stage of culture, we do not know ahead of time, we have only means of tentative guessing, what is the significance of plot conceived as the soul of action. We are not in the position of putting these people into relation with some received or religious or predicted concept of significance—as Sophocles, Vergil, Dante were. We are working the other way round: we have to find out in the process of the experience itself. We are about the great business of the novel, to create out of manners and action motive, and out of the conflict of the created motive with the momentum to find the significance: an image of the theoretic form of the soul.

To accomplish this art of psychology, this art of the psyche, this driving form and drifting form (as the stars drift) is perhaps the characteristic task of the novel in a society like that of the nineteenth century: a society without a fixed order of belief, without a fixed field of knowledge, without a fixed hierarchy; a society where experience must be explored for its significance as well as its content, and where experience may be created as well as referred. This is the society where all existing orders are held to be corruptions of basic order; or, to put it differently, where, in terms of the confronted and awakened imagination, the creation of order has itself become a great adventure. This is what Anna and Levin have, great personal adventures in the creation of order: an order is the desperate requirement each has for the experience each bodies forth.

Let us look at a few examples in the Second Part of the relation between manners and momentum and of the force under the momentum breaking through. There is the gradual spread of the scandal of Anna and Vronsky from rumor to declaration to conflagration. At first Anna *uses* the manners of the fashionable set to promote her relations with Vronsky, then she *breaches* manners to solidify them, and at last—with her husband, with society, with Vronsky—she throws manners away, and the force which has been there all along takes over although she does not as yet wholly know it. When asked at Betsy's party what she thinks of repairing the mistakes of love after marriage, she answers: " 'I think,' said Anna, playing with the glove she had taken off, 'think . . . of so many men, so many minds, certainly so many hearts, so many kinds of love.' " After that party her husband, home to read, finds himself uneasy at the situation there tacitly (by manners) acknowledged between Anna and Vronsky. They have breached the formal role of the husband of a pretty wife, and he must speak to her in order to correct their estimate of the situation. As he thinks and walks the floor we see there is something more. When one set of manners impeaches another set—when the twilight assaults the broad day—an ambiguity appears. He who had always worked with reflections of life, and had shrunk away from life itself as something irrational and incomprehensible, now found himself "standing face to face with life." He had walked a bridge over the chasm of life and now the bridge was broken. Thus he is forced outside his official manners, is forced to think of *Anna's* own life for the first time. The plans he makes are all official, to communicate a firm decision and to exact obedience. But when Anna appears, glowing, a conflagration on a dark night, he found he was assaulting an impenetrable barrier and was reduced to begging. She had closed the door into herself, and he knew it would remain closed. As for Anna, his assault found her armored with an impenetrable falsehood and was strengthened, Tolstoy says, by an *unseen force*. His very speaking confirmed the new force and focussed it on Vronsky. In attempting to deceive him she makes the mistake of being natural, candid, light-hearted, qualities which in the circumstance are effects of the unseen force. In the new life between Karenin and Anna, Anna could lie awake feeling the brilliance of her own eyes, but Karenin found himself powerless because the spirit of evil and deceit which possessed her possessed him too. He could only implore and jeer.

When Anna and Vronsky perfect their new life in adultery they find they have murdered the first stage of their love. "Shame at their spiritual nakedness crushed her and infected him." Without the aid, rather the enmity, of decorum, manners, institutions, they cannot cope with the now visible force that binds *and* splits them. Being what they are—that is, being by Tolstoy condemned to full and direct experience—they cannot let the force pass. Vronsky tries to cover up with kisses. Anna tries, and puts off trying, to join together the shame, rapture, and horror of "stepping into a new life." She tries for and cannot find an order in thought. But in her dreams, when she was not protecting herself from her thoughts, she sees the hideous nakedness of her position. She dreams of two husbands, two Alexeys, two happinesses, and the dream weighed like a nightmare because it dramatized the impossibility of the only solution. As for Vronsky there is what happened when he went to see his mare, Frou Frou, the day before the race. The mare's excitement infected Vronsky. "He felt that his heart was throbbing, and that he, too, like the mare, longed to move, to bite; it was both dreadful and delicious." Swift never did this better; and Tolstoy does it without bitterness, though the scene is one which contains most of the occasions for human bitterness. What Vronsky wanted was Anna like the horse. But like the horse, Anna must be used in reckless pastime, or not at all. Take away the pastime, and the recklessness becomes uncontrollable and all the beautiful anarchy in the animal—all the unknown order under orders known—is lost. So, as with Anna, Vronsky failed to keep pace with Frou Frou and broke her back.

While Anna and Vronsky are bodying forth reality, Kitty is being cured of one reality by immersion in another. She is away, taking the waters. Tolstoy gives the tale of her cure lightly and ironically, but it is nevertheless accomplished by very hazardous means, and furnishes interesting analogies to what happened to Vronsky, Anna, Karenin, and in a way, also, to Levin who is immersing himself in the idyll of the simple life on his estate. Almost Kitty becomes a "pietist," a professional doer of good, a conspicuous instrument of false charity: a filler-up of the void of life with the "manners" of sincerity, virtue, and faith in the phase where life is left out. One hardly knows whether it is Mme. Stahl or Mlle. Varenka who better represents the negation of vitality. Both are unconscious charlatans of charity: the one for occupation, the other for duty. Kitty is taken in by both, and being a creature of vital impulse, herself tries the role of charalatan of charity from her heart. She has reached a moment of conversion, but not to recognition of life or God, rather to puerile substitutes for them, when she is rescued by the sick man Petrov's hysterical "love" for her combined with the return of her father full of health and humor and buoyancy. Petrov's "love" she recognizes, though she does not put it into words: "one of those things which one knows but which one can never speak of even to oneself so terrible and shameful would it be to be mistaken." Through her father, through the contagion of life he spreads, she sees Mme. Stahl's short legs and hears the feeble laughter of Varenka. And in the little crisis of these recognitions, she is converted *back* to life.

The figure of Varenka remains only as a threat, the threat of something the opposite of reality. This is the threat of public life, of life in public: the threat of turning the heart into an institution: the situation so desired by Karenin, in which one no longer feels what one ignores; when without conscious hypocrisy or deceit one ignores both the nature and the springs of human action, when all natural piety is transformed into the artifact of piety. There is no sympathy in it, much less mimesis, only empty histrionics: the vanities of spiritual ill-health mistaken for the pangs of vocation.

In all this Tolstoy never leaves us in the dark. It is only Kitty, the little Princess, who is led astray into thinking here is a career, or a new life, with these creatures who take no part in the momentum which sweeps them along. It takes only the lyric stagger of her "lover" Petrov, repeated to show it was doubly meant, a stagger for disease and a stagger for love, and the genuine momentum of her father the old Prince to pull her back into the stream. If we the readers remember in what language Tolstoy introduced Varenka we should ourselves never have been deceived. A creature without youth, nineteen *or* thirty, "she was like a fine flower, already past its bloom and without fragrance, though the petals were still unwithered." She is one of those who have nothing to suppress, no matter what the situation.

It may be, of course, that Tolstoy wrote all this to express his instinctive hatred of professional bad health: the bad health that keeps on living and makes of the open air a morass. These people also however make a parallel to the true purpose of the book: they cover up the encroaching reality of death much as Dolly and Karenin cover up what is for them the vanishing reality of life. The difference is that the sick and the charlatans succeed: they are equal to what they admit of their condition, and so take power over the living (nobody can so dominate a situation as the confirmed invalid); while Dolly and Karenin are never equal to their situation and still struggle with it, however pitifully or pretentiously, and lose power over others as over themselves with each successive act. The difference may be small from another perspective, but from Tolstoy's perspective it is radical. That is why the figure of Nikolay Levin passes, a small harsh whirlwind, across the scene: the very whirl-wind of a man preparing and building into the reality of his death: tall, with stooping figure, huge hands, a coat too short for him, with black, simple, and yet terrible eyes: this figure shouting at the doctor and threatening him with his stick.

Tolstoy has many skills in the dialectic of incarnation. Here is one where the incarnation is of raw force itself, but it must be thought of in its setting. Consider how he surrounds the affair of Anna and Vronsky —the seduction, pregnancy and declaration—on the one side with the true idyll of Levin in the spring and on the other side the false idyll of Kitty at the watering place. It is across Vronsky and Anna that Kitty and Levin reach. At the very center lies Frou Frou, the mare, with her broken back, struggling up on her forelegs, then falling: all because Vronsky could not keep pace with her. Vronsky kicked her with his heel in the stomach. "She did not stir, but thrusting her nose into the ground, she simply stared at her master with her speaking eyes."

Vronsky's unpardonable act was no accident; neither was it done by intention. It was rather that, at a moment of high arbitrary human skill, at a moment of death-risk and momentary glory, the center of all eyes and the heart of an almost universal act of mimetic participation—at that moment something like fate broke the rhythm. Yet Vronsky was right: "for the first time in his life he knew the bitterest sort of mis-fortune, misfortune beyond remedy, and caused by his own fault." What is beyond remedy is beyond judgment: is its own justice; and if it is nevertheless caused by Vronsky's own fault, it is because the fault is universal. It is the fault that inheres in Kitty and Levin, in Dolly and Stiva, Anna and Vronsky alike: the fault of not keeping pace. This does not seem hard to understand in its general symbolic reach, that it may happen or that it may not that a breach of pace may be fatal. It is a harsher act of imagination to grasp the actuality of the absolute intimacy *and* the absolute inadequacy—the deliciousness *and* the dread—in human relationship; precisely what must be grasped if that phase has been reached.

But what is even more terrifying about Tolstoy's honesty—or let us say what is more astonishing about his genius—is that he could have broken the back of a mare in the midst of the crisis in the passion of Anna and Vronsky without either adding or diminishing *human* significance but rather deepening the reality. It is as if in this image he had gotten into the conditions of life from which the conditions we know of emerge: into conditions purer and conditions more intolerable: into an order which includes all human disorders.

These are affairs, as Tolstoy like Dante knew, of which the sane mind makes no report except in symbol, however they may remain thereafter the very growth of the mind. So it was with Vronsky. His friend Yashvin the rake understood it best, "overtook him with his cap, and led him home, and half an hour later Vronsky had regained his self-possession." The death of Frou Frou had become a part of him, no longer separately recognized.

Like the death of Frou Frou, so it is with the passions that inhabit our heroes. The passion of the force will pass but not the force, and if the passion has not wrecked the hero (as it does Karenin) the force will be stronger after the passion has passed than before. That is why the notion of purification is attached to the passion of tragic action. Society, nature, and the individual in society and nature, have three common arrangements to take care of the situation when genuine passion has passed. There is the arrangement for outlets in the demi-monde or twilight world. There is the arrangement for the cultivation of passion for its own sake, which suits those afraid of being *otherwise* occupied. And there is the arrangement that when the passion passes those who have been joined in it will find themselves insuperably bound—unless a fresh passion of the force supervene. Both for Anna and for Levin, with their different aspirations, none of these arrangements is enough. Or rather, for Levin none of them will do at all, and for Anna they will all do in their turns. But both need the identification of force with love, the one outside society and nature, the other through society and nature. Anna needs to become herself standing for everybody, Levin needs to become everybody in order to find himself represented. That is why both Anna and Levin are subject to fearful jealousies. Their rebirth into new life is never complete and the identification of force with love is never complete. Thus the force remains free, capable of assuming all possible forms. That

is why Anna dreads in Vronsky and Levin in Kitty the positive enactment
of what is at constant potential in themselves. Their jealousy is that they
crave each other's possibilities, and hence each is bound to muster out of
the force that moves them a new burst of passion in the hope that this
time the new birth will take place but in the hidden certainty that it
will not.

Vronsky, even more than Anna, as their love becomes more of a scandal,
is deprived of the social phases of "force" and is required to envisage it
as if naked, and an enemy. The worm of ambition in him which had
been covered in the first stages of love is now uncovered by the scandal
of love. He understands perfectly what his friend the successful general
means when he says, "Women are the chief stumbling-block in a man's
career. It's hard to love a woman and do anything." He understands but
he answers softly that the general has never loved, and he understands
even better when the general returns it, "We make an immense thing of
love, but they are always *terre à terre*." It is what he understands, and
keeps out of sight, that gives him a hard expression when Anna tells him
she is pregnant. He is thinking of all that is lost, and of the duel that
must come. Anna does not understand that and gives up all hope that his
love will be enough for her, though in the same breath of her mind she
tells him that it will be. She sees he has already been thinking and will
not tell her all he thought. She is, she tells him, proud, proud, proud—
but she cannot say what she is proud of; and Vronsky if he had spoken
must have said the same thing. They get at so differently what lies
between them that they wholly misunderstand each other, but never for
a second do they fail to grasp the force that compels the misunderstanding.

As for what happens to Karenin there is no better image than the
lawyer whom he consults about a divorce: he plucks four moths out of
the air, as if he were the law engorging the individual. Unlike Anna and
Vronsky, who are deprived of them, Karenin is more and more taken
over by the brutality of the social phases of "force." He makes one final
effort to reverse himself—as do Anna and Vronsky—when Anna, in child-
birth, thinks herself dying. Then all three reverse and renounce their
roles, and do so in deep analogy to Levin and Kitty at the true death of
Levin's brother Nikolay where they gain great access to their true roles.
It is the image of death—the attractive and repulsive force of death—
which takes over each of them. There is something in the rhythm of death
which for Vronsky, Anna, and Karenin elicits a supreme failing effort to
keep pace, as there is for Levin in his brother's death. For each, it is as
far as they can go in their opposed directions.

Indeed it is Anna's literally incomplete death-scene which is the death in which rebirth takes place. She makes a histrionic mimesis of death because of the two women within her. Thinking, in her last spasm of social guilt, to kill one, actually she kills the other. No, not by thinking does she do this, unless it is something outside the mind that thinks. Rather she, the whole of her, takes advantage of the vision of death to find out what can be seen through it. Her mistake is only initial. The rebirth is accompanied by an exorcism, which she sees and feels but which, so great is the force of the world, she does not at once recognize for what it is. She has become single; it seems to be by renunciation; actually it is by an access of devotion—for she is not a woman gifted with renunciation, and her first practice of it shows as irritation and inability, as something to overcome and something to perfect. Had Vronsky not come, had he not rushed in, and stroked her cropped hair, calling her a pretty boy, she might never have found out in actuality what her new singleness was. Instead of positive desperation she would have ended in self-contemptuous despair. There would have been nothing to break down, only the collapse of a dry shell. As it is, she begins at once, against the world-and-his-wife and contemptuous of both, the long course of building her own desperation, the positive desperation of her own cause, to the point where her own strength but not that of her cause should be exhausted.

That is the nature of her tragedy, that her own strength cannot be equal to her cause. The independence of the individual is never equal to the cause of independence. And the flaw is as it should be, both in her and in the nature of things, and not at all less guilty for that (or if you like, less innocent): a flaw in any case, a human need, which as it finds its mode of action and creates its motive becomes less and less the kind of flaw that asks for the forgiveness of understanding and is more and more revealed as a single, eminent aspect of the general nature of things which brings the mind to compassion.

How otherwise—how if it is not this train that has been set going—can we look at the irony of the pure, lawful, and successful love affair of Levin and Kitty as anything but cheap and puerile "moralism"?—that is, not irony at all. Levin in new life, Levin on wings, has also singled his life, has made an act of devotion, to which he will necessarily turn out inadequate, not so much because of inadequate strength but because the cause itself (in the form of his original impulse) will desert him. The very, brutal force of the world and his wife which will bring ruin to Anna and Vronsky because they contest it, is the force Levin leans on—his cause—and it is a force hardly less reliable taken as a cause than as the enemy. No institution and no individual may ever be more than a partial incarnation of the underlying or superior force; nor can any set of individuals and institutions taken together. It is only Stiva or the peasant with the pretty daughter-in-law whom Levin had seen pitching hay who can use or abuse this force indifferently: with the kind of faith that makes no enquiries and would not know a vision if it saw one. For Stiva, there is always a way out, not death. For the peasant girl—she is herself a way out, and death is a matter not yet experienced. These are the creatures not subject to individual rebirth, they are the nearest thing to permanence: momentum or recurrence.

But the shoe of Anna's rebirth pinches sharpest, under the impact of symbolic death, on Karenin and Vronsky: the one with his head in the hollow of Anna's elbow, the other with his face in his hands: the one suffering total and permanent spiritual change, the other suffering total humiliation followed by recovery through violence: the one inwardly transcending his society, the other rejecting his society and both to be ever afterwards victimized by it—though one, Karenin, is put in contempt by society, and the other, Vronsky, is made a hero so to speak outside society. Karenin can never get back into society and is in a misunderstood position above it. Vronsky can never leave society behind him: it goes with him: he is a kind of pet public outcast. They have passed, by humiliation and self-contempt, through their relations to Anna's symbolic death, to the roles most nearly opposite to those in which we first saw them.

That is, to each of them comes a deep reversal of role through a direct, but miscomprehended, experience of the force of life in the phase of sex under the image of an incomplete death. We shall see the deaths completed diversely. Meanwhile we see Anna, Vronsky, Karenin, and Levin tied in the hard knot of individual goodness, and each, in that goodness, in a different relation to the manners and momentum of society. I mean, by goodness, that each has been reborn into a man or woman for once, and at last, proper to his or her own nature. Each was *virtu*, and to the point of excess, but—such is the power of Tolstoy's imagination—without loss of humanity. Each, seen beside the self, is more the self than ever. Levin, seen in society, is no more representative of it than the other three, who are seen against it.

It is for this goodness that they pay the cost. The good, said Aristotle, is that which all things aim at, and when an aim has been taken everything flies that way—whether the target was indeed the good or not. We see Levin in doubt and delight about everything, desiring not to desire, as we see Vronsky equally in doubt, but so full of *ennui* that he desires desire. We see that Anna's problem is to maintain the state of crisis in love, to be always a young girl in love, and that Vronsky's problem is to find substitutes, caprices of action, to prevent *ennui* from absorbing crisis. In Vronsky's house all were guests, in Levin's all were part of the household; and so on. Tolstoy gives us hundreds of comparisons and analogies of the two honeymoons. But perhaps the most instructive is the comparison of Veslovsky at Levin's and at Vronsky's. This young man with unseemly eyes, fat thighs, and hand-kissing habits was very much a gentleman of the bed-chamber: altogether in place at Vronsky's, very much a part of the general pretense at occupation. Vronsky ignores in him what had genuinely put Levin in a rage, and Anna was amused at him where Kitty was ashamed. Kitty and Levin made a fight for life within the fold, Anna and Vronsky fight in abuse of the fold; and a little in the background Dolly surrenders to life within a broken fold.

Each of them is inadequate to him or herself as a solitary actor; and perhaps this is nowhere shown so clearly as in the image of Dolly making her solitary visit to Anna sitting in the coach, afraid to look in her glass, daydreaming herself a perfect paramour. Again we see it in Dolly in her darned gown listening with aversion and distrust to Anna talk of birth-control. She knows suddenly that in the very numbers of her children is her safety: not in perspective, future or past, but in numbers, in everyday life. Dolly is the monitor of all that is living: she has paid the cost of goodness without ever having had it, and in so very deep a way that no fresh start—neither rebellion nor new effort along old lines—could ever get it for her. She is neither good nor evil; neither hopeless nor desperate. She believes in high principles, and that they must not be forgotten, but in every act of her being she knows the necessity, if she is to survive, of the alternate assertion and abuse of these principles. The compassionate gesture of her visit to Anna is symbolic of all this; and it is the kind of peak of meaningfulness she can reach at any time, with no need for crisis. So we begin to see what she is doing in this novel: she is to be recognized, not understood. But we should never have believed her, or in her, had we seen her in such a moment at the beginning; nor would she have believed in herself. She would have been a bad Varenka, a hypocrite unendurable. It was right that she had to be brought round by Anna, just as it is right now that her presence should remind Anna of all the life she was smothering. But best of all is to think of Dolly with the road dust in the creases about her eyes, imagining at the end of her daydream of illicit love, what the expression on Stiva's face would be, when, like Anna to Karenin, she flaunted her infidelity in his face.

This image of Dolly may have come to Tolstoy as an afterthought, as a debt to his novel he had not known he was incurring and which he had therefore all the more obligation to pay. He had thought of Rachel, but not of Leah. But with the other image in this part of the book—the death of Nikolay—it is the other way round. This is the death that lived in Tolstoy all his life, for which he made three great images of which this is the first and greatest—the others are "Ivan Ilyitch" and *The Living Corpse*. Death is the inevitable thing from which there is no freedom by recognition but only by enactment. Where Anna (as Dolly saw) has learned a new gesture, to half close her eyes on what is threatening her and cannot be dealt with, Tolstoy himself has to force a steady gaze on death physical, spiritual, and dramatic (poetic, dialectic, rhetorical). He has to mime death. He has to show in fact that death, as well as good, is what all things aim at; that death is the moving *and* the fixed background of life. He knows and must show that it is a commonplace truth and illusion that men die well. The whole commonplace is there in the physical—the terribly physical—death of Nikolay: and in the longing for death that surrounds it.

This death—the most innocent and most mature in all fiction—though it has nothing to do directly with the plot is yet a center of attractive force presiding over its whole course. Everything else is drawn to it, across a gap. It is this attractive force that begins to complete the actions of each of our persons, those actions which were focussed in the partial deaths endured by Anna and Levin in the middle portion of the book, and which were initiated by the death of Frou Frou at the first crisis in the action: it is the solitary and menacing incarnation of all these. And it should be well noted that in this death everything is as near the physical as possible without affront to the spiritual and the dramatic. The turbulence is all of something watched by Kitty or felt by Levin. It is death as raw force, a concrete, focal, particular epiphany of the raw force of death. It is the after part of every forethought.

Surely that is what is somehow in Levin's mind when, in making his one call on Anna in her Coventry, he sees her face as stone and more beautiful than ever, the very Medusa-face of life (Henry James's phrase) to which for a moment he succumbs. Altogether these nine or ten pages of Levin's vision of Anna are a high example of what may be meant in the novel by full drama. As in the modern stage drama, a great deal depends on what has gone before, now summarized and brought to a fresh and conclusive action against a background which may and will come forward when the action is done: when the violent inner light of conflagration in Anna is changed to the lightning that momentarily obscures the stars for Levin. That is what the dramatic action is for, to pull the whole background forward. It is the background in which they are all implicated, and in which the action is a series of parallels and a series of analogies which show all our principal persons in deeply but narrowly different responses to the same force: each lawful, each valid, complementing each other like ice and water, or night and day, converging like slush or twilight, like midnight and noon. Each is brought to a clarity, of which the meaning is seen, not alone in relation to the other persons, but also with respect to the sweep of things: the sweep which moves with the strange intimate noise which Shakespeare calls the endless jar of right and wrong in which justice resides. It is against this that Anna's face was stone and more beautiful than ever.

There is a nakedness in this sort of experience for Anna which ends in death, and an unarmored defencelessness for Levin which begins in birth. It leaves both of them without the protection or clothes of the intellect. And there is a harshness in the compassion required of total response to each—the compassion of peace with a sword—which is possible only to a saint or a great artist. Such response touches what is under our behavior, and what comes into our behavior, which whether we shun it or salute it, remakes, while the contact lasts, our sense of relation with ordinary life. We cannot live at crisis, at the turning point, but must make out of it either a birth or a death in the face of ordinary life. This is what happens to morality in art. It is an image of passing one way or the other; which may explain what Eliot had in mind when he observed that as morals are only a preliminary concern to the saint so they are only a secondary concern to the artist. That is the condition, between the preliminary and the secondary, of harsh compassion that made Tolstoy reject his novels, including this one, along with Shakespeare. He rejected the uncopeable truth, because he wanted to remake the world piecemeal in terms of morality as a central authority. In the novels he wanted only the mimesis of morality as a central experience, both in the world and in the crisis of individuals who were somehow, because of the crisis, removed from it.

The novels wanted to show the tacit, potential crisis which gave the ordinary world meaning, and which in turn put individuals to the test. It is in contest and concert with the ordinary world that crisis is reached and given worth; and it is into the ordinary world that things break through and are bodied forth, visibly in crisis, actually all along. The last two parts of *Anna Karenina* put into parallel and analogy such recognitions as these. Under pressure of the action even the parallels seem to become analogies, to be in proportional relation to each other: as in the stream of consciousness—the articulate hysteria—in which

Anna's last hours are recorded, which is both parallel and analogous to Levin's final conversion in company with the beetle under the dusty shade of the poplars at noon.

For a major parallel which is also analogy, let us look at the whole structure in the next to last part of the book. We begin with Kitty's delayed confinement and from it see Levin moved through Moscow's "society," intellect, and club life, to reach that other form of delayed or arrested vitality which is Anna, and in which he is for a moment absorbed. Then through quarrel and jealousy we are moved sharply to the scream of birth for Kitty and the plunge to death for Anna: the birth which for Anna meant death not herself, which to Kitty meant new life not herself, and which to Levin were one and the same. Between the two sets of movements there is a chapter in which an independent evil spirit grew up in Anna because there was a delay in her affairs, just as there was an independent new life in Kitty in the delay of *her* affairs. The one ends in senseless rage, the other in senseless joy. In either case it is the uncopeable power not themselves which moves them, and to each it shows with the terrible ambiguity of an immediate experience.

Surely it is not providential that before returning to Anna and her death, Tolstoy carries us to Petersburg, the city of government and decorum and manners, and gives us, so we may make our own irony, images of what happens when people insist on coping with their own troubles in terms of the unilluminated ordinary world. We see all this in Stiva pursuing his double errand, to get himself a better job and to get Anna her divorce. To get the job he has to descend into humiliation. To prevent himself from giving the divorce, Karenin, with Lidia aiding, has to descend to a false appeal to a false force pretending to govern a false society: he descends to the clairvoyance of a charlatan, to an "induced" change of heart. By betrayal of his own traditions, Stiva gets his job; so does Karenin refuse the divorce. Anna is not a matter of genuine consideration. In this analogy, Tolstoy presents all that is left, in these people, of the true force: he sees that Stiva and Karenin have become all manners and no men.

Nor is it providential, it is the very essence of the prepared drama, that we return from Stiva in Petersburg to find Anna in Moscow, herself clutching at manners—in the form of quarrels, jealousies, formal emotions —in the one place where manners cannot act but only cover up ugly action—the place where people are outside society, but where, since so little else is left except the raw emotion of the self, appearances must be kept up. It is their manners, failing, that keep Anna and Vronsky from joining their emotions. They neither do their part nor keep pace. It is when her manners wholly fail that Anna brims over, sees herself clear, and comes on that unintermediated force which makes her suffer, and it is in desperate pursuit of some manners into which she can deliver that suffering that she finds her death: precisely as she thought she had done so long ago in her false death. Her tragedy is that she has destroyed too much of the medium, too many of the possibilities, of actual life, to leave life tolerable, and she has done this partly by dissociating manners from the actual world and partly by losing her sense of the sweep of things. Thus her last turning point, her last effort at incarnation, was death.

With no less of the force in him that drove Anna, Levin turned the other way. He too had been at the point of death and for months at a time, but through the death of his brother and the delivery of his wife found himself alive instead. It could have been the other way; Levin and Anna were aimed equally at life or at death. Human life cannot stand the intensity of Anna, but works toward it; human life requires the diminution of intensity into faith and of faith into momentum which is Levin. The one is very near the other. Only Anna's face was stone and more beautiful than ever. Yet it is in the likeness not the difference that the genuineness and the dialectic of Tolstoy's incarnation lies.

Tolstoy's "The Death of Ivan Ilytch" and Jamesian Fictional Imperatives

by Edward Wasiolek

I

The reader who has been brought up on the conventions of the technique of the modern novel, on the refinements of points of view, complex involutions of time, symbolic and mythic levels, and on the imperative to be dramatically objective, must read the later works of someone like Leo Tolstoy with a sense of discomfort. His content is massively moral and dogmatically expressed; his art is distressingly lacking in ambiguity and levels of meaning; and he obtrudes himself unabashedly in his narratives.

The disjunction between Tolstoy's later technique and contemporary literary predispositions—to Tolstoy's disadvantage—was brought to me forcefully by a student's comment on *The Death of Ivan Ilytch*. The student found that his enjoyment of this long story was spoiled by what he called Tolstoy's "arbitrariness." The tale of a provincial judge who passes from a pleasant and proper life to death, by way of great physical and moral suffering from a trivial accident, seemed to the student and to others in the class grossly unreal. Tolstoy's lesson of changed awareness of the value of life under the bludgeon of pain and terror was to them clumsily manipulated, remote from real life, and highly debatable in moral value. Quite simply, they wanted to know why Ivan Ilytch had to suffer such pain, implying in their question that his sufferings were unrealistically disproportionate to the probabilities of his character. They argued, in answer to their own question, that Tolstoy had not represented reality as it was, but as he wished it to be. He was, in short, arbitrary.

That Tolstoy's art is manipulated and remote from real life, at least in one sense, is true; that this makes bad literature is debatable. The charge

"Tolstoy's 'The Death of Ivan Ilytch' and Jamesian Fictional Imperatives" by Edward Wasiolek. From *Modern Fiction Studies*, VII (1961), 314-324. Copyright © 1961 by the Purdue Research Foundation. Reprinted by permission of the Purdue Research Foundation and the author.

assumed, explicitly or implicitly, it to be. Every assumption about
[exp]erience carries with it its own law of aesthetic appropriateness. This
[ma]y sound very similar to James's granting to every author his subject;
[the] difference, and it is great, is that James insists that it be executed in a
[ver]y special way.

II

If we judge Tolstoy, in *The Death of Ivan Ilytch*, by his own assump-
[tio]ns about experience—and the modern reader is a dogmatist if he does
[no]t—Tolstoy's art is anything but arbitrary. Ivan Ilytch's suffering, his
[pa]in, and the behavior of others toward him, as well as the techniques
[us]ed to express these, follow with irreproachable logic certain assumptions
[T]olstoy makes about experience. What are these assumptions? The first
[an]d perhaps the most important is that the meaning of life can be
[u]nderstood and formulated and that human behavior can be judged as
[g]ood or bad. The second assumption, peculiar to this story, is that a
[li]fe built wholly and exclusively on self-pleasure will lead to certain
[in]evitable consequences in the behavior of people. *The Death of Ivan
Ilytch* is the chronicle of a life badly lived among lives that are badly
[l]ived. At first, everything for Ivan Ilytch goes as he had arranged it,
[p]leasantly and properly. From successes in school, he goes to successes in
[h]is profession, in society, in play, and in love. He is a kind of Russian
[e]veryman; he gets his degree, starts up the occupational ladder, marries
[t]he right kind of girl, gets the right kind of friends, the right kind of
[f]urniture, and then everything goes wrong because of a little accident.
While hanging some drapes, he slips and hits his side, and subsequently
a dull pain becomes an insistent discomfort, and the discomfort, excruciating pain. Ivan Ilytch spends the last three days of his life screaming
with pain. Moral and physical pain, loneliness and terror, and finally
death are the wages of Ivan's pleasant and proper life.

Why is Tolstoy so hard on Ivan? He is to be sure vain, trivial, pleasure-
loving, but he is also not so much different from most of us. Why does
Tolstoy bludgeon him with so much for so little? Ivan asks himself the
same question, late in the story, alone with the knowledge that he is
dying. He cries out to God: "But what is it? What have I done to
Thee? What is it for?" Is not the punishment too much? Must we not,
then, while granting Tolstoy all his skills of relentless analysis and irony
charge him with being arbitrary? Is not the judgment he places on Ivan
a kind of moral aberration of an old man who had recently gone through

stems from a predisposition of the modern reader to a special view of
experience in fiction and of techniques appropriate to that view. Not only
is the view predisposed against the representation of what "ought" to be,
but it is also predisposed against the representation of experience as
something caught and formulated into definite meaning. It is a view of
experience that is timorous before norms of any kind, moral or intellectual; character, in this ivew, is believable only when it is ever defining
itself in new and changing contexts, and meaning is acceptable only
when it is ever contingent on the massive complexity and endless qualification of particular experience.

Henry James, whose theory and practice have been an important but
not exclusive determinant of this view, expresses it in this way in "The
Art of Fiction": "Experience is never limited, and it is never complete;
it is an immense sensibility, a kind of huge spiderweb of the finest silken
threads suspended in the chamber of consciousness, and catching every
air-borne particle in its issue." Significantly caught experience in fiction
for James lies in seeing life not with the delimiting systematizing and
abstract faculties of the mind, but with the retina of the mind's sensitive
reflection of life's coruscations: "It goes without saying that you will not
write a good novel unless you possess the sense of reality; but it will be
difficult to give you a recipe for calling that sense into being. Humanity
is immense, and reality has a myriad forms." The successful work of
fiction, for James, does not interpret experience, and even less prescribes
what it should be. Rather, it is a simulacrum of reality, an "immense and
exquisite correspondence with life."

The techniques which have been a consequence of this view of artistic
experience are conditioned by a horror of conceptual formulation and of
authorial intrusion. James's insistence on "rendering" rather than "stat-
ing" is still a crisp formula for this predisposition. The reader does not
receive the author's statement of experience; rather, he, with a sensitivity analogous to that of the author, is asked to participate in the
act of seeing. "Meaning" is not given in the work itself in any explicit,
generalized sense, and its formulation involves necessarily the reader as
one of its variables.

The opposite is true of Tolstoy's method. The representation of
experience is interlarded with the author's comments, which constantly
interpret and explain what the representation "means." Tolstoy demands
more acuteness of understanding than acuteness of vision. He is sure of
his meaning and does not hesitate to fix it in generalization and control
it by direct intrusion. The significance of Ivan Ilytch's life has no
penumbra of ambiguous qualification surrounding it. Ivan Ilytch shares

neither the contingent nature of James's characters, who are at every moment becoming something more; nor, to take a more contemporary example, the indeterminate nature of Faulkner's characters, who, though finished becoming, are never finished being understood by interpreters within the novel. For each the meaning of the lives represented is indeterminate and contingent; for one, upon the dramatic context; for the other, upon who is doing the understanding. For both "meaning" in the sense of something explicit and definite, as in Tolstoy, would be a post-aesthetic process arrived at by the reader on the basis of his own seeing and interpretation. There is no core of stated authorial meaning, which the representation supports by illustration and which the reader is asked to receive or even to penetrate.

Since the very principle of definition implies a formulatable essence, it is impossible to catch in definition a Jamesian character. He is always in some dynamic relationship with the situation he finds himself in. Maisie is one kind of person at the beginning of the novel, another kind at the end, and something subtly distinct in all the dramatic situations that intervene. The dependence of the meaning of her character on changing dramatic situations explains, I believe, the sharply divergent interpretations of her that have been published. She is neither a case of childhood purity triumphing over a corrupt environment, nor a victim of her environment, passively submitting to the corrupt moral air she breathes. Maisie is simply not finished. At the end of the novel she is quite clearly not responding to her environment in the same way she had done at the beginning. She has taken on a faint coloration of the methods used by the people around her—she is, for example, beginning to fight for her own ends—but these methods are not corrupt in themselves. They are a necessary consequence of the consciousness of maturity. Whether she will take on a deeper hue of the morality of those about her is dependent upon situations not yet presented and upon her interaction with these situations. As twentieth century readers we see readily that writers like Faulkner and James are using narrative techniques appropriate to the way they see experience, and we accept with ease, if not with inevitability, their view of experience. We see less readily Tolstoy's techniques as the necessary consequence of the way he saw experience; we see least readily that such a view of experience is artistically palatable.

James himself, with conviction that was but a shade from dogmatism, never questioned his own assumptions about the form experience should take in a successful piece of fiction. Although seemingly generous in his championing of the author's right to choose his "idea," his subject, and

insistent on the reader's obligation to respect that choic[e] theless, quite rigid in his unquestioning assumption fictional experience was "executed" experience, so as bristling correspondence the endless qualification of ex flected in a sensitive consciousness. "Oh, I grant you," he one hand,

> your starting point, because if I did not I should seem to pre[s] and heaven forbid I should take that responsibility. If I pr you what you must not take, you will call upon me to tell yo you must take; in which case I shall be prettily caught. More till I have accepted your data that I can begin to measure you standard, the pitch; I have no right to tamper with you[r] then criticize your music.

But on the other hand, he says, "In proportion as in what s offers us we see life *without* arrangement do we feel that we a the truth; in proportion as we see it with arrangement do v we are being put off with a substitute, a compromise and c[o] When faced with the example of one who is bold in his " but who is at the same time an unquestioned genius, Leo Tols could only dismiss him as a "splendid accident." Of Tolstoy, in his essay "Turgenev and Tolstoy": "His own case is prod[i]g his example for others dire: disciples not elephantine he can on[l] and betray."

If we assume, with someone like James, that the complexi perience is too great to be fixed in logical statement and generalization, then someone like Tolstoy, who believes that lif understood, its laws characterized, and the actions of men judg inevitably appear "arbitrary," in the student's words, and "arran James's words. It is clear, however, that the term "arbitrary" imp assumption about experience from which the author in question and, more important, an assumption that is put forth, at least imp as a "law." We arrive then at the curious position of calling an work arbitrary when it fails to obey certain assumptions about e ence, which by their very nature must be arbitrary unless we ar sumptuous enough to believe that our view is sanctified by infallibi would argue simply that the assumptions about experience by v artistic works are to be judged are those which are implied in the in question. An author is arbitrary, then, not when he violates someone else thinks is experience, but when he violates what he him

a religious conversion? It looks that way, for the acts and the judgment do not fit.

I do not believe, of course, that the flaw is there. The judgment is not arbitrary; the suffering of Ivan is not accidental, no more so than the callousness of people to each other and the abstract relations that obtain between them. What happens in the story happens because it had to happen that way. How the people of this society live, argue, and treat each other is all inevitable. Take what detail you will in the story, and you will find that it is there—not because Tolstoy wanted it there— but because it follows on the laws by which these people live: and they live for pleasure and not for pain. If you assume a world in which pain is inevitable (and it is inevitable if for no other reason than death), and if you assume a society built on the pursuit of pleasure, wholly and exclusively—and Tolstoy sets up the society in this extreme way—then everything that happens in *The Death of Ivan Ilytch* happens with the necessity of a formal syllogism.

Take, for example, Ivan Ilytch's relations with his wife. They are happy and then they become estranged. At one point Ivan Ilytch can hardly tolerate his wife; at a later point she can hardly tolerate him. The happiness and estrangement, and Ivan's inability to support his wife and she him, follow from the kind of people they are. Ivan marries her because she fits into his plans for a pleasant and proper life. She comes from a good family, is not bad looking, has some property, and, most important of all, the people he respects look with approbation on the match. The marriage, at first, with its conjugal caresses, new furniture, crockery, and linen goes well. But from the first month of pregnancy, something new, unpleasant, and unseemly shows itself: "His wife began to be jealous without any cause, expected him to devote his whole attention to her, found fault with everything, and made coarse and ill-mannered scenes." Ivan deals with his wife's erratic behavior by formalizing his relations with her: he spends much of his time away at work; and when compelled to be alone with her, he has a third person present.

All this is inevitable, as is Praskovya Fyodorovna's attitude toward Ivan Ilytch when it is his turn to cry out for compassion, for the involvement of another being in his suffering. As the increasing pain Ivan Ilytch suffers is, in a series of futile medical examinations and treatments, diagnosed as coming from a floating kidney and a vermiform appendix, Praskovya Fyodorovna mutes into silence Ivan Ilytch's increasing request for compassion by formalizing her relations with him in the same way he

had done with her. As her behavior in pregnancy had appeared to Ivan
Ilytch as inexplicable, capricious, and threatening to his well-planned and
happy life, so too Ivan Ilytch's mysterious illness appears to her as
perverse, unseemly, and threatening to her own well-being. Each treats
the other as he had been treated. The more insistent the cry for compassion, the more determined the efforts to have none of the increasing
disagreeableness. It is no accident, in the logic of this moral world, that
Ivan Ilytch's moral and physical pain augment in direct proportion to
the increase of his wife's and daughter's happiness. On the morning
when his condition takes its final turn for the worst and when the last
days of agonized screaming are to begin, his wife's and daughter's fondest
hopes are realized in the proposal of the young examining magistrate.

A life based on the pleasure principle, based wholly and exclusively on
it, cannot, without contradiction, admit voluntarily any pain; and faced
with demands to admit some particle of disagreeableness, which in Tolstoy's view of mature life is unavoidable and indeed desirable, such a life
will substitute for real acceptance pretended acceptance. It will in short,
formalize the emotion, abstracting it from real involvement. This is
what Ivan Ilytch does when faced with the request for involvement in
his wife's pain, and this is what she does when Ivan Ilytch stretches out
his hand with pain to be shared. And this is what all the characters—
with the exception of Gerasim and Ivan Ilytch's son—are doing. The
abstract relations that obtain between the characters of the story are not
there because Tolstoy wants to generalize about abstract relations. The
abstract relations, the terrible impersonality of Ivan Ilytch's life, the
vicious opportunism that Tolstoy exposes among Ivan Ilytch's colleagues
at the time of his death are all a consequence of the law of this society as
is almost every other element of the tale.

So too is the technique. The story is not structured in the fussy, self-
conscious, contrived manner of so much of the work of twentieth century
novelists; but it lends itself, nevertheless, to inexhaustible structural
refinements. The structure is there for a purpose, deepening the insights
into character and motive, and itself formed by the demands of the law
Tolstoy has assumed for this society. I'll give only one small example,
taken from the first paragraph of the story. We first learn about Ivan
Ilytch's death by the obituary Pyotr Ivanovitch reads to his colleagues.
In the obituary Ivan Ilytch's wife announces her affection and grief to
the world in the formalized and conventional diction characteristic of
such announcements. The item tells us not only that Ivan Ilytch is dead,
but it tells us something about how he lived with his wife, and it sounds
the first note of a whole gamut of abstract human relationships that are

depicted in the tale. When Ivan Ilytch is sick, he is a vermiform appendix for the doctors, a bad sport for his card-playing friends, and an irascible husband for his wife. When he is very sick, he is an embarrassment to everyone, like some bad smell in a room that everyone tries to ignore. When he dies, he is an opportunity for promotion for some, and a relief to others. Never is he a person for others, or even to himself. Tolstoy shows how the process of abstraction penetrates into every gesture, feeling, action, word, and syllable of this society.

The announcement of Ivan Ilytch's death comes as an interruption of a legal argument over the jurisdiction of some case. It comes in an interval similar to those, as we learn later, which Ivan Ilytch had loved, when in the judicial chambers he had smoked, drunk tea, chatted a little about politics, a little about general topics, a little about cards, but most of all about official appointments. Ivan Ilytch's life is, in effect, sketched in miniature in the opening scene: his lively conversations in the judicial chambers between cases; his passion for card playing; his concern with promotion; his relations with his wife and friends; and his concern for the furniture and decorations of his apartment. The attitudes and actions of his friends and wife, the hypocritical disparity between their real feelings and their public gestures, are in perfect accord with the laws by which Ivan Ilytch had lived. They act toward the fact of his death in exactly the way he would have acted toward theirs.

Although the techniques Tolstoy uses are radically different from the imperatives of our age, he has all the technique he needs, and, most important, they are appropriate to his intention. What characterizes his technique is a clear, unambiguous control of the meaning he intends. Many of the narrative details function almost as inductive instances of stated generalizations. The casual reader will remember the author's direct commentary on the implications of what such and such a character is saying. He will remember, for instance, Tolstoy's explanations, in the opening scene where Ivan Ilytch's death is announced, of the real feelings and thoughts of those who go through the forms of regret. Many of such explanations, analyses, and judgments seem needlessly obvious, but Tolstoy's art, though always careful to control sharply meaning, meets the reader at various levels of sophistication. On the most sophisticated level his art operates with a subtlety that grants nothing to James's art and is yet able to communicate without ambiguity.

If we grant Tolstoy his assumptions about the meaning of experience, the action represented in *The Death of Ivan Ilytch* follows with probability and even necessity. We may still ask, however, if these assumptions are reasonable. Is it possible to find people, let alone a whole society, so completely dominated by the principle of self-pleasure as is found in the mechanism of Ivan Ilytch's world? Is it not more realistic to see even the most self-interested person as possessing some capacity for compassion? Is it not more realistic, in short, to take a less abstract view of experience? It is not possible to find a whole society or even a substantial number of people who are as exclusively dominated by the principles of self-pleasure as Tolstoy has characterized the people in the world of Ivan Ilytch. But it is possible to agree with Tolstoy that since the tendency to self-interested pleasure is a feature of life as we know it, the *possibility* of a society totally and exclusively dominated by this principle does indeed exist. Tolstoy has traced out in *The Death of Ivan Ilytch* the inevitable consequences of a real tendency in human nature; that this tendency is not numerically validated by reality, as we know it, is irrelevant. By leaving behind the endless qualification of particular experience, Tolstoy was able to do what is perhaps the most distinctive trait of Russian fiction, to trace out the extreme, but logically possible, reaches of a human characteristic. We do not have character represented in *The Death of Ivan Ilytch* as it presents itself phenomenologically, but as it is theoretically possible in the human condition.

III

Isabel Archer in *The Portrait of a Lady* exemplifies, at first glance, a problem analogous to that of Ivan Ilytch, but shows at the same time how far Tolstoy is from the fictional imperatives of James's practice. The law of her life, at least as she is first presented, is a naïve and innocent miscalculation of her capacity to be free and a consequent misunderstanding of evil. One might speak of this miscalculation as a kind of romanticism, which determines her fate as the law of self-interested pleasure determines Ivan Ilytch's life. But James reveals an indetermination, uncharacteristic of Tolstoy, about the operation of this law and its effect upon Isabel Archer. Although Isabel Archer suffers the consequences of her naïve view of experience, she does not illustrate ineluctably and passively these consequences to the end, as does Ivan Ilytch the consequences of the pleasure-seeking principle; and the reason she does not is because James is not interested in the problem of Isabel's romanticism, but in the character of Isabel Archer conceived in the massive complexity of real life. She learns, in contrast to Ivan Ilytch, to confront the consequences of her miscalculation and in confronting them to pose a different, though not wholly different, law of character.

At the end of the novel Isabel Archer is a different woman, posing an altered law of character, living in a moral context that is a compound of past experiences and future capabilities. The meaning of her experience from this point on is left indeterminate, for future character can take form only in contexts yet to be made. In direct contrast, nowhere in the narrative of Ivan Ilytch's life do we have the sense that Ivan Ilytch participates, by choice and re-evaluation of his values, in the formation of his character. Rather his character is a static illustration of the problem set by Tolstoy at the beginning. It is the problem and not the character of Ivan Ilytch that is dynamic. At the very moment when Ivan Ilytch sees that the life he has led was false, Tolstoy's interest in him is over; it is at that moment that Henry James would have found the situation dramatically interesting and would have begun to explore its implications and effect upon the character of Ivan Ilytch. James, working with different assumptions of how experience is to be seen and portrayed in fiction, would have explored the dramatic interaction of Ivan Ilytch's perception, his assimilation of this perception, and the effect of it upon Ivan Ilytch in new contexts of experience.

Neither Ivan Ilytch nor Isabel Archer and Maisie are inaccurately portrayed. They are each a consequence, skillfully worked out, of what each author assumes to be the significant contour of experience. James was generous in insisting on the author's right to choose his subject matter, but he was close to dogmatism in his unquestioning belief that the subject matter must be pictured and not interpreted. To follow experience in its endless qualification by situation was for him to see life; to fix experience in some generalization was to be blind to life.

Since the techniques of fiction exemplified by the work of Henry James are the dominant modes of our day and since these dominant modes have infected not only the work of younger writers—who would today, for instance, write with the massive intrusiveness of Tolstoy?—but also the work of critics, it is important, I think, to look hard at what our intuitive taste tells us is great literature. I suppose every age, and ours no less, is ever in danger of elevating to universal law what may be the preferences of the day. Mark Schorer, for example, has told us that "technique is everything," restricting technique to the particular techniques of writers like Conrad and James. Then on the basis of these particular techniques, he has found writers of the pre-Flaubertian and Jamesian tradition to be deficient in technique. I am persuaded that technique is not everything, certainly not what Mr. Schorer understands as technique. Too many bad novels have technique in his sense. The difference between *Lord Jim* and *Chance* is not technique—*Chance* has too much of that—but imagination, vision, perception. The modern insistence on technique when it ceases to be a description of the method of particular writers and becomes an imperative for all can result in the critical bluntness of the kind that resulted when Percy Lubbock—whom Allan Tate has called "the best critic who has ever written about the novel"—found *War and Peace* inferior to *Madame Bovary* and the novels of James because it had technical faults.

By criteria broader than the imperatives of our day, Tolstoy has all the technique he needs. The differences in his practice from what we may consider to be good novel writing today arise from no clumsiness on his part or from no primitive quality in his work, but from different assumptions about experience. Our own critical interpretations and evaluations, both of writers of our century and those of previous centuries, ought to be concerned with drawing out the nature of such assumptions, Unless we do that, we are ever in danger of applying alien standards to works of the past. In the final analysis, of course, technique, despite the shibboleths of our time, is always less important than the artist's view of experience, less important than his vision, intuition, imagination—all unpopular critical terms today.

The Last Judgment: Tolstoy's Last Works

by Leo Shestov

Other men seem not to have noticed
that those who truly embrace philosophy
concern themselves with nothing else
but dying and death.

Plato, *Phaedo* 64 A

Aristotle says somewhere that every one has his own particular world in his dreams, while in his waking state he lives in a world common to all. This statement is the basis, not only of Aristotle's philosophy, but also of all positive scientific philosophy, before and after him. Common sense also looks upon this as an indisputable truth. Can man give up self-evident truth? Certainly not. Nobody, not even God Himself, can ask this of him. *Deus impossibile non jubet.* God does not ask the impossible. That is a self-evident truth which is admitted equally by common sense, by science, and even by the Catholic Church, impregnated with mysticism though it may be.

But death takes no heed of this. It has its own truths, its own self-evidence, its possibilities and its impossibilities, which do not agree with our ordinary ideas, and which we, therefore, cannot understand. Only a few exceptional men have succeeded, in rare moments of extreme tension and excitement, in hearing and understanding the mysterious language of death. This understanding was given to Tolstoy. What did death reveal to him? What were the impossibilities which were changed into possibilities for him? Death does, as a matter of fact, unlike common sense, demand the impossible of man. In spite of Aristotle, it drags him out of the world common to all. How does this happen? How can the impossible become possible?

Among Tolstoy's posthumous works there is a short, unfinished story called *The Diary of a Madman.* The subject is very simple. A rich land-

"The Last Judgment: Tolstoy's Last Works" by Leo Shestov. From *In Job's Balances* by Leo Chestov (Dent & Sons' spelling), trans. G. Coventry and C. A. Macartney (London: J. M. Dent & Sons Ltd., 1932). All rights reserved, 1932, by J. M. Dent & Sons Ltd. Reprinted, with omissions, by permission of J. M. Dent & Sons Ltd.

owner, having learned that an estate was for sale in the province of Penza, makes up his mind to go down, have a look at it and buy it. He is very pleased about it; according to his calculations, he will be able to buy it at a very low figure, almost for nothing. Then, *suddenly,* one night at an hotel on the way, without any apparent reason, he is seized by a horrible, insufferable anguish. Nothing in his surroundings has changed, nothing new has happened, but until now everything had always inspired him with confidence, everything had seemed to him to be normal, necessary, well-regulated, soothing; he had felt the solid earth beneath his feet and reality on all sides of him. No doubt, no questions! Nothing but answers! Then suddenly, in an instant, in the twinkling of an eye, everything is transformed as though by a magic wand. Peace, answers, the solid earth, consciousness of right, and the easy feeling of lightness, simplicity and certainty which springs from this—all suddenly disappear. Around him are nothing but looming questions with their inevitable train of importunate anxiety, of doubt, and senseless, gnawing, invincible terrors. The ordinary means by which these painful thoughts are usually routed are completely ineffectual.

> I tried to think of things which interested me; of the acquisition of the estate, of my wife. Not only did I find nothing pleasant in these thoughts, but they were all as nothing to me. The horror of my wasted life overshadowed everything. I tried to go to sleep. I lay down, but no sooner was I on my bed than terror roused me again. And anxiety! An anxiety like one feels before one is going to be sick, but it was moral. Fear, anguish—we think of death as terrible, but when we look back upon life, it is the *agony of life which overwhelms us!* Death and life seemed in some way to be confounded with one another. Something tore my existence to rags, and yet could not succeed in tearing it completely. I went once more to look at my fellow-sleepers; I tried again to get to sleep; but terror was ever before me, red, white, and square. Something was tearing, but it still held.

Thus Tolstoy pitilessly strips himself before our eyes. There are few writers who show us truths like these. And if one wants, if one is able to see this truth—for even naked truth is not easy to see—then a whole series of problems arise which are out of all relation with our ordinary thoughts. How are we to apprehend these groundless terrors which so suddenly appeared, red, white, and square? In the world which is common to us all, there is not and cannot be a "suddenly"; there can be no action without a cause. And its terrors are not red, nor white, nor square. What happened to Tolstoy is a challenge to all normal, human consciousness. Now it is Tolstoy who has been suddenly and causelessly seized by terror; to-morrow it may be another, then a third, and one fine day it will be the whole of society, the whole of mankind who will be attacked. If we take seriously what we are told in *The Diary of a Madman* there is no third alternative; either we must repudiate Tolstoy and cut him off from our midst as lepers and others suffering from contagious diseases were cut off in the Middle Ages; or else, if we consider his experiences justifiable, we must be prepared for others to undergo the same, for the "world common to us all" to fall to pieces and men to begin to live in their own separate worlds, not in dreams but in their waking moments.

Common sense, and science which derives from it, cannot hesitate for a moment before this dilemma. Tolstoy is in the wrong with his senseless anxieties, his unreasonable terrors, and his mad uncertainty. It is "the world common to us all" which is right, with its solid beliefs, its eternal, satisfying truths, clear, defined, and accessible to all. If the person concerned had not been a world-famous writer, his fate would have been quickly decided; he would have been exiled from society as a dangerous and unhealthy member. But Tolstoy is the pride and glory of Russia; it is impossible to treat him like this. Although what he says appears utterly meaningless and unacceptable, one goes on listening to him, one goes on reckoning with him.

"To-day," he continues,

> they took me before the provincial council for a mental examination. Opinions were divided. They argued, and finally decided that I was not mad. But that was because I constrained myself not to speak frankly during the medical inspection. I was not frank because I am afraid of the lunatic asylum. I am afraid that there they would not allow me to accomplish my madman's work. They declared that I was subject to fits and other things of the sort, but that I was of sane mind. *They certified this, but I know that I am mad.*

It is beyond question that *he* is right, not *they*. All his life Tolstoy was aware that there was something in his soul driving him out of the world common to all. He tells us that it had happened to him before, although not often, to experience crises like that which occurred on the road to Penza. From childhood upwards, he would suddenly find himself overwhelmed on quite trivial occasions by intolerable terrors which would brutally deprive him of all joy in life and of all sense of the normality and natural balance of existence. . . .

The pleasures, preoccupations, and all the innumerable business affairs of life naturally distracted Tolstoy's attention from his extraordinary visions for many years. And then, as he tells us, he had an instinctive dread of the madhouse, and an even greater dread of madness, of having to live in his own individual world instead of in the common world. Therefore he made desperate efforts to live like every one else, and to see only what is contained within everyday limits.

The Diary of a Madman is in a sense the key to Tolstoy's work. . . . Only death and the madness of death are able to awaken man from the nightmare of existence. This is what Tolstoy's *Diary of a Madman* also tells us—not the short unfinished story which bears this title, but the whole of what he wrote after *Anna Karenina*. His "madness" lay in the fact that everything which had formerly seemed to him to be real and to have a solid existence, now appeared illusory, whereas all that had seemed illusory and unreal now seemed to him the only reality.

The review the *Russian Archive* published in 1868 an article by Tolstoy which, for no reason that I know, has never been republished since; it is called "A Few Words about *War and Peace*." It contains some extremely significant passages showing Tolstoy's attitude towards serfdom. He had been reproached with not having sufficiently depicted the character of the times in *War and Peace*. "To these reproaches," Tolstoy declares,

> I should reply as follows: I know quite well what are the characteristics of the times, which are supposed to be wanting in my novel: the horrors of serfdom, the burial of women alive, the flogging by men of their grown sons, Saltychike,[1] etc., but I do not consider that this character, as we imagine it to-day, conforms to reality, and therefore I did not want to describe it. I have studied letters, memoirs, and hearsay, but have not found that these horrors were more frequent then than now or at any other period. People loved in those days, were jealous, sought truth, virtue, or were the slaves of their passions just as now; the intellectual and moral life was the same— often, indeed, more refined than to-day, especially in the upper classes. If we represent these times to ourselves as particularly cruel and brutal, it is only because the novels, stories, and legends of that period have only preserved what was exceptionally brutal or strikingly savage.

Tolstoy was forty years old when he wrote these lines. It is the age when the intellectual powers reach their zenith. In Tolstoy, at that age, the days of Arakcheev awaken no horror, no disgust; yet we remember that as a child he gave way to mad despair on seeing a little boy beaten or hearing his nurse and the steward quarrelling. He certainly knew what to think of Arakcheev and his men, he also knew what serfdom was and the condition of the peasants under the despotic rule of the landed proprietors; but he did not want to "see" it; reason, which should know

---

[1] The mistress of Arakcheev, Alexander I's favourite. She was killed by peasants, who were driven to desperation by her tyranny and cruelty.

all things, forbade. Why? Because such a vision would have been useless. It would have destroyed that *ordo et connexio rerum* which had established itself historically in the face of so many difficulties, and upset the common world outside whose boundaries there exists nothing but madness and death. Unvarnished truth, that truth which runs contrary to the vital needs of human nature, is worse than any lie. This is what Tolstoy thought when he wrote *War and Peace,* when he was still entirely possessed by Aristotle's ideas, when he was afraid of madness and the asylum and hoped that he would never have to live in an individual world of his own. But when he was obliged to say to himself, "They certified that I was sane, but I know that I am mad"; when he felt himself expelled from the world common to all, then he was obliged, willy-nilly, to look at things with his own eyes and not with every one else's. Then the character of Arakcheev's day appeared to him quite otherwise. Formerly he had spoken of "the refined existence of the upper classes." Later he spoke of the cruel, coarse, and debased "uppermost classes."

The outward seeming is spick and span and elegant, but beneath this beautiful appearance there are folly, emptiness, vile cruelty, narrow, inhuman selfishness. The Rostovs, Bezukhovs, and Bolkonskis change before our eyes into Sobakevich, Nozdrev, and Chichikov. There is no longer even Gogol's laughter, only his tears.

In another short story, also unfinished, "The Morning after the Ball," written in 1903, when the author was seventy-five years old, Tolstoy, with obvious intention, confronts his old and new visions. The story is in two parts; the first describes, with an art unequalled in Russian literature before or since, a gay, elegant, and amusing ball. It is a really marvellous ball: there are music and dancing, there is champagne, the young people are of the highest class, charming and aristocratic; naturally there is also a charming young lady there and a young man who is in love with her; it is he who tells the story. An hour after the ball, the narrator, still gay, excited, and possessed by his "refined" emotions, is witness of quite another scene in the street; a Tartar deserter is being made to run the gauntlet. And this is being done at the orders of the colonel, the father of the charming young girl, the very man who, to the universal delight, himself had danced the mazurka with his daughter at the end of the ball, displaying such charm and old-world gallantry. I have said that the scene at the ball is described by Tolstoy with inimitable art; the torture of the Tartar is described with no less strength and feeling. I will not quote extracts, for the story is well known. The important point is to compare and contrast the two ways of looking at reality. And considering the whole of Tolstoy's work, one might say, metaphorically of course and with certain reservations, that in his youth Tolstoy described life as a fascinating ball; and later, when he was old, it was like a running of the gauntlet. When he was old, it was not only the time of Arakcheev and Nicholas I which seemed to him like a mad and oppressive nightmare; he could not even endure our own comparatively mild ways. His own family became unendurable to him, that family which he had described in such idyllic colours in *Anna Karenina*. And he saw himself under an aspect as hideous as that of the people with whom he lived. As it is said in Scripture, one must hate one's father and mother, wife and children, and even oneself; there is evidently no other way for the man who is shut out from the world common to us all. . . .

He who wants to learn the truth must first learn the art of reading works of literature. It is a difficult art. To know how to read is not enough. It is for this reason that rough drafts, and notes thrown hastily on paper, are so valuable. A sketch, a few words, a half-formed thought, can often tell us more than a finished work; the man has not yet had time to adapt his visions to the demands of society. The introduction which was to prepare the way, and the conclusion which rounds it off, are alike missing. The brutal, naked truth rises to its full height, like a rock above the waters, and no one has yet attempted to "justify" its stark savagery, neither the author himself nor his sedulous biographer.

This is why I have lingered so long over *The Diary of a Madman,* an unfinished and incomplete story. Tolstoy in his finished works obstinately insists that he is working for the cause of common sense; that his one object is to strengthen, men's faith in common sense. Only once, in this short sketch, did he allow himself to call what happened in his soul by its true name. "They certified that I was sane; but I know that I am mad." This confession gives us the key to what is most important and significant in Tolstoy's hidden life.

We must not, however, forget that Tolstoy was not always in this state of "madness," even during his last years. There were only passing attacks; sometimes he lived in his own particular world, sometimes in the world common to all. Wild unreasoning terrors suddenly welled up, God knows whence; they disappeared, overthrowing and breaking the treasures which reason had amassed; they dissipated themselves and vanished, God knows how or whither, as abruptly as they had arisen. And then Tolstoy became a normal man once more, he was like every one else, except for certain strange ways, pale reflections of the storms which had passed or which were brewing. Hence the inequalities of his character and actions, the flagrant contradictions on which his many enemies have maliciously insisted. Tolstoy was even more afraid of madness than of death, yet at the same time he hated and despised his normal state with his whole soul. And his restless, impetuous inconsequence reveals more to us than the even and reasonable consistency of his accusers.

Many people, in the effort to calm themselves and dissipate the uneasiness which seizes them on reading Tolstoy's works, have thought to explain his struggles and his wild outbursts as the result of his fear of death. They think that such an explanation would free them once and for all from every difficulty and would also re-establish in their old strength the solutions which he had rendered null and void. This proceeding is not new, but it is effective. Aristotle had already suggested it when, with firm hand, he traced a definite line to mark the limit beyond which human endeavour and inquiry must not go. The ultimate mystery must not be approached, the idea of death must not be allowed to take possession of the human soul.

But Plato taught otherwise. . . .

Eight years after *The Death of Ivan Ilych,* Tolstoy wrote *Master and Man.* These two stories are, in spite of their surface dissimilarity, so intimately connected with one another that they seem to be only variations on a single theme. Since Tolstoy had been forced out of the common way by the terrors which he had described to us in *The Diary of a Madman,* one single thought, one single problem pursued and obsessed him. If Plato is right in saying philosophers "concern themselves with nothing but dying and death," . . . then we must admit that few of our contemporaries have so wholly devoted themselves to philosophy as Tolstoy. Tolstoy begins by describing to us, in these two stories, a man in the ordinary circumstances of existence, circumstances which are well known and universally admitted. Then suddenly, in *Master and Man* (the catastrophe is even less prepared than in *The Death of Ivan Ilych*), he transports his characters to that solitude which could not have been more complete in the bowels of the earth or in the depths of the sea. Vassili Andreivich Brekhunov is a "self-made man," a rich villager, of the corporation of merchants, proud of his intelligence and of the fortune which he has won. He owes nothing to any one but himself, to his own talents, his own energy, for everything that he possesses; and he is, moreover, convinced that he possesses a great many excellent things. He genuinely despises those who have not succeeded in carving out their own path through life; misfortune and incapacity are synonyms in his eyes. He would probably repeat with others: "Trust in God, but look out for yourself," but in his mouth these words would mean: "God's duty is to help

those who do not sit with folded arms." If he had had a theological education he would have said: *Facienti quod in se est Deus infallibiliter dat
gratiam,* and he would protest against those who affirm that *Deum necessi-
tare non posse.* But he does not know Latin and expresses the same ideas
in Russian with no less emphasis. The man worthy of the name is the
one who has the means to make himself beloved of God by his own efforts.
Masses, fat wax candles, and all the rest are not for a miserable moujik
like the workman Nikita, who earns with difficulty a few kopeks to supply
his immediate needs. But he, Vassili Andreivich, can do anything. By
his own energy and intelligence he has assured his welfare here below
and his eternal salvation above.

The consciousness of his righteousness, indeed of his election, never
leaves him. He even cheats with conviction. Two days before the festival
which marks the opening of the story, Marfa, the servant Nikita's wife,
has come to Vassili Andreivich and has obtained from him white flour,
tea, sugar, the eighth of a measure of brandy, three roubles' worth altogether, besides five roubles in money. She has thanked him for all this
as though he had done her a special favour, although at the lowest com-
putation he owed Nikita twenty roubles for his work.

"Are we agreed on our bargain?" Vassili Andreivich had said to Nikita: "if
you want anything you shall have it from me, and you shall pay me in labour. I am not like others where you must wait, make out bills and then
pay fines into the bargain. No, I am a man of honour. You serve me and I
will not desert you." As he spoke thus Vassili Andreivich was quite sincerely
convinced that he was Nikita's benefactor, so persuasive were his arguments
and so wholeheartedly did all those who depended on him, beginning with
Nikita himself, support him in the opinion that, far from exploiting other
people, he was loading them with benefits.

Tolstoy insistently underlines this gift which Vassili Andreivich possessed
of being able to convince himself and others of his rectitude. It was a
precious gift. To it Vassili Andreivich owed the comfort of his position.
A few pages later on Tolstoy quotes another example of his talents. He
is trying to sell Nikita a worthless horse.

"Well, take the bony horse; I won't charge you much for him," cried
Brekhunov, feeling agreeably excited and joyfully seizing the opportunity to
drive a bargain, which he loved of all things.
"Give me fifteen roubles or so instead, it will buy one at the horse fair,"
said Nikita, who knew quite well that the bony beast which Vassili Andreivich was trying to pass off on him was worth seven roubles at the outside,
and that it would be reckoned against him at twenty-five. He would not see
the colour of his money again for many a long day.

"It is a good horse. I want your good as well as my own. Word of honour! Brekhunov deceives no one. I would rather lose on the bargain myself. I am not like others. I give you my word that the horse is a good one," he cried in the special tone which he used in order to talk over and deceive buyers or sellers.

Brekhunov, as we have seen from these extracts, was no ordinary man. Being a merchant, he could only make use of his great powers over himself and others for a modest end, bargaining. But if fate had seen fit to put him in a more exalted position, if he had had the necessary education, his voice, which was now only used to confuse his fellow merchants in their ideas, to deceive buyers and sellers, would certainly have been used for other purposes. Who knows to what he might not have persuaded the masses which he could then have addressed? The secret of talent lies in the ability to work upon men. Conversely, success, general approbation, is the atmosphere which talent needs for its development. Crowds need leaders, but leaders also need crowds.

Tolstoy knew this; the hero of his story was no ordinary character; he had a powerful will and a clear intelligence, in his own way he was a genius. Such is the personality which Tolstoy will now tear out of his natural setting and put abruptly into the midst of new conditions, facing him with the absolute solitude which we have already met in *Ivan Ilych*.

Nikita goes out with Brekhunov and together they are caught in a snowstorm. But Nikita's agony in the snow is of no interest either to Tolstoy or to us. Perhaps Brekhunov is right when he prepares to abandon his faithful servant and says: "It doesn't matter to him whether he dies or not. What was his life like? He won't regret his life. But I, thanks be to God, I still have something to live for!" Nikita prepares to die as he has lived, peacefully, with that calm submission which, losing itself in the grey uniformity of the surrounding world and obeying eternal laws, makes no particular individual impression which can be seized and retained in the mind of the observer. Tolstoy himself cannot guess at what happens in Nikita's mind when life ceases and death begins in it under the snow which covers him. Perhaps this is why Nikita lives and Brekhunov dies. Tolstoy wanted to confront life with death; but a rich life, full to the brim, confident in itself and its sacred rights and without even a suspicion that an implacable enemy infinitely stronger than itself is watching it at every turn. Even when it turns out that master and man have lost their way and that they will have to pass the night buried under the snow, Brekhunov will not admit that his reason and his talents, which have already got him out of so many difficult situations, will betray him now; that in a few hours his stiffened hands will let fall the *potestas clavium,* which gave him the proud right to look upon the future with the same confidence as the present.

This is what he is thinking of while Nikita, in his thin clothes, drowses under the falling snow and tries to protect his shivering body against the raging of the bitter wind. Brekhunov is warmly clad, as yet he does not feel the cold, and from past experience is confident he never will.

> ". . . What did we possess in my father's time? Nothing much; he was no more than a rich peasant. An inn, a farm; that was all. And I, what have I collected in fifteen years? A shop, two inns, a mill, barns for grain, two farm properties, a house and its outbuildings all under iron roofs." He thought of all that with pride. "It is quite different from my father's time. Who is now famous throughout the whole district? Brekhunov! And why? Because I never lose sight of business. I work. I am not like others who are always sleeping or else running their heads into some foolishness or other."

Brekhunov continues for a long time to sing the praises of these reasonable, active principles, the source of all "good" on earth. And I repeat: if Brekhunov had received a superior education, he would have been capable of writing an excellent philosophical or theological treatise, which would have made him famous, not only in his own district but throughout all Russia and Europe.

But here we come to the second part of the story, where an unexpected reality suddenly supervenes and affords the critique of this treatise which Brekhunov might have written.

In the middle of this reasoning Brekhunov began to doze.

> But he suddenly felt a shock and awoke. Whether it was that the horse had tugged at a few straws from behind his head, or whether it was the effect of some internal uneasiness, he suddenly awoke and his heart began to beat so violently and quickly that it seemed as though the whole sledge were trembling beneath him.

This was the beginning of a whole series of events of which Brekhunov had no suspicion in spite of his long life, his powerful intelligence, and his rich experience. Around him was the boundless plain, boundless, at least, to him, and snow, cold, and wind, Nikita, already numbed by the cold, and the shivering horse. He felt unreasonable but insistent and overmastering terror. "What to do? What to do?" This is the regular question which every man asks when he finds himself in a difficult situation. It presents itself to Brekhunov, but this time it seems completely absurd. Hitherto, the question had always held the elements of its own answer, it had at least always shown him the possibility of an answer. But this time it held nothing of the sort. The question excluded all possibility of an answer; there was *nothing to be done*.

Brekhunov was no coward. He had been in many difficult places in his lifetime, and had always been ready to fight any adversary, even one stronger than himself. But his present situation was such that it would have been impossible to imagine anything more terrible. The enemy was formidable and—this was the worst part of it—completely invisible. Against what could he direct his blows? Against whom could he defend himself? Brekhunov's reason could not admit that such a thing was possible.

When they had stopped at Grichkino, an hour earlier, everything had seemed so comfortable, so natural, so easy to understand. One was able to talk, to listen to other people, drink tea, give orders to Nikita, drive the bay. And now there was nothing to be done but to look on and feel oneself freeze. Where is truth, where is reality? Over there at Grichkino, or here on this plain? Grichkino had ceased to exist for ever; must one then doubt the reality of its existence? And with it the reality of the existence of all the old world? Doubt everything? *De omnibus dubitandum?* But did great Descartes really doubt everything? No, Hume was right: the man who has once doubted all things will never overcome his doubts, he will leave for ever the world common to us all and take refuge in his own particular world. *De omnibus dubitandum* is useless; it is worse than storm and snow, worse than the fact that Nikita is freezing and that the bay is shivering in the icy wind.

Always so strong, so clear-minded, Brekhunov tries, for the first time in his life, to take refuge in dreams.

> He began once more to reckon up his profits, the sums which were due to him. He began to boast to himself again, and to take pleasure in his excellent situation; but at every moment fear slipped into his thoughts and interrupted their pleasant flow. Try as he might to think of nothing but his accounts, his transactions, his revenues, his glory and his wealth, fear little by little took possession of his whole soul.

It will seem strange that Brekhunov, like King Solomon in Ecclesiastes, told over the tale of his riches and his glory. But this was just what Tolstoy wanted, and he knew what he wanted. If the great king himself had been in Brekhunov's place, the situation would not have been changed in any way. Riches and glory added nothing to Brekhunov's strength, nor diminished in any way that of his invisible adversary. For the lowly and humble Nikita it was much easier. "He did not know whether he was dying or whether he was falling asleep, but he was equally ready to do either."

All his existence, utterly devoid alike of glory and wealth, had accustomed Nikita to the thought that he was not his own master, that he must not ask any one to render him an account, or to explain what was happening. He had never understood anything, and he continued not to understand; there was not much difference. But for Brekhunov it was quite another matter. He was accustomed to being his own master, and to having clear and distinct explanations given him; everything indefinite and indeterminate was intolerable to him. To live in the unknown is to live under a strange power which slays or spares us as it will. Can one have confidence in it? Why should it have mercy on us? It will certainly condemn us. One cannot believe any one or anything, except oneself. And in any case, before believing one must ask *cui est credendum*—whom shall we believe? You must not be surprised that Brekhunov takes to talking Latin and quoting St. Augustine, for it was certainly no more surprising than everything else which was happening to him.

And Brekhunov, gathering together all his strength for the last time, firmly declared: "I will never believe in this silence, in this forsaken solitude, in the snowstorm, the shivering horse, freezing Nikita, this cold and dreary desert, and this infinite waste." Reason was still alive within him, and reason which had always taught him what to do would guide him again. There was still some possible answer, although a lying terror was whispering to him that he must yield.

Brekhunov decides to abandon Nikita and take his chance, mounts the horse and goes off in search of the road.

This was undoubtedly a reasonable decision; the only reasonable decision. Was he to die, caught by the cold, like a dog, he, Brekhunov, who for so many years had filled Russia and Europe with the fame of his inns, his house, his barns with their iron roofs?

Brekhunov makes a last, supreme effort to defeat his invisible foe. But what he does, what he is forced to do, in no way resembles what one would call "action". He urges on his horse, which obeys him docilely, but his strength of mind, in which he had always had so much confidence, now betrays him. Without noticing it, he continually changes the direction of his march. Everything overwhelms him, he is trembling more from fear than from cold now—a quite absurd and unreasonable fear of every tussock which appeared through the snow. To his distracted eyes every outlined object was as a phantom. He suddenly found himself placed in circumstances so contrary to his usual reasonable, positive nature, that everything appeared to him stupid and absurd as in a fairy tale. But where is truth? In that old world, with that old reason where everything is clear and comprehensible, or here? Until now there had been nothing hostile or terrible or mysterious in that tussock or in those dried grasses. They had been subject to man and useful to him. What then, is the force that suddenly takes possession of them? Why do they inspire him with such terror? And not they alone; this immense, mournful desert appears peopled with phantoms who until now, as he had positively known, did not exist and could not exist.

> Suddenly a terrible cry rang in his ears and everything trembled and moved beneath him. Vassili Andreivich clung to the neck of his horse, but the neck trembled and the cry rang out again, more terribly still. For a few minutes Vassili Andreivich could not take heart again, could not understand what had happened. But all that had happened was simply that the horse had neighed with all its powerful voice, either to give itself courage or else, perhaps, to call for help. "Oh, curse you," said Brekhunov, "how you frightened me!" But even when he understood the real cause of his terrors, he did not succeed in overcoming them.

The last chance of safety disappeared, terror invaded his soul and took possession of it. Explanations which had formerly driven away all his doubts and fears were now powerless and brought him no comfort. "One must think, one must be calm," said Brekhunov to himself; but in vain. He had already crossed the fatal border line, he was cast off for ever from solid earth, where order reigns and laws and methods which have been securely established for the ascertaining of truth. The phantoms with which the desert is peopled will disappear no more, whether or no he succeeds in explaining that the dried grasses are nothing but a vegetable growth and the cry of terror no more than the neighing of his horse. And, moreover, are these descriptions accurate? Has that black bush not got some occult force which had escaped Brekhunov's sagacity until now? . . .

Brekhunov falls from his horse into a snowdrift, the horse goes on and leaves him alone, utterly alone in the snow. "The forest, the farmsteads, the inns, the house under its iron roof and the barns . . . will his heir —what," he thinks, "will become of these? But what is happening? This cannot be." Suddenly he remembers the tuft of grass which the wind had shaken and which he had passed twice already. "Such a terror invaded him then that he could not believe in the reality of all that was happening to him. He thought, "Is not this a dream?" And tried to awake. But it was not a dream."

He tried to remember the theories of knowledge which even a few hours earlier had given him the power to distinguish between the real and the visionary, dreams from waking; but these principles, hitherto so clear and definite, had effaced themselves and could no longer guide him. They defined nothing, taught nothing, and could not deliver him. Then he gave up all scientific theories and remembered that he had one last resource left to which he had not resorted until now, having felt no need of it, and having kept it in reserve for a last emergency.

"Queen of Heaven, Holy Father Nicholas, Lord of Renunciation. . . ." He thought of the Mass, of the ikon with its dark face in the gilded frame, of the candles which he sold for this ikon, the candles which were immediately brought back to him, hardly burnt at all, and which he hid in a drawer of his writing table. Then he began to pray to this same St. Nicholas that he would save him, and promised him a Mass and candles.

But he immediately and very clearly understood that this face, those ornaments, the candles, the priest, the Mass might all be very important, very necessary even, over there in church, but that they could not help him in any way, that there had not been and was not any connection between the candles and the religious ceremonies, and his present situation.

But what does this new reality call to mind? Nothing that Brekhunov knows, except dreams. Brekhunov's powerful and well-balanced understanding can imagine nothing, it feels itself lost in the midst of the dreams which press in on reality, he struggles like a madman and does just the opposite of what could help him. "Only, no confusion! No haste!" He repeats to himself these well-learned and tried rules of reasonable action and methodical search. But his terror grows, and instead of looking for the road, calmly and carefully, according to rule, he begins to run, falls, picks himself up again, falls once more and loses the last remnants of his strength. Thus he arrives, quite by accident, at the sledge where Nikita is lying. There, at first, from old habit, he makes proof of great activity. Then suddenly a complete change comes over him, such as could not have been deduced by any ordinary rules, from his empirical character.

Before Nikita, who, as it seems to him, is about to die, in the face of inevitable death, Brekhunov suddenly resolves to break completely with his past. Whence this decision comes, and what it means, Tolstoy does not explain; and presumably he does well, for the fact admits of no explanation; in other words, we can establish no connection between the force which drives a man towards the unknown, and the facts that we have previously known about him. This break means, in the words of Plato and Plotinus, "a flight from the known," and any explanation, in so far as it tries to re-establish broken ties, is only the expression of our wish to maintain the man in his former place, to prevent him from accomplishing his destiny.

"Vassili Andreivich," Tolstoy tells us, "stood for some moments in silence, and then, *suddenly,* with the same decision with which he used to clinch a successful bargain by a hand-shake, he took a step backwards, rolled up the sleeves of his coat and set about rubbing life back into Nikita's half frozen body." Can you explain this "sudden" and "suddenly" from which spring the decisions of those who are forsaking the common world? Brekhunov suddenly descends from the height of his glories to warm that worthless peasant Nikita. Is it not an obvious absurdity? But it is still to a certain extent the old Brekhunov; one feels his need to do something, in order not to have to look IT in the face. In the words which he addresses to Nikita we still catch a ring of the old boasting tones, the old self-glorification. Brekhunov still tries instinctively in his old way to escape the inevitable. He is still afraid to let drop from his trembling hands the *potestas clavium* which obviously no longer belongs to him.

"Ah, there you are! You are all right! . . . And you talk of dying. Don't get up, keep warm. That's what we do, we cunning ones. . . ." Vassili Andreivich begins to hold forth. But he could not go on in the same strain. And he was obliged to throw this act, too, overboard. "That's what we do . . ."—this phrase might have been of some use to him formerly, but now, after the decision of this autocratic "suddenly," it is of no use at all, even though crowned by supreme self-abnegation. Something else is wanted, something quite different.

> To his great astonishment he was unable to go on, for his eyes filled with tears and his lower jaw began to tremble. He stopped talking and could only swallow the lump in his throat. "I have been frightened," he thought to himself, "and now I am very weak." But this weakness was not unpleasant; it caused him a peculiar feeling of joy such as he had never previously known.

Brekhunov rejoiced in his weakness; the same Brekhunov who all his life had gloried in his strength, according to the laws of common humanity, persuaded that he was not and could not be happy except in his full strength; and in this conviction he had disputed the *potestas clavium,* the power to bind and loose, with Heaven itself. This joy which was born of weakness, was the beginning of the miraculous, inconceivable, enigmatic change which we call death. Brekhunov, Tolstoy tells us, tries once more to get back for a moment into the old world; he boasts to someone that he has saved Nikita, that he has sacrificed his life to him; but these abrupt stirrings of the old consciousness, the consciousness of strength, become shorter and shorter and eventually cease altogether. Then there remains in him only the joy of his weakness and his liberty. He no longer fears death; strength fears death, weakness does not know this fear. Weakness hears the appeal coming from the place where, long pursued and despised, she has found her eventual refuge. Brekhunov renounces, eagerly and with feverish haste, his inns, his barns, and all the great ideas, including the *potestas clavium*, which had gathered in his soul and been the boasts of the other, the learned, Brekhunov. And now an admirable mystery is revealed to him. " 'I come, I come,' he cried joyfully with his whole being. And he felt that he was free and that nothing held him back any more." And he went, or rather he flew on the wings of his weakness, without knowing whither they would carry him; he rose into the eternal night, terrible and incomprehensible to mankind.

The end of *Master and Man* turned out to be a prophecy. Leo Nicolaievich Tolstoy also ended his days on the steppe, in the midst of storms and tempests. Thus destiny will end. The glory of Tolstoy was spread abroad throughout the whole world while he still lived. And yet, in spite of that, soon after his eightieth birthday, which was celebrated in the four quarters of the globe, in every language—an honour which no one before his day had enjoyed—he yet left all and fled from his home one dark night, not knowing whither or wherefore. His works, his glory, all these were a misery to him, a burden too heavy for him to bear. He seems, with trembling, impatient hand, to be tearing off the marks of the sage, the master, the honoured teacher. That he might present himself before the Supreme Judge with unweighted soul, he had to forget and renounce all his magnificent past.

Such, in fact, is the revelation of death. Down here on earth, all that was of importance, but here one wants something quite different. . . . "Let us flee to our dear fatherland . . . for thence are we come, and there dwells our Father." (Plotinus, *Enn.* I, vi, 8.)

Chronology of Important Dates

N.B.—Dates are given in the old style (Julian calender). In the nineteenth century the Julian calender was twelve days and in the twentieth century thirteen days behind the Gregorian calender used in the West.

1828	August 28—Tolstoy born at Yasnaya Polyana.
1830	Death of Tolstoy's mother.
1836	Family moves to Moscow.
1837	Death of Tolstoy's father.
1841	Death of Alexandra Osten-Saken, legal guardian of the Tolstoys. Children move to Kazan.
1844	Tolstoy enters Kazan University, Department of Eastern Languages.
1845	Transfers to the Faculty of Law.
1847	Leaves the University and returns to Yasnaya Polyana.
1849	Takes examination for degree at University of Petersburg. Withdraws after passing first two subjects and returns to Yasnaya Polyana.
1851	April—Leaves for the Caucusus with his brother Nicholas.
1852	January 3—Passes examination for noncommissioned officer. Writes "The Raid." *Childhood* published in *The Contemporary*, No. 9. Begins *Novel of a Russian Landowner* (unfinished) and *Boyhood* (finished 1854).
1853	Begins *The Cossacks* (finished 1862). "Notes of a Billiard Marker."
1854	Promoted to Ensign. Transferred to Crimea.
1855	Begins *Youth* (finished 1856). *Sevastopol in December, Sevastopol in May. Sevastopol in August 1855.* Trip to Petersburg where he meets leading literary figures.
1856	Promoted to Lieutenant. Resigns and returns to Yasnaya Polyana. "The Snowstorm," "Two Hussars."
1857	Travel to France, Germany, and Switzerland. "Lucerne." "Albert" (finished 1858). July 30—Arrives in Petersburg. Returns to Yasnaya Polyana.
1859	"Three Deaths" (written preceding year), "Family Happiness." Founding of Yasnaya Polyana School and work as teacher of peasant children.
1860	July 2—Leaves for Europe. Meets Herzen in London.

1861   April 13—Returns to Petersburg. Settles in Yasnaya Polyana.
                Begins *The Decembrists* (unfinished), *Polikushka* (finished
                1862).

1862   September 23—Marries Sofya Behrs. Duties as mediator after
                the liberation of the serfs. Works on "Kholstomer" (finished
                1885).

1863-69   *War and Peace.* June 28, 1863—first of thirteen children born.

1869   September—Trip to purchase estate. Spends a night in Arzamas
                ("Diary of a Madman"—written in 1884).

1870-72   Works on a novel about the era of Peter the Great (unfinished).

1871-75   Pedagogical activity at Yasnaya Polyana. *Primer* and first four
                Readers.

1873-77   *Anna Karenina.*

1878-79   Works on a novel about the era of Nicholas I (unfinished).

1879-80   *Confession* and *Critique of Dogmatic Theology.*

1881   "What Men live By." Family moves to Moscow.

1882   "What I Believe." Buys house in Khamovniki (Moscow).

1885-86   Stories for the *Intermediary*, founded by V. G. Chertkov after
                befriending Tolstoy.

1886   *Death of Ivan Ilych. Power of Darkness* (performance for-
                bidden by censorship).

1890   *The Fruits of Enlightenment. The Kreutzer Sonata* (publica-
                tion only permitted in 1891 in the *Collected Works*). *The Devil*
                (published posthumously). Begins "Father Sergius" (finished
                1898) and *Resurrection* (1899).

1891   Renounces author's rights to his work after 1881.

1891-93   Helps in famine-relief work in province of Ryazan.

1892   Divides property and possessions among wife and children.

1894-95   *Master and Man.*

1896   Begins *Hadji Murad* (finished 1904).

1898   *What is Art?* Famine-relief work in Tula Province.

1899   *Resurrection* published to raise money for transporting Du-
                khobors to Canada.

1900   *The Living Corpse.* "Thou shalt not kill." Acquaintance with
                Gorky.

1901   Excommunicated by Orthodox church. Illness. Residence in
                Crimea.

1902   June 27—Return to Yasnaya Polyana.

1903   "Reminiscences" begun. "After the Ball." Works on "The
                Forged Coupon," "Shakespeare and the Drama."

1908   Universal celebration of eightieth anniversary.

1910   October 28—Leaves Yasnaya Polyana. November 7—Dies at
                Astopovo. November 9—Buried at Yasnaya Polyana.

Notes on the Editor and Authors

RALPH E. MATLAW, the editor, is Professor of Russian at the University of Chicago. He has written on, and translated, major and minor figures in Russian literature, including Dostoevsky, Turgenev, Pushkin, Apollon Grigor'ev, and V. F. Odoevsky.

SIR ISAIAH BERLIN, Professor of Social and Political Theory at Oxford, Fellow of All Souls, is author of *The Hedgehog and the Fox,* a study of Tolstoy (1953), *Historical Inevitability* (1954), a series of articles on Russian literature in the 1840s (*Encounter,* 1955), and other seminal works.

RICHARD P. BLACKMUR (1904-1965), taught at Princeton University. His essays on the novel, poetry, and criticism were collected in volumes such as *The Double Agent* (1935), *The Expense of Greatness* (1940), and *Language as Gesture* (1952).

REGINALD F. CHRISTIAN teaches at the University of Birmingham.

ALBERT COOK, Professor of English at the University of New York at Buffalo, has written on many forms of literature. His works include *The Meaning of Fiction* (1960) and *The Dark Voyage and the Golden Mean: A Philosophy of Comedy* (1949).

BORIS EIKHENBAUM (1886-1959), an outstanding Russian scholar, wrote the best book extant on Tolstoy, but unfortunately could cover only the period until 1880 by the time of his death. He was also the foremost authority on Lermontov, and in addition to a dozen books wrote hundreds of articles on Russian verse and prose and on literary theory.

KÄTE HAMBURGER, Professor of Literature at the Technische Hochschule, Stuttgart, is the author of *Thomas Mann und die Romantik* (1932), *Schiller* (1947), *Die Logik der Dichtung* (1957), and other works.

GEORG LUKÁCS (b. 1885), Europe's foremost man of letters and Marxist critic, has written a score of books, including *Die Theorie des Romans* (1920), *Goethe und seine Zeit* (1947), and a monumental work on aesthetics, the first two volumes of which have appeared so far.

DMITRI SERGEEVICH MEREZHKOVSKI (1865-1941), Russian poet, critic, and novelist, is best remembered for his novels *Julian the Apostate* (1896) and *Leonardo da Vinci* (1901).

RENATO POGGIOLI (1907-1963) was Professor of Russian and Comparative Literature at Harvard. He was an editor of *Inventario,* in which he published "Teoria dell'arte d'avanguardia," translated widely into Italian from Russian and English, and wrote *The Phoenix and the Spider* (1957), *The Poets of Russia* (1960) and *The Spirit of the Letter* (1965).

Leo Shestov (L. I. Schwarzman, 1866-1938), author of *Tolstoy and Nietzsche* (1900), *Dostoevsky and Nietzsche: The Philosophy of Tragely* (1901), *The Apotheosis of Groundlessness* (1905), *Kierkegaard and Existential Philosophy* (1936), and other works, is one of the finest stylists in Russian literature.

Edward Wasiolek is Professor of Russian and English Literature at the University of Chicago. His works include *Dostoevsky, The Major Fiction* (1964).

Edmund Wilson, America's foremost man of letters, has published many critical volumes, beginning with *Axel's Castle* (1931).

Selected Bibliography

(Works only in Russian have been omitted.)

Berlin, Isaiah. *The Hedgehog and the Fox: An Essay on Tolstoy's View of History.* New York, Simon and Schuster, 1953. A brilliant short essay on Tolstoy's view of history and its relation to his work, particularly *War and Peace.*

Christian, Richard F. *Tolstoy's* War and Peace. Oxford, Clarendon Press, 1962. An analysis of the evolution of the novel, its structure and style, containing much source material otherwise not available in English.

Du Bos, Charles. *Approximations.* Quatrième Serie. Paris, Correa, 1930. A study of Tolstoy's moral and spiritual development as evidenced in his work.

Farrell, James T. *Literature and Morality.* New York, Vanguard Press, 1947. Contains a series of articles on *War and Peace.*

Gibian, George. *Tolstoy and Shakespeare.* The Hague, Mouton and Co., 1957. A brief but thorough consideration of Tolstoy's attitudes toward Shakespeare and the drama in general.

Goldenveizer, A. B. *Talks with Tolstoy.* Richmond, 1923. Contains only part of the original Russian version, a repository of Tolstoy's pronouncements on art, literature, and life.

Gorky, Maxim. *Reminiscences of Tolstoy.* London, The Hogarth Press, 1934. A moving and splendid description of Tolstoy in brief glimpses.

Lubbock, Percy. *The Craft of Fiction.* New York, Peter Smith, 1947. Two excellent essays, marred by the notion that the two main novels would have been even better if Tolstoy had written them according to Lubbock's notions rather than to his own.

Mann, Thomas. "Goethe and Tolstoy" in *Essays of Three Decades.* New York, Alfred A. Knopf, 1947. A famous essay on literary giants and the nature of art.

Poggioli, Renato. *The Phoenix and the Spider.* Cambridge, Harvard University Press, 1957. Contains a suggestive psychological-literary analysis entitled "A Portrait of Tolstoy as Alceste."

Simmons, Ernest J. *Leo Tolstoy.* Boston, Atlantic, Little Brown, 1947. The standard biography in English.

Steiner, George. *Tolstoy or Dostoevsky: An Essay in the Old Criticism.* New York, Alfred A. Knopf, 1959. A pretentious and inaccurate book with occasional striking insights and juxtapositions.

Struve, Gleb. "Tolstoy in Soviet Criticism." *The Russian Review,* April 1960. A concise review of the vagaries and achievements of Tolstoy criticism in the last fifty years. The entire issue of the *Review* is devoted to Tolstoy.

Zweig, Stefan. *Master Builders: A Typology of the Spirit.* New York, Viking Press, 1939. A stimulating and well considered biography of Tolstoy based on Tolstoy's artistic works.

European Authors in the Twentieth Century Views Series

BAUDELAIRE, edited by Henri Peyre—S-TC-18
BRECHT, edited by Peter Demetz—S-TC-11
CAMUS, edited by Germaine Brée—S-TC-1
DANTE, edited by John Freccero—S-TC-46
DOSTOEVSKY, edited by René Wellek—S-TC-16
FLAUBERT, edited by Raymond Giraud—S-TC-42
HOMER, edited by George Steiner
   and Robert Fagles—S-TC-15
IBSEN, edited by Rolf Fjelde—S-TC-52
KAFKA, edited by Ronald Gray—S-TC-17
LORCA, edited by Manuel Duran—S-TC-14
MALRAUX, edited by R. W. B. Lewis—S-TC-37
THOMAS MANN, edited by Henry Hatfield—S-TC-36
MOLIERE, edited by Jacques Guicharnaud—S-TC-41
PROUST, edited by René Girard—S-TC-4
SARTRE, edited by Edith Kern—S-TC-21
SOPHOCLES, edited by Thomas Woodard—S-TC-54
STENDAHL, edited by Victor Brombert—S-TC-7

British Authors in the Twentieth Century Views Series